JEREMIAH *for* **EVERYONE**

Also available in the Old Testament
for Everyone series by John Goldingay

Genesis for Everyone, Part I

Genesis for Everyone, Part II

Exodus and Leviticus for Everyone

Numbers and Deuteronomy for Everyone

Joshua, Judges and Ruth for Everyone

1 and 2 Samuel for Everyone

1 and 2 Kings for Everyone

1 and 2 Chronicles for Everyone

Ezra, Nehemiah and Esther for Everyone

Job for Everyone

Psalms for Everyone, Part I

Psalms for Everyone, Part II

Proverbs, Ecclesiastes and the Song of Songs for Everyone

Isaiah for Everyone

JEREMIAH *for* EVERYONE

JOHN GOLDINGAY

Published in the United States of America in 2015
by Westminster John Knox Press, Louisville, Kentucky

Published in Great Britain in 2015

Society for Promoting Christian Knowledge
36 Causton Street
London SW1P 4ST
www.spck.org.uk

Unless otherwise indicated, Scripture quotations are the author's
own translation.

British Library Cataloguing-in-Publication Data
A catalogue record for this book is available from the British Library

ISBN 978-0-281-06138-9
eBook ISBN 978-0-281-06787-9

Typeset by Graphicraft Limited, Hong Kong
First printed in Great Britain by Ashford Colour Press
Subsequently digitally printed in Great Britain

eBook by Graphicraft Limited, Hong Kong

Produced on paper from sustainable forests

CONTENTS

CONTENTS

CONTENTS

ACKNOWLEDGMENTS

The translation at the beginning of each chapter (and in other biblical quotations) is my own. I have stuck closer to the Hebrew than modern translations often do when they are designed for reading in church so that you can see more precisely what the text says. Thus although I prefer to use gender-inclusive language, I have let the translation stay gendered if inclusivizing it would obscure whether the text was using singular or plural—in other words, the translation often uses "he" where in my own writing I would say "they" or "he or she." Sometimes I have added words to make the meaning clear, and I have put these words in square brackets. When the text uses the name of God, Yahweh, I have kept the name instead of replacing it with "the Lord" as translations usually do. And I've transliterated some other names in a way that's different from the way translations traditionally do, partly to make it easier to work out the pronunciation (e.g., Jehoiakin, not Jehoiachin). At the end of the book is a glossary of some terms that recur in the text, such as geographical, historical, and theological expressions. In each chapter (though not in the introduction) these terms are highlighted in **bold** the first time they occur.

The stories that follow the translation often concern my friends or my family. While none are made up, they are sometimes heavily disguised in order to be fair to people. Sometimes I have disguised them so well that when I came to read the stories again, I was not sure at first whom I was describing. My first wife, Ann, appears in a number of them. A few months after I started writing The Old Testament for Everyone, she died after negotiating with multiple sclerosis for forty-three years. Our shared dealings with her illness and disability over these years contribute significantly to what I write in ways that you may be able to see but also in ways that are less obvious.

Then, a year or so before I started writing this particular volume, I fell in love with and married Kathleen Scott, and I'm grateful for my new life with her and for her insightful comments on the manuscript, which have been so careful and illuminating that she practically deserves to be credited as coauthor.

I'm also grateful to Matt Sousa for reading through the manuscript and pointing out things I needed to correct or clarify and to Tom Bennett for checking the proofs.

INTRODUCTION

As far as Jesus and the New Testament writers were concerned, the Jewish Scriptures that Christians call the "Old Testament" *were* the Scriptures. In saying that, I cut corners a bit, as the New Testament never gives us a list of these Scriptures, but the body of writings that the Jewish people accept is as near as we can get to identifying the collection that Jesus and the New Testament writers would have worked with. The church also came to accept some extra books such as Maccabees and Ecclesiasticus that were traditionally called the "Apocrypha," the books that were "hidden away"—a name that came to imply "spurious." They're now often known as the "Deuterocanon-ical Writings," which is more cumbersome but less pejorative; it simply indicates that these books have less authority than the Torah, the Prophets, and the Writings. The precise list of them varies among different churches. For the purposes of this series that seeks to expound the "Old Testament for Everyone," by the "Old Testament" we mean the Scriptures accepted by the Jewish community, though in the Jewish Bible they come in a different order, as the Torah, the Prophets, and the Writings.

They were not "old" in the sense of antiquated or out of date; I sometimes like to refer to them as the First Testament rather than the Old Testament to make that point. For Jesus and the New Testament writers, they were a living resource for understanding God, God's ways in the world, and God's ways with us. They were "useful for teaching, for reproof, for correction, and for training in righteousness, so that the person who belongs to God can be proficient, equipped for

1

every good work" (2 Timothy 3:16–17). They were for everyone, in fact. So it's strange that Christians don't read them very much. My aim in these volumes is to help you do so.

My hesitation is that you may read me instead of the Scriptures. Don't fall into that trap. I like the fact that this series includes much of the biblical text. Don't skip over it. In the end, that's the bit that matters.

An Outline of the Old Testament

The Christian Old Testament puts the books in the Jewish Bible in a distinctive order:

> Genesis to Kings: A story that runs from the creation of the world to the exile of Judahites to Babylon
> Chronicles to Esther: A second version of this story, continuing it into the years after the exile
> Job, Psalms, Proverbs, Ecclesiastes, Song of Songs: Some poetic books
> Isaiah to Malachi: The teaching of some prophets

Here is an outline of the history that lies at the books' background. (I give no dates for events in Genesis, which involves too much guesswork.)

1200s	Moses, the exodus, Joshua
1100s	The "judges"
1000s	King Saul, King David
900s	King Solomon; the nation splits into two, Ephraim and Judah
800s	Elijah, Elisha
700s	Amos, Hosea, Isaiah, Micah; Assyria the superpower; the fall of Ephraim
600s	Jeremiah, King Josiah; Babylon the superpower
500s	Ezekiel; the fall of Judah; Persia the superpower; Judahites free to return home

400s	Ezra, Nehemiah
300s	Greece the superpower
200s	Syria and Egypt the regional powers pulling Judah one way or the other
100s	Judah's rebellion against Syrian power and gain of independence
000s	Rome the superpower

Jeremiah

To judge from the length of his book, Jeremiah was the most significant prophet of the last years of Judah's independent life, up until the nation was overcome by the Babylonians in 587 BC. During his lifetime, the great king Josiah sought to bring about a reform of Judah's religious and community life, but the reform had no lasting effect. Politically, Josiah's reign saw Babylon replace Assyria as the Middle Eastern superpower, but Judah resisted Babylonian control of its life. More than one Babylonian invasion of Judah followed. Jeremiah sees these events as not merely the consequence of unwise political policies but as the consequence of unwise religious and social policies. Behind Babylon's invasion he sees the hand of God.

Jeremiah's ministry lasted over forty years, and he spent the bulk of it warning Judah about the chastisement that would come unless it turned back to God. He thus had to keep warning Judah about a catastrophe that didn't happen, and he lost credibility as years passed. His book tells many stories about his experiences as a prophet, so it represents a cross between a book such as Isaiah that focuses on passing on a prophet's words and the sections of 1 and 2 Kings that tell stories about prophets such as Elijah and Elisha. The person as well as the message is important, because people's treatment of Jeremiah indicates their response to God. In this connection, even more vivid than the stories about him are the accounts of the way he was driven to pray by the way people treated him.

The book interweaves reports of his prophecies, stories about his experiences, and accounts of his prayers in a way that can seem random, though sometimes one can see reason in the sequencing of the material. It brings home the interwovenness of Jeremiah's preaching and praying and the people's response to him and thus to God. The book of Jeremiah can't be divided into sections in the clear way that the book of Isaiah can—though chapters 1–25 are mostly concerned with the teaching of Jeremiah; 26–45, with stories about Jeremiah; and 46–51, with his indictments of other nations (these are similar to Isaiah 13–23). Chapter 52 is a tailpiece that repeats the story at the end of 2 Kings relating how Jerusalem was taken and Jeremiah's prophecies are thereby proved true. But here is a rough outline:

Chapters 1–25 Jeremiah's Message

1	His summons by God
2–6	Judah's apostasy, waywardness, and punishment
7–10	Further warnings, focusing on false trust
11–20	The rejection of God's message and the persecution of God's messenger
21–24	Further warnings from the time of Zedekiah
25	His review of his twenty-three years of ministry from his call to 604

Chapters 26–35 Jeremiah's Life: The Demand of God's Message (i)

26–29	Three parallel stories emphasizing that the more stubbornly people resisted Jeremiah's message, the worse their trouble
30–33	Stories showing that the darkest hour is the dawn of hope: God doesn't intend judgment to be the end
34–35	The choice: be like the nation, which continues to rebel and must be judged (34), or be like the few who keep their commitments (35)

Chapters 36–45 Jeremiah's Life: The Demand of God's Message (ii)

Chapters 46–51 Prophecies about Other Nations

Chapter 52 Postscript: The Fall of Jerusalem

The chief events during Jeremiah's ministry were as follows:

640   Josiah becomes king.

626   God summons Jeremiah to be a prophet.

621   The discovery of a Torah scroll in the temple gives new impetus to reform in Judah designed to throw off Assyrian-style theology and worship (2 Kings 22–23).

612   Nineveh, the Assyrian capital, falls to the Babylonians.

609   King Josiah is killed in a military action designed to support the Assyrians.

609   Jehoahaz is made king; the Babylonians replace him with Jehoiaqim.

601   Jehoiaqim rebels; the Babylonians invade Judah.

597   Jehoiaqim again rebels, and the Babylonians again invade.

Jehoiaqim dies; Jehoiakin succeeds.

The Babylonians take Jerusalem, deport Jehoiakin, and replace him with Zedekiah.

587   Zedekiah rebels; the Babylonians again invade, capture Jerusalem, and destroy the temple. Judahites again rebel, kill the Babylonian governor, and flee to Egypt, taking Jeremiah with them.

There were many other prophets in Judah in Jeremiah's time, including Zephaniah, Nahum, and Habakkuk. Apart from prophets who had books named after them, there was also the woman prophet Huldah, whom Josiah consulted when the Torah scroll was discovered; she was perhaps on the king's staff, as Jeremiah wasn't. There were also a number of "false prophets" such as Hananiah, people who devised their own messages that were in conflict with what God actually wanted to say.

JEREMIAH 1:1–19

More a Summons than a Vocation

[1]The messages of Jeremiah son of Hilqiah, one of the priests of Anatot in Benjamin's territory, [2]to whom Yahweh's message came in the days of Josiah son of Amon, king of Judah, in the thirteenth year of his reign, [3]and came in the days of Jehoiaqim son of Josiah, king of Judah, until the end of the eleventh year of Zedekiah son of Josiah, king of Judah, until Jerusalem's exile in the fifth month.

[4] Yahweh's message came to me:
[5] "Before I formed you in the womb I acknowledged
       you,
   before you came out from the womb I set you
       apart.
   I made you a prophet concerning the nations."
[6] I said, "Oh, Lord Yahweh—
   really, I don't know how to speak,
       because I'm a young man."
[7] But Yahweh said to me,
       "Don't say, 'I'm a young man.'
   Because you're to go out to anyone to whom I
       send you,
   and speak anything that I command you.
[8] Don't be afraid of their faces,
       because I'll be with you to rescue you"
       (Yahweh's declaration).
[9] Yahweh put out his hand and touched my mouth,
       and Yahweh said to me,
       "I'm putting my words into your mouth.
[10] See, I'm appointing you this day
       over the nations, over the kingdoms,
   to uproot and pull down, to destroy and overthrow,
       to build and plant."
[11] Yahweh's message came to me:
   "What are you looking at, Jeremiah?"
       I said, "I'm looking at the branch of a watcher tree."

¹² Yahweh said to me,
    "You've done well to look at it.
Because I'm watching—
    over my message, to put it into effect."
¹³ Yahweh's message came to me a second time:
    "What are you looking at?"
I said, "I'm looking at a boiling pot,
    with its mouth facing from the north."
¹⁴ Yahweh said to me,
"From the north evil will open out
    on all the residents of the country.
¹⁵ Because here am I summoning
    all the families of the northern kingdoms
    (Yahweh's declaration).
They'll come and put his throne, each one,
    at the opening of Jerusalem's gates,
against all its walls around,
    and against all Judah's cities.
¹⁶ I'll pronounce my decisions to them,
    for all their evil, in that they've abandoned
        me.
They've burned sacrifices to other gods,
    bowed down to things their hands made.
¹⁷ You, you're to put your belt around your waist,
    get up and speak to them
    anything that I myself command you.
Don't shatter in front of them,
    lest I shatter you in front of them.
¹⁸ I—here I am, making you
    a fortified city today,
an iron pillar
    and bronze walls against the entire country
    (for Judah's kings and its officers,
    for its priests and the people of the country).
¹⁹ They'll battle against you but they won't overcome
        you,
    because I'll be with you (Yahweh's declaration)
    to rescue you."

Last week I took part in a conference on God, the church, and disability. One participant was a woman who has been ordained a priest, but she has a speech impediment that makes it hard to understand what she says, and she has had difficulty finding a position in a parish. Another was a paraplegic man who spends much of his time selling candy in the street, but he has raised thousands of dollars by doing so and has supported five needy children in India and Africa with the proceeds; he's also visited India and Africa to meet them. He was hard to understand, too, but he had a vibrant testimony mostly given through his father. How could these people have the courage to believe they had a ministry to exercise?

The question arises for Jeremiah because he's just a young man—maybe in his twenties, maybe even younger. A culture such as **Israel**'s recognizes that wisdom lies with people more senior. Who's going to listen to someone so junior? While not disputing that Jeremiah is correct in principle, God isn't constrained by the way things usually work. He likes to choose the younger brother rather than the older one (in the West he might make the point in the opposite way, by using someone who's "past it"). What will count isn't whether Jeremiah has had time to develop wisdom but whether God gives him things to say. The point is made vividly by **Yahweh**'s talk of deciding on Jeremiah before his birth, before any gifts he might develop have had a chance to form. Even then, Yahweh "acknowledged" him, made a commitment to him, and set him apart. Like Saul of Tarsus when Jesus appears to him, Jeremiah has little alternative to becoming God's agent. There's no suggestion that God's call corresponds to the inclination of the person called. He's the master whether the servant likes it or not.

Another advantage of choosing a young man is that he has no marital or family commitments and will be able to exercise a ministry that persists over forty years, as far as we know the longest of any prophetic ministry. The point is implicit in the opening to the book, which gives a date of 626 for his initial receiving of a message from Yahweh and indicates that it continues until after Jerusalem's fall to the **Babylonians** in 587. It actually continued after that event, but the point about mentioning the city's fall and its people's **exile** is that these events were the vindication of his prophecies over all those decades.

I myself had an experience of God's calling me to a ministry, but Jeremiah's account of his call isn't designed to encourage us to see our experiences as analogous to Jeremiah's. Rather the opposite. It's here to push people into taking seriously the prophecies that will follow. They're not like the words of other preachers or self-styled prophets. The fact that God had to overcome Jeremiah's unwillingness is another indication that he isn't prophesying because he has an ambition to be a prophet or thinks he has prophetic gifts. He's under compulsion. The community cannot afford to ignore him. God doesn't necessarily call people because they have the appropriate gifts—again, it may be rather the opposite. Other prophets whom we'll meet, such as Hananiah, look more gifted, but they're not actually God's mouthpiece.

Jeremiah is to be a prophet concerning the nations in several senses, but the expression "the nations" often refers to whatever is the imperial power of the day, and a major focus of his preaching will be the trouble that the upcoming great power, Babylon, will bring to **Judah**. It'll be by its agency that Yahweh will destroy Jerusalem and uproot its people. Babylon will turn out to be the pot of trouble that will boil over from the north, the direction from which invaders usually came to Judah. It'll also be by means of the next imperial power, **Persia**, that Yahweh will later see to the city's rebuilding and its people's replanting. The watcher tree is the flowering almond, which blossoms early after winter as if it's waking up and watching for spring, so it provides a parable for what Yahweh is doing over his message, even when it doesn't look like it.

It's an impossibly demanding task imposed on a man who doesn't want it. But Jeremiah isn't just pushed out into the battlefield without support. God will be with him. In the Bible, it doesn't mean that people feel that God is with them and that things will be OK. It means God is with them in a way that brings protection, whether or not they feel God is with them.

JEREMIAH 2:1–11

On the Cliff's Edge

¹ Yahweh's message came to me:
² Go, proclaim in Jerusalem's ears:
    Yahweh has said this:
    I've kept in mind for you the commitment of your
        youth,
        your love as a bride,
    your following me through the wilderness,
        a country not sown.
³ Israel was holy to Yahweh,
    the firstfruits of his harvest.
    All the people who ate of it would be guilty;
        evil would come upon them (Yahweh's
        declaration).

⁴ Listen to Yahweh's message, Jacob's household,
    all the families of Israel's household.
⁵ Yahweh has said this:
    What wrongdoing did your ancestors find in me,
        that they went far away from me,
    went after emptiness and became emptiness,
⁶ but didn't say, "Where is Yahweh,
    the one who brought us up from the country of
        Egypt
    and enabled us to go through the wilderness,
        through a country of steppe and pit,
        a country of drought and deep darkness,

a country through which no one passed
    and where no human being lived?"
7 I enabled you to come into a country of farmland,
    to eat its fruit and its good things.
But you came and defiled my country;
    you made my possession an outrage.
8 The priests didn't say, "Where is Yahweh?";
    the people controlling the teaching didn't
      acknowledge me.
The shepherds rebelled against me,
    the prophets prophesied by the Master,
and followed beings that couldn't achieve anything.
9 Therefore I'll contend with you more (Yahweh's
    declaration)
    and contend with your grandchildren.
10 Because cross over to the shores of Cyprus and see,
    send off to Qedar and observe well,
    see if something like this has happened.
11 Has a nations changed its gods,
    when those are not gods?
But my people have changed my splendor
    for what doesn't achieve anything.

Some years ago we had a visiting preacher in seminary chapel who talked about the church in the West as being in exile. In the past the church sat at the center of society's life. Our holidays linked with Christian festivals, and the nation's life was expected to reflect Christian values. Shops mostly closed on Sundays. But the church has been thrown out from the center of national and intellectual life. It's in exile. The preacher was a Brit who lives in Canada, and I think his description applies to the church in Europe. The profile of the relationship of church and society in the United States has been different. Some of those marks of being a "Christian nation" never applied; in other ways the Christian faith has been more central to national life. Yet that centrality is disappearing fast in the United States, too. The number of people for whom the church counts and the ways in which the church counts are steadily decreasing.

While the church hasn't been sent into exile, it's on the verge of that happening, and it doesn't recognize the fact. They say you can put a frog in cold water and gradually boil it, and the frog won't jump out but will let itself be cooked. Fifty years ago the church in the United States could identify with its culture because the culture broadly accepted Christian values, but the culture has gradually become more and more secular (for instance, in its attitude to money and celebrity). The church has continued to identify with the culture and hasn't noticed the change in the water temperature. It isn't in exile yet, but it's living in a time like Jeremiah's, when the **exile** is near, and Jeremiah's analysis of **Judah**'s position is instructive for the church.

One reason for Judah's decline was that it had given up on its gospel. The idea of a gospel doesn't start in the New Testament—the expression comes from the Old Testament. The gospel is the good news, the story of what God has done for us. Judah has forgotten its story. Cities are commonly personified as women, so Jeremiah can portray Jerusalem's action as like a wife's unfaithfulness to her husband. He will soon note that Jerusalem's people can even teach a thing or two to **evil** women (women who are already involved in sexual immorality?). Turning a blind eye to some of the people's early indiscretions, Jeremiah can draw a contrast between its stance at the beginning of its relationship with **Yahweh** and the infidelity that now characterizes Judah. It had been Yahweh's special possession, and Yahweh had protected it jealously. But soon the ancestors of the present generation turned to other spiritual resources (the book of Judges tells the story).

Admittedly "spiritual resources" is a compliment. These other deities were not resources at all. They were empty. They had no power. The ancestors' behavior was paradoxical. On the way to the promised land they had proved Yahweh's capacity to provide and protect, but inexplicably they then stopped looking to Yahweh and looked in the same direction as the people of Canaan; perhaps they assumed the Canaanites knew what they were doing. They stopped asking, "Where is Yahweh?" In this context it's not a question suggesting unfaith but one suggesting faith—as when we speak of "seeking God," which doesn't mean we think God is hiding. Much responsibility rests with the leadership—priests, whose responsibility included instructing people in the **Torah**; community leaders ("shepherds"); and prophets. The whole business was a mystery. You could go west across the Mediterranean and east to Arabia (Qedar) and find nothing like it. Yahweh speaks not only like an aggrieved husband but like someone who has been betrayed by a business partner and brings an accusation in front of the elders in the community court.

For the church, there's a tragic paradox here. What we need is to be brought out of ourselves by seeing our lives set in the context of a bigger picture, a bigger story, the gospel story. But it's possible to be so overwhelmed by our emptiness, our isolation, and our insignificance that we don't pay attention to this bigger story. All we want to do both inside and outside of church is think about ourselves and our needs. Scripture and the gospel may seem boring and irrelevant. So we turn God into someone whose focus is on meeting those needs. We try to short-circuit the process whereby God gives content and meaning to our lives, making God a quick fix for our needs. But quick fixes don't work. The only fix that works is the gospel story and the Scriptures where we find that story. But in worship we've often given up on those. We may use the same words our forebears used, the words *God* and *Lord* and *Jesus*, but the content we read into them comes from the contemporary context. A new age person could come into much Christian worship and be quite happy with nearly all of what we say, sing, and do. We are scratching where we itch. But when you have a serious itch, you need more than scratching to put it right.

Jeremiah tells people they need to turn back. We need to turn away from our preoccupation with ourselves and our individual journeys to God and God's journey. We need to turn from our preoccupation with ourselves to God and turn from our individual stories to God's story. Jeremiah wants the people to do so, to remember their gospel story again and see how it relates to their needs. He isn't saying, "Forget about your needs, about the need for your crops to grow, and just think about God." He's saying that they need to bring their needs and the gospel story together.

JEREMIAH 2:12–37

Looking for Spiritual Resources

¹² Be devastated at this, heavens,
    shudder, be utterly desolate (Yahweh's
      declaration).
¹³ Because my people have done two evil things:
    they've abandoned me, the fountain of running
      water,
  to dig themselves cisterns, breakable cisterns,
    that cannot [hold] water.
¹⁴ Was Israel a servant, or someone born in a
    household—
  why has he become plunder?
¹⁵ Lions roar over him,
    they've lifted their voice.
  They've made his country a devastation;
    his cities are burned, without resident.
¹⁶ The people of Memphis and Tahpanhes
    will also break your skull [Jerusalem].
¹⁷ Isn't it this that does it to you,
    your abandoning of Yahweh your God
      at the time when he was enabling you to go on
      your journey?

18 So now what [gain] is there for you in a journey to
        Egypt
      to drink the Nile's water?
    What [gain] is there for you in a journey to
        Assyria
      to drink the Euphrates' water?
19 Your evil should discipline you,
      your turning away should reprove you.
    Acknowledge and see how evil and bitter it is,
      your abandoning of Yahweh your God.
    And you have no awe before me
      (a declaration of the Lord Yahweh Armies).
20 Because of old you broke your yoke,
      tore off your straps, and said, "I won't serve."
    Because on every hill and under every green tree
      you're lying down as a whore.
21 I—I planted you as a top-class vine,
      all of it reliable seed.
    So how have you changed in relation to me
      into the turnings of a foreign vine?
22 Because even if you wash with soap
      and use much detergent for yourself,
    your waywardness is inscribed before me
      (a declaration of the Lord Yahweh).
23 How can you say, "I've not become defiled,
      I've not followed the Masters."
    Look at your journey into the Ravine,
      acknowledge what you've done there,
      a swift camel twisting her ways,
24   a donkey accustomed to the wilderness,
    sniffing the wind in her desire—
      who can reverse her craving?
    None who seek her get tired;
      in her season they find her.
25 Hold your foot back from being shoeless
      and your throat from being dry.
    But you say, "It's desperate,
      because I love strangers, I shall follow them."

16

²⁶ Like a thief's shame when he's found out,
    so Israel's household was shamed.
They, their kings, their officials,
    their priests, their prophets,
²⁷ were saying to a piece of wood, "You're our
        father,"
    to some stone, "You gave me birth."
Because they turned their back to me,
    not their face.
At the time when evil happened to them
    they'd say, "Arise, deliver us."
²⁸ But where are your gods
    that you made for yourself?
They should arise if they can deliver you,
    at the time when evil happens to you.
Because your gods have become
    more than the number of your cities, Judah.
²⁹ Why do you contend with me
    when all of you have rebelled against me?
    (Yahweh's declaration).
³⁰ To no effect did I hit your children;
    they didn't accept discipline.
Your sword consumed your prophets
    like a destroying lion.
³¹ This generation,
    consider Yahweh's message!
Did I become a wilderness to Israel,
    or a country of deep darkness?
Why did my people say, "We've wandered,
    we won't come to you anymore"?
³² Can a girl disregard her jewelry,
    a bride her adornments?
But my people disregarded me,
    days without number.
³³ How well you've made your way in seeking love
        [Jerusalem];
    therefore you've even taught evil women your
        ways.

17

³⁴ Further, on your garments is found
 the blood of the lives of needy innocent people
 (you didn't find them breaking in).
 Because despite all these things,
³⁵ you've said, "I'm innocent,
 his anger has surely turned from me."
 Here I am, taking a decision against you,
 because of your saying, "I haven't offended."
³⁶ Why do you go about so much,
 changing your way?
 Through Egypt you'll be shamed again,
 as you were shamed through Assyria.
³⁷ Through this you'll again come out
 with your hands on your head.
 Because Yahweh has rejected the ones you trust,
 and you won't succeed through them.

I just read about a couple who traveled to India because they couldn't have a baby. The British medics were puzzled about the reasons, as both husband and wife seemed to be physiologically OK. In India the couple sought some traditional treatments, but they were also told that the problem was their lack of faith and their lack of prayer. They were advised to visit the shrine of a great Sufi saint in Delhi, where they tied a ribbon to the saint's mausoleum and wept at the shrine. A few months later the woman conceived and gave birth to a healthy baby.

People in **Judah** in Jeremiah's day would understand the longing to have a baby, the willingness to go some lengths to succeed in doing so, and the willingness to explore alternative spiritual resources in this connection. Indeed, a Judahite couple would feel the point more strongly. Having children wasn't only the fulfillment of a natural human instinct but also key to their future as a family and to Judah's future as a people. Indeed, it was key to fulfilling their religious vocation. To put it in Christian terms, if Judah dies out, there'll be no people from whom a messiah can be born. In Jeremiah's day, the point is sharper than it has been previously because the Northern Kingdom of **Ephraim** to which most of the twelve clans belonged had ceased to exist (in Jeremiah, the name **Israel** often refers to Ephraim). Jeremiah himself came from Anatot, only three miles north of Jerusalem but across the border into the area of the clan of **Benjamin**, which was technically part of Ephraim. So Jeremiah is in a strong position to draw attention to the price Ephraim paid for its behavior. The people of **Yahweh** is shrinking rather than growing. Was Israel originally like a bond servant, someone who had had to sell himself into service or someone born to a family whose members were already servants? If not, why is he being treated as somebody who doesn't count?

The Ephraimites had known that they needed to grow as a people and that they needed food to eat, and the pressures of their needs made them turn from Yahweh to the **Masters**, the traditional gods in their culture who had a reputation for making families, crops, flocks, and herds grow. Jeremiah's image for their action is that they made two mistakes, committed two **evils**. They abandoned Yahweh, who's like a well of fresh water, and dug themselves water cisterns, which people relied on if they had no well or the well ran dry. Cisterns collected rain water, which was by no means as nice as fresh water, and anyway they might leak—with devastating implications, deathly implications. Your water is gone, and it may be months before it rains. How stupid it would be to give up a natural spring and choose to rely on a cistern, and specifically a cistern that leaks.

Not that people saw themselves as seeking the help of other gods rather than Yahweh. In theory they saw these other "gods" as Yahweh's servants or underlings. So they blithely accompanied their temple worship by journeys down into the nearby Hinnom Ravine, the place whose name eventually generates the name Gehenna. It was a hellish place, all right.

19

They engaged in rites there designed to make contact with dead family members, to seek their advice and help. These rites included the sacrifice of children, a costly offering indicating a commitment that might win a god's help. Jeremiah calls it shedding the blood of innocent people, which usually denotes action such as the execution of a prophet or of a person such as Naboth in order to appropriate his land (1 Kings 21). If someone is killed when committing a robbery, it counts as manslaughter rather than murder. In this context Jeremiah is making a sardonic comment about human sacrifices. They were acts of murder.

Won't Judah learn the lesson? It's advancing hell-bent toward the same cliff from which Ephraim jumped. Memphis (one of the greatest of Egyptian cities) and Tahpanhes (the first big Egyptian city you reach when traveling from Judah) stand for Egypt as a whole. Judah had long been playing politics in seeking support from **Assyria** or Egypt and changing sides when it seemed a good idea. It constitutes another form of unfaithfulness to Yahweh. He was supposed to be the one they trusted for their political life as well as for their crops and their fertility, but it was hard to live that way.

JEREMIAH 3:1–4:4

Go Together Like a Horse and Carriage

¹Saying: If someone dismisses his wife, she goes from him, and she comes to belong to another man, can he return to her again? Will that country not be totally defiled? And you [Jerusalem] have been whoring with many lovers. Would you return to me?

> ²   Raise your eyes to the bare places and look—
>   where have you not been laid?
>   By the roads you sat for them,
>   like a Bedouin in the wilderness.

You defiled the country
 with your whoredom and evildoing.
³ Showers held back,
 there was no rain,
but you had the brazenness of a whore;
 you refused to be shamed.
⁴ But now have you not called to me,
 "Father, you're the partner of my youth!
⁵ Does he hold onto things forever
 or keep watch for all time?"
There—you have spoken;
 you have done what was evil, and succeeded.

⁶Yahweh said to me in the days of King Josiah: Have you seen what Israel did, she who turned? She was going up every high mountain and under every green tree and whoring there. ⁷I said, "After she's done all these things, she'll return to me." But she didn't return. And her faith-breaking sister Judah saw. ⁸I saw that because of the acts of adultery that Israel committed, she who turned, I dismissed her and gave her divorce document to her, but her sister, Judah, she who broke faith, wasn't afraid. She went and acted as a whore, too. ⁹It came about that because of the frivolity of her whoring she profaned the country; she committed adultery with stone and wood. ¹⁰But even in all this, her sister, faith-breaking Judah, didn't return to me with her whole spirit but rather with falsehood (Yahweh's declaration).

¹¹Yahweh said to me: Israel who turned has shown herself more faithful than Judah, who broke faith. ¹²Go, proclaim these words to the north. Say, Return, Israel who turned (Yahweh's declaration); I won't make my face fall against you, because I'm committed (Yahweh's declaration), I don't hold onto things forever. ¹³Only acknowledge your waywardness, that you've rebelled against Yahweh your God and scattered your journeys to strangers under every green tree, and not listened to my voice (Yahweh's declaration). ¹⁴Return, children who are turning away (Yahweh's declaration), because I'm your master. I'll take you, one from a city, two from a family,

and bring you to Zion. [15]I'll give you shepherds in accordance with my will and they'll shepherd you with acknowledgment and good sense. [16]When you increase and are fruitful in the country in those days (Yahweh's declaration) people will no longer say, "Yahweh's covenant chest!" It won't come to mind: they won't be mindful of it or pay attention; it won't be made again. [17]At that time they'll call Jerusalem "Yahweh's throne," and all the nations will gather to it, to Yahweh's name, to Jerusalem. People will no more follow the determination of their evil mind. [18]In those days Judah's household will go to Israel's household, and they'll come together from the northern country to the country that I enabled your ancestors to possess.

[19]I myself had said: How [gladly] I'd put you among my children and give you a desirable country, the loveliest possession of the nations. I'd said you'd call me "Father," and not turn from following me. [20]Actually, [as] a woman breaks faith with her lover, so you broke faith with me, Israel's household (Yahweh's declaration).

[21]   A sound makes itself heard on the bare places,
            the Israelites' weeping that pleads for grace.
        Because they've misdirected their way,
            they've disregarded Yahweh their God.
[22]   Return, children who turn away;
            I'll heal your turnings.
        "Here we are, we are coming to you,
            because you are Yahweh our God.
[23]   Yes, what comes from the hills belongs to falsehood,
            uproar from the mountains.
        Yes, in Yahweh our God
            is the deliverance of Israel.
[24]   But the shameful has consumed
            our ancestors' labor from our youth,
        their sheep and cattle,
            their sons and daughters.
[25]   We must lie down in our shame,
            our disgrace should cover us.

> Because we've offended against Yahweh our God,
>   we and our ancestors from our youth until today.
> We haven't listened
>   to the voice of Yahweh our God."
> ^{4:1} If you turn, Israel (Yahweh's declaration),
>   turn to me,
> and if you remove your abominations from in front
>   of me
>   and don't wander,
> ² but swear "As Yahweh lives,"
>   in truth and in faithful decision making,
> nations will pray to be blessed by him,
>   and will exult in him.
> ³ Because Yahweh has said this to Judah's people and
>   to Jerusalem:
> Till the tillable land for yourselves,
>   and don't sow among thorns.
> ⁴ Circumcise yourselves for Yahweh,
>   remove the foreskin from your mind,
> people of Judah and residents of Jerusalem,
>   lest my wrath comes out like fire,
> and burns with no one putting it out,
>   because of the evil of your deeds.

One of my first memories of being a wet-behind-the-ears young parish minister is an interview with a couple who wanted to get married in our church though they were not members of it. We filled in the appropriate forms, and they described themselves as single, but it eventually transpired that the groom was divorced; he took the view that he could therefore describe himself as single again. I never knew whether he was trying to be deceptive, but the Anglican church doesn't use language that way; after divorce you do not become "single" again. And in those days divorced people couldn't remarry in church. My recent memory of a related question involves one of our bishops commenting that she wouldn't usually marry someone who was twice-divorced, but she'd done so more than once recently. Times have changed.

There's an odd rule in the **Torah**, in Deuteronomy 24, about remarriage. It lays down that if a divorced woman remarries but is subsequently divorced again or widowed, her first husband may not have second thoughts and agree to restart the marriage (we don't know why **Israel** had that rule, but it would be a disincentive to adultery and a disincentive to impetuous divorce). Here God raises the question whether he's bound by such a rule in his relationship with his people. I've heard it said that John Calvin doesn't see God as bound by his own rules, though I've not been able to find the quotation. But in any case Jeremiah is here dealing with a metaphor. It's nevertheless a metaphor that brings home vividly the breadth of God's grace toward **Judah**. Initially God implies that it would of course be impossible for God to have Jerusalem back. A "woman" who has been so unfaithful and has by implication been divorced couldn't come back to her first "husband" and be taken again by him. Such an action is the more unthinkable if someone goes through the motions of coming back and appeals to aspects of God's character such as mercy that should make it possible to have her back, but does so even though the return isn't genuine. Judah is actually worse than **Ephraim** because it has failed to learn from what happened to Ephraim. Yet ironically Judah is right in its expectation that God will surely have it back. Jeremiah refers to God's commitment; one of the ideas suggested by the Hebrew word is of someone staying faithful even when the other party has forfeited any right to faithfulness.

When **Yahweh** declares that the people of Judah must come back to him, he reworks the point. The word for *master* is *ba'al*, which is both the word for an alternative god (a **Master**) and the ordinary word for a husband. The Old Testament doesn't regularly use this word for a husband—the word *husband* in English translations usually represents the ordinary Hebrew word for a man, as the word *wife* usually represents the ordinary Hebrew word for a woman. The advantage of this usage is that it avoids giving the impression that a husband is his wife's owner or master. But when a passage is referring to God's husbandly relationship to Israel, that connotation is appropriate. So reminding Israel that Yahweh is its *ba'al* reminds it that he's its master or owner and also that he has the place in its life that it's inclined to give to alternative gods.

As its master or owner or husband, Yahweh will see that Israel gets looked after.

JEREMIAH 4:5–31

The Big One

5　Declare in Judah, make it heard in Jerusalem,
　　　　say, "Sound the horn in the country."
　　Proclaim, confirm it, say,
　　　　"Gather up, let's go into the fortified cities!
6　Raise a banner toward Zion,
　　　　take refuge, don't stay."
　　Because I am going to bring evil from the north,
　　　　a great wounding.
7　A lion has gone up from its thicket,
　　　　a destroyer of nations has set out.
　　He's gone out from his place
　　　　to make your country a devastation.
　　Your cities will be wasted,
　　　　without resident.
8　On account of this, put on sackcloth,
　　　　lament and howl,
　　"Yahweh's angry blaze
　　　　isn't turning from us."
9　On that day (Yahweh's declaration)
　　　　the king's spirit and the officials' spirit will expire.
　　The priests will be devastated,
　　　　the prophets will be dumbfounded.

¹⁰ And I said, "Oh, Lord Yahweh,
    really you've totally deceived this people and
      Jerusalem,
in saying, 'There'll be peace for you,'
    whereas the sword has reached their throat."

¹¹ At that time it will be said
    concerning this people and concerning Jerusalem:
On the way to the daughter of my people
    a searing wind comes,
from the bare places in the wilderness,
    not to winnow, not to fan.
¹² A wind too full for these things comes on my behalf;
    now I myself announce decisions against them.
¹³ There: one will go up like clouds,
    his chariots like a whirlwind.
His horses are swifter than eagles—
    oh, alas for us, because we are destroyed!

¹⁴ Wash your spirit of evil, Jerusalem,
    so that you may find deliverance.
How long will you let your wicked intentions
    stay within you?
¹⁵ Because a voice declares from Dan,
    it lets wickedness be heard from Mount Ephraim.
¹⁶ Make mention to the nations;
    there—let it be heard against Jerusalem.
Watchers are coming from a far-off country,
    they'll give voice against Judah's cities.
¹⁷ Like people guarding the fields
    they've come against it all around,
because it has rebelled against me
    (Yahweh's declaration).
¹⁸ Your way and your deeds
    have done these things to you.
This is the evil that has come to you,
    because it's bitter, because it has reached your
      heart.

19 My pain, my pain, I writhe, the walls of my heart,
      my heart howls within me, I cannot be still.
   Because you've heard, my soul,
      the sound of the horn, the battle shout.
20 Wounding upon wounding is proclaimed,
      because the entire country is destroyed.
   Suddenly my tents have been destroyed,
      in an instant my tent cloths.
21 How long shall I see a banner,
      listen to the sound of the horn?

22 Because my people are stupid,
      they haven't acknowledged me.
   They're dense children;
      they're not people who understand.
   They're clever at doing evil
      but they don't know how to do good.

23 I looked at the earth and there—it was empty, void;
      and at the heavens—there was no light in them.
24 I looked at the mountains and there—they were
         quaking,
      and all the hills were moving to and fro.
25 I looked and there—no human being,
      and every bird in the heavens had fled.
26 I looked and there—the farmland was wilderness,
      and all its cities were burned,
   on account of Yahweh,
      on account of his angry blazing.
27 Because Yahweh has said this:
   The entire country will become desolation
      (but I won't make an end).
28 On account of this the earth mourns,
      the heavens are dark above.
   Because I have spoken, I have made a scheme;
      I haven't relented, I won't turn from it.
29 At the sound of horseman and bowman
      the entire city is fleeing.

They've gone into the woods,
    climbed onto the rocks.
The entire city is abandoned,
    there's no resident in it, not one.
30 So you who are going to be destroyed,
    what do you do when you dress in scarlet,
when you adorn yourself in gold adornment,
    when you broaden your eyes with mascara?
It's in vain that you look beautiful;
    your lovers have rejected you, they seek your life.
31 Because I've heard a voice like someone in labor,
    distress like someone having her first baby,
the voice of Ms. Zion—
    as she gasps, she stretches out her hands:
"Oh, alas for me,
    because my life faints before my murderers!"

One time when my elder son and his family visited us in California, there was an earthquake of the kind that you can feel but that doesn't cause much damage, though it causes some unease if you're used to the stability of London. The television noted that there might be aftershocks but then unwisely pointed out that the shaking might alternatively be the pre-shock of a big earthquake. That was enough for my daughter-in-law, who declared that there was no way we were venturing on the freeway today. It was five years ago, and there has been no earthquake since, which is a bit worrying because small earthquakes act as a release mechanism. Perhaps destructive energy is building up, and any day the "big one" will come.

It will give you a foretaste of the desolation God will bring when he acts in judgment, says Jeremiah. Will the big one be God's judgment? Maybe it would be nice to think so; it could be interpreted as providing evidence that we live in a moral universe. Admittedly, we know history doesn't always work out that way, any more than individual lives do.

Jeremiah isn't working backward from an actual event to an explanation. Maybe he's working backward from a vision of something that's going to happen and looking for the causes that will explain it. Alongside the vision of an earthquake is the more literal vision of an army advancing on the country, which will mean that people need to take refuge in fortified cities—supremely Jerusalem itself—rather than staying in their unwalled villages. In another image, the situation resembles one where a predatory lion is attacking the village, threatening people's animals and children and their own lives. Or it resembles the scorching sirocco wind that withers crops. The invaders look like people guarding the fields from marauders—which hints at how they'll soon be treating the fields as their own. It won't be a total end; Yahweh's commitment to Jerusalem makes that impossible. But it will be a horrifying devastation.

So people should start grieving over this coming disaster. Their leadership won't know what to do about the situation. Audaciously, Jeremiah makes God responsible for promises of peace that prophets have falsely given in God's name, and he accuses God of deceiving the people. Jeremiah himself is overwhelmed at the horror of what he knows is coming. There's some poignancy about his declaration; the trouble is coming on the city that is "the daughter of my people." But he's also gripped by an awareness of the horrifying nature of Jerusalem's way of life, its willful refusal to let God be God and its extraordinary stupidity. The residents of a city such as Jerusalem would often have the sense to run away rather than wait for an invader to kill them; they can come back later when things have quieted down. Instead, Jerusalem is like a woman making herself look attractive, as if it could still win over the murderers who were once its allies but are now intent on being its destroyers.

If we knew enough about the pressures building up under the earth, we could perhaps predict when the big one will come. We couldn't avert it, but we could try to be ready. Here is where the metaphor breaks down. The point of Jeremiah's preaching is to get Jerusalem to clean up its act. While Yahweh has made **decisions** about Jerusalem's future and won't relent or turn from them, he stays infinitely flexible. If the people turn, Yahweh will respond. It's never too late to turn and find deliverance.

JEREMIAH 5:1–19

If You Can Find Anyone

1 Explore Jerusalem's streets, do look and get to
   know,
      seek in its squares, if you can find anyone,
   if there's someone exercising authority
      seeking truthfulness, and I'll pardon it.
2 Even when they say, "As Yahweh lives"—
      therefore they swear in falsehood.
3 Yahweh, do your eyes not look for truthfulness?—
      you struck them but they didn't feel sick.
   When you consumed them,
      they refused to accept constraint.
   They made their faces harder than rock;
      they refused to turn.
4 I myself said,
      those are only the poor who act foolishly,
   because they don't acknowledge the way of
      Yahweh,
      the authority of their God.
5 I'll go to the important people
      and speak with them,
   because those people acknowledge the way of
      Yahweh,
      the authority of their God.
   Yet those people had altogether broken the yoke,
      torn off the straps.

⁶ Therefore the lion from the forest has struck them,
 the wolf from the steppes destroys them,
the leopard is lying by their towns;
 anyone who goes out from them will be torn to
  pieces.
Because their rebellions are many,
 their turnings are multiple.
⁷ For what reason should I pardon you?—
 your children have abandoned me and sworn
  by no-gods.
I filled them and they committed adultery;
 they troop off to the whorehouse.
⁸ They were horses in heat, lusty;
 they were bellowing, each for his neighbor's wife.
⁹ Shall I not deal with these things
 (Yahweh's declaration),
or myself not bring redress
 against a nation that's like this one?

¹⁰ Go up among its vine-rows and destroy them,
 (but don't make an end).
Remove its branches,
 because those people don't belong to Yahweh.
¹¹ Because Israel's household and Judah's household
 have totally broken faith with me (Yahweh's
  declaration).
¹² They've acted deceptively toward Yahweh,
 and said, "He isn't the one.
Evil won't come upon us,
 we won't see sword or famine."
¹³ The prophets—they'll be but wind,
 the message isn't in them; so it will be done to
  them.
¹⁴ Therefore Yahweh, God of Armies, has said this:
 Because you people have said this thing,
here I am, putting my words in your mouth as fire
 [Jeremiah]:
 this people are the wood, and it will consume them.

¹⁵ Here I am, bringing a nation from afar against you,
  Israel's household (Yahweh's declaration).
It's an enduring nation,
  it's an age-old nation,
a nation whose tongue you don't know;
  you can't listen to what it speaks.
¹⁶ Its quiver is like an open grave;
  all of them are warriors.
¹⁷ It will consume your harvest and your food;
  it will consume your sons and daughters.
It will consume your sheep and cattle;
  it will consume your vine and fig.
It will destroy your fortified cities,
  in which you trust, with the sword.

¹⁸But even in those days (Yahweh's declaration) I won't make an end of you. ¹⁹And when they say, "On account of what did Yahweh our God do all these things to us?" you [Jeremiah] are to say to them, "As you abandoned me and served alien gods in your country, so you'll serve foreigners in a country that isn't yours."

Last night we watched a Woody Allen movie called *Match Point* about a man who commits adultery and murder but by pure luck gets away with it. The last shots of the movie make clear that he'll always live with the burden of what he's done. In this sense he will pay for his wrongdoing. But in terms of public justice the movie is dark. Wrongdoers get away with things. It's a converse of the way earthquakes don't necessarily happen to people who deserve them. The adulterer and murderer was someone from an ordinary background who had managed to get on well in life and then marry into a wealthy British family. Was this a significant factor in his downfall? An op-ed piece in today's newspaper discusses whether our leaders are more corrupt now that we are a meritocracy.

Jeremiah starts from some related questions. How prevalent is the turning away from **Yahweh** in Jerusalem? He imagines

Yahweh's inviting some research on the question. The findings will be of great consequence. A saying in the Talmud (Jewish teaching from the Church Fathers' time) declares, "If **Israel** repents for one day, forthwith the son of David will come. . . . If Israel would keep a single Sabbath in the proper way, forthwith the son of David will come." Here Yahweh similarly says that one person's living a truthful life will give him reason to pardon the whole community. One should not press the point; Jerusalem eventually fell notwithstanding the truthful life of someone such as Jeremiah. But the presence of some truthful people in a community can give God the excuse to show mercy to it. The trouble is, God knew there were no such people.

Is it just the poor? Jeremiah wonders. Given the earlier reference to whether people are truthful in the way they exercise **authority**, maybe he's thinking of the heads of families that have become poor; one can imagine the pressure they feel that leads them into dishonesty. My mother used to express surprise when prominent, important, intelligent people were convicted of some crime; she thought their intelligence would make them not act that way. In reality it just makes them cleverer as criminals. Jeremiah thinks like my mother, but he looks and finds that the truth is gloomier. Never trust people because of the positions they're in. We are still shocked when some politician or president or CEO gets convicted for wrongdoing. You'd think we had learned by now not to trust anyone.

The scholarly world sometimes follows Jeremiah in assuming that adherence to traditional religious practices such as those associated with the Canaanites constitutes "popular religion" in **Judah** as opposed to "official religion." The Old Testament also makes clear that Israel's religious leadership as much as its ordinary people were involved in such practices. His later reference to the prophets illustrates the point; there were many more prophets encouraging Judah in its spiritual adultery (and promising that the future would work out well) than prophets like Jeremiah urging reform (and warning

Its waves toss but don't overcome,
    they roar but don't pass over.
23 But this people has a mutinous, rebellious mind;
    they've mutinied and gone.
24 They haven't said to themselves,
    "We must be in awe of Yahweh our God,
who gives the rain, the early and later rain at its
       time,
    who keeps for us the weeks set for harvest."
25 It's your wayward acts that have diverted these
       things,
    your offenses that have withheld good things
       from you.
26 Because faithless people were found among my
       people,
    like someone who watches in a bird-catchers' hide.
They've set up a means of destruction
    so they may capture people,
27   like a basket full of birds.
So their houses are full of deceit;
    thereby they've grown great and rich.
28 They've become fat, become sleek;
    further, they've passed over evil words.
In decision making they haven't given decision for
       the orphan,
    so that they might be successful,
    and they haven't exercised authority for the
       needy.
29 Shall I not deal with these things (Yahweh's
       declaration),
    or myself not bring redress
    against a nation that's like this one?
30 A devastating thing, a horrifying thing
    has happened in the country.
31 The prophets prophesy falsely,
    the priests rule on the basis of their own power,
and my people like it so—
    but what will you do at the end of it?

35

^{6:1} Take refuge, Benjaminites,
    from Jerusalem's midst!
Sound the horn in Tekoa,
    raise the signal at Bet-hakkerem!
Because evil looms from the north,
    a great wounding.
² I'm destroying Ms. Zion, lovely and refined:
³   shepherds and their flocks will come to you.
They've pitched their tents against you all around,
    they graze each one his own.
⁴ "Prepare battle against it,
    we'll attack at noon!"
"Hey, the day is declining,
    the evening shadows get long.
⁵ Up, we'll attack at night
    and destroy its fortresses."
⁶ Because Yahweh Armies has said this:
Cut down the trees,
    build a ramp against Jerusalem.
It's the appointed city,
    in its midst all of it is oppression.
⁷ Like a well's flowing with its water,
    so it flows with its evil.
In it violence and destruction makes itself
      heard,
    sickness and injury are in front of me
      continually.
⁸ Be disciplined, Jerusalem,
    lest my soul withdraws from you,
lest I make you a devastation,
    a country not inhabited.
⁹ Yahweh Armies has said this:
Like a vine they are to glean and glean
    the remains of Israel.
Put your hand again
    like a grape-picker over the branches.
¹⁰ To whom shall I speak,
    and testify so they listen?

No, their ear is uncircumcised,
  they can't give heed.
No, Yahweh's message has become for them
  an insult; they don't delight in it.

I had an odd experience yesterday. My wife initiated a quite ordinary and reasonable conversation about moving around some of the furniture and repainting the walls and replacing the dining furniture that's falling apart. I responded abruptly to some of her comments (but then I'm capable of sounding brusque when I don't actually feel aggressive). Later I had a headache, and later still, an odd feeling of anxiety inside. In the middle of the night I realized what was happening. The stability of our home is part of my security in a way I hadn't realized. I can cope with changes in individual items, but suddenly the whole house seemed to be in the air. It took me a while to understand the dynamics of my reactions. The links between my ears and my inner being were not working properly.

Jeremiah has a striking image for that experience. It's as if people's ears are uncircumcised. He's spoken in chapter 4 of their minds needing to be circumcised. There's a blockage stopping things getting into the mind from the ears. Whether you picture the blockage located in the ears or the mind, it means that communication fails. It's a vivid image for stupidity. Often it's obvious what we should or shouldn't do, yet we often fail to live in light of the obvious. The Hebrew expression for "without sense" is more literally "without a mind" (even more literally "without a heart," because Hebrew commonly associates the heart with thinking, forming attitudes, and making **decision**s). It's as if people have perfectly good eyes but won't let themselves see things (as my mother used to say, "There's none so blind as people that *won't* see").

It's so obvious what they ought to see: that as the great creator, **Yahweh** deserves people's awe and obedience. In the

Western world, we'd need urging to take God into account rather than explain everything in sociological, scientific, or psychological terms. In **Israel**'s world, people knew that deities needed to be taken into account; the question was which deity to approach or how to think of God. In theory, people knew Yahweh was God and was the great creator as well as the Lord of Israel's history, but they combined belief in Yahweh with religious practices that conflicted with that belief. They had self-contradictory views of Yahweh. Jeremiah pushes them back to some basics. Yahweh is the great creator, the one who asserted **authority** in setting boundaries for the sea and thus ensuring that the land where people live was secure. Yahweh's authority is both solemn news and good news.

They need further to take into account that Yahweh's activity as creator involves more than setting the world on a secure foundation at the beginning (and then maybe absenting himself, treating subsequent history as one continuous Sabbath). Yahweh is involved with the providing for human needs in an ongoing way. For the harvest to work, you need rain in the right quantities at the right times. You need rain in the fall to soften the ground for plowing and sowing, and you need rain in winter and spring to make the crops grow. As creator, Yahweh had promised that the cycle would work out as part of his relationship with Israel, but it has failed to do so. On this occasion at least (Jeremiah says) it's not "just one of those things." It's a purposeful withholding by Yahweh in response to the people's withholding and their turning to other deities, as if Yahweh is saying, "OK, try that out, and see how it works for you." It's also a response to the way they've treated one another. It's one thing to catch animals and birds for food, but that's how they've treated one another.

The harvest's failure won't turn out to be their only problem. Jeremiah again imagines an army advancing from the north. God is commissioning this attacking army. It may attack by day or by night, but attack it will.

JEREMIAH 6:11–30

The Perilous Position of Prophet and Priest

¹¹ So Yahweh's wrath—I'm full of it,
    I'm weary of holding it in.
Pour it on the child in the street
    and on the group of youths, together.
Because both man and woman will be captured,
    the elder with the one advanced in years.
¹² Their houses will pass to other people,
    fields and wives together.
Because I shall extend my hand
    against the residents of the country
    (Yahweh's declaration).
¹³ Because from their smallest to their greatest,
    every one of them is greedy for loot.
Prophet and priest alike,
    every one of them is acting falsely.
¹⁴ They've healed my people's wound too easily,
    saying, "Things are well, they're well,"
    when they're not well.
¹⁵ They've been shameful, because they've committed
      an outrage;
    they neither manifest any shame
    nor do they know how to be disgraced.
Therefore they'll fall among the people who fall;
    at the time when I deal with them, they'll
      collapse
    (Yahweh has said).
¹⁶ Yahweh said this:
Stand by the roads, and look,
    ask about the old paths.
Which is the road to good things?—
    walk on it, and find peacefulness for yourselves.
But they said, "We won't walk there,"
¹⁷   so I raised up lookouts for you:
"Pay heed to the sound of the horn,"
    but they said, "We won't pay heed."

¹⁸ Therefore listen, you nations,
and acknowledge, you assembly, what will be
against them.
¹⁹ Listen, earth:
here am I.
I'm going to bring evil on this people,
the fruit of their intentions.
Because they haven't paid heed to my words,
and my teaching—they've rejected it.
²⁰ What use to me is incense that comes from Sheba,
or fine cane from a far-off country?
Your burnt offerings don't find favor,
your sacrifices aren't pleasing with me.
²¹ Therefore Yahweh has said this:
Here am I; I'm going to set obstructions for this
people;
they'll collapse because of them.
Parents and children together,
neighbor and friend—they'll perish.
²² Yahweh has said this:
There, a people is going to come from a northern
country,
a great nation will arise from earth's remotest parts.
²³ They take hold of bow and javelin;
violent it is, they don't have compassion.
Their sound is like the sea that roars,
they ride on horses.
It's deployed like a man for battle,
against you, Ms. Zion.
²⁴ "We've heard news of them, our hands fail,
pain has taken hold of us, anguish like a woman
giving birth.
²⁵ Don't go out into the fields, don't walk by the roads,
because the enemy has a sword, terror is all around."
²⁶ My dear people, put on sackcloth, roll in the dust,
make for yourself the mourning for an only child,
bitter lament,
because suddenly the destroyer will come upon us.

40

> ²⁷ I've made you an assayer among my people,
>   a refiner, so that you may assay their ways.
> ²⁸ All of them are the most mutinous people,
>   people who live by slander,
> bronze and iron,
>   all of them are people who destroy.
> ²⁹ The bellows are scorched by fire,
>   the lead has come to an end.
> In vain the smelter smelted,
>   and the evil ones were not separated out.
> ³⁰ Reject silver, people have called them,
>   because Yahweh has rejected them.

Today we had a bumper crop of birthdays to celebrate at church; I was tempted to ask people to stand up if they were not having a birthday this week. As a wondrous coincidence, the Gospel reading was the story of a birthday party. Unfortunately it was Herod's birthday party, when his stepdaughter Salome gets him to present the head of John the baptizer to her. John was a prophet and had rebuked Herod for wresting Salome's mother from her previous husband, his brother. You may pay with your life for being a prophet, as Jesus later did.

The prophets and priests Jeremiah speaks of were in no such danger. Jeremiah wasn't the normal sort of prophet you'd meet in **Judah**; a Jeremiah or a John the baptizer was the exception, not the rule. Many prophets were more like pastors, the sort of people you'd consult in the temple when you needed advice or guidance, or who'd minister to you when you came there to pray about an illness or some other form of trouble. And you'd likely offer them something for their ministry. While the prophet Micah speaks scathingly about prophets who give you guidance in return for money (see Micah 3:11), one can hardly insist that in principle prophets should not be supported financially for their ministry. Likewise priests were supported through the people's offerings; the **Torah** allocated a share of them for priests and their families.

But once you're financially dependent on the people you minister to, you're under huge pressure to tell people what they want to hear. Who's going to pay a prophet for telling them that they deserve to be sick and need to go home and repent? It was action of that kind that cost John the baptizer his life.

Further, being a prophet or priest puts you into a position of power and prestige, and it's easy to enjoy that position and be more concerned for exercising your power than for serving God or serving people. Jeremiah spoke earlier of prophets' prophesying falsely and priests' ruling on the basis of their own power, and he associates prophet and priest with the same greed for loot that characterizes the community as a whole. They assure people that things are going to be fine when it's not so. They ought to get people to acknowledge the shamefulness of their lives and thus escape the trouble that will come; then things will be fine. Instead they assimilate to the people, and they'll share in their fate.

There's thus a collusion between the community's spiritual leaders and the community as a whole. "My people like it so," **Yahweh** has already noted. In the short term, the arrangement works. But (Yahweh goes on to ask), "What will they do at the end of it?" The words make me think of the mortgage fiasco of the 2000s. With hindsight it was obvious that the bubble must eventually burst, but the watchdogs failed to face the fact and press the community to face it. We were all greedy for loot, stupid people, senseless people who willfully avoided using our brains, eyes, and ears. So everything collapsed.

The equivalent experience for Judah has involved a collapse of the cycle of rain, growth, and harvest, and it will involve invasion and defeat. Jeremiah has come to share Yahweh's view of his people. He's appalled at what he sees throughout the community and has come to share Yahweh's conviction that wrath must fall on the community and to see that the decades and centuries of deferring judgment must come to an end. And when the moment comes, there'll be no one who can escape—parents and children, young and old, husbands and wives, important people and ordinary people. Everybody is affected by the way they've made the accumulation of loot at other people's expense the cornerstone of their life. They may offer costly, sacrificial worship (unlike our worship at church today, which is free), but this worship simply irritates Yahweh. While the worship was prescribed by Yahweh's **teaching**, the "old ways" that this teaching prescribed covered more than worship. While getting people to live together on the right basis doesn't please Yahweh when it's unaccompanied by costly worship, costly worship unaccompanied by living together on the right basis is no more pleasing.

JEREMIAH 7:1–20

The Prophet Who's Forbidden to Pray (1)

[1]The message that came to Jeremiah from Yahweh: [2]Stand in the gate of Yahweh's house and proclaim this message there. You're to say, Listen to Yahweh's message, all of Judah who are coming through these gates to bow down to Yahweh. [3]Yahweh Armies, Israel's God, has said this: Make your ways and your deeds good, and I'll let you dwell in this place. [4]Don't trust for yourselves in words of falsehood, "These [buildings] are Yahweh's palace, Yahweh's palace, Yahweh's palace." [5]Rather, make your ways and your deeds truly good. If you really make [right] decisions between an individual and his neighbor, [6]don't exploit alien, orphan, and widow, don't shed an innocent person's blood in this place, and don't follow other gods with evil results for yourselves, [7]I'll let you dwell in this place, in the country that I gave to your ancestors from of old, forever. [8]There: you're trusting for yourselves in words of falsehood that won't achieve anything. [9]Is there stealing, murder, adultery, swearing falsely, and burning sacrifices to the Master, and following other gods that you didn't acknowledge, [10]and you come and stand in front of me in this house over which my name has been proclaimed and say "We are rescued"—so

as to do all these outrages? [11]Has it become a cave for thugs in your eyes, this house over which my name has been proclaimed? Actually I—yes, I've been looking (Yahweh's declaration).
[12]Because you can go to my place that was at Shiloh where I let my name dwell before, and look at what I did to it in the face of my people Israel's evil. [13]So now because of your doing all these things (Yahweh's declaration), and I've spoken to you, speaking urgently, but you haven't listened, and I've summoned you but you haven't responded, [14]I'll do to the house over which my name is proclaimed, in which you're trusting, the place that I gave to you and your ancestors, as I did to Shiloh. [15]I'll throw you out from my presence as I threw your brothers out, Ephraim's entire offspring.
[16]You, don't plead for this people, don't lift up a cry or plea for them, don't intercede with me, because I'm not listening to you. [17]Aren't you seeing what they're doing in Judah's cities and in Jerusalem's streets? [18]The sons are collecting wood, the fathers are lighting the fire, and the women are kneading the dough, to make loaves for the Queen of Heaven and pour libations to other gods, to provoke me. [19]Is it me they're provoking (Yahweh's declaration)? Is it not themselves, to bring shame on their faces? [20]Therefore (the Lord Yahweh has said this): Now. My anger, my fury is going to pour out on this place, on human beings, on animals, on the trees in the countryside, and on the fruit of the earth. It will burn and not go out.

My first Old Testament mentor once told us about his first visit to the new cathedral in Coventry in the center of England. The old cathedral, like much of the city, was devastated by bombing in the Second World War. The new cathedral is the only one in Britain built from scratch over nearly a century. It stands next to the ruins of its predecessor. My mentor told us how he went up to the lectern and found to his disbelief that its Bible was open at Jeremiah's warning: as I did to that place, so I'll do to this one.

The sanctuary at Shiloh, north of Jerusalem in the territory of **Ephraim**, had once been an important one. It was where

Hannah had prayed for a son and where the prophet Samuel had been based. By Jeremiah's day it was evidently a ruin, though for **Judah** its importance had been eclipsed by that of Jerusalem itself. Yet Jerusalem could go the same way if its people continue to live the way Ephraim lived and were invaded by the **Assyrians.**

Jeremiah delivers his message at the temple in Jerusalem. The temple complex wasn't as large as the enclosure around the Dome of the Rock today, but it was similar in function in that its courtyards provided a natural meeting space. As is the case in the context of Jesus' ministry, it's a natural destination for a preacher who wants to be heard, though also a dangerous one because the authorities will also be there. Hebrew has no technical word for "temple"; it uses the ordinary word for a house or a palace. The temple is the "house" where **Yahweh** lives, but as a house fit for a heavenly King, it can also be called a palace. People think that the presence of Yahweh's palace in Jerusalem guarantees the city's security. What king is going to let his palace be destroyed, let alone take an initiative to destroy it? The heavenly king of **Israel**, is the answer.

Even more shocking is the heavenly king's own instruction to Jeremiah not to plead for a holding back from this action. A prophet mediates between king and people. He brings the king's message to the people, but he also brings the people's words to the king. Being a prophet meant being admitted to the king's cabinet, the body in heaven that makes **decision**s about what should happen on earth and how decisions should be implemented. So Jeremiah is in a position to transmit information on the cabinet's decisions but also to represent the people's interests in the cabinet meetings. It's a useful image for understanding what we're doing when we pray. We're not merely in a one-on-one conversation with God but taking part in a meeting that God is chairing. The image helps us see why prayer sometimes works and sometimes doesn't: the meeting will sometimes be able to heed our urgings but sometimes will have reason to make a different decision from the one we want. But if we don't speak, then the decision we want certainly won't get made.

Jeremiah is told not to speak. The president of the cabinet has heard enough about the life of the people he represents. There's no basis or reason for any more talk about giving them more time. This doesn't mean Jeremiah has to agree and shut up. Maybe he'll still insist on representing his people. We don't know. That consideration points to why this story is unfolding as it is. Bringing the people this frightening news that Yahweh has told Jeremiah not to pray for them anymore constitutes another attempt to get through their thick skulls. "Can't you see: your attitude is so horrifying, I can't even pray for you anymore. *Now* will you turn back to Yahweh?"

Jeremiah goes on to tell us more specifically the way they were turning away. We know from archeological discoveries that as well as making images of Yahweh, people in Israel assumed that Yahweh had a consort. Among the Canaanites and the Assyrians the Queen of Heaven was the wife of a top god. People in Judah thought of Yahweh's consort the same way. Proper belief in Yahweh had been laid over that traditional Canaanite belief but had never obliterated it. Further, a century of Assyrian domination of Judah had put political and cultural pressure on Judah, which had assimilated to the assumptions of its imperial overlords. Only in the **Second Temple** period in light of the new covenant of which Jeremiah 31 speaks will Judah really come to worship Yahweh alone and give up making images. Meanwhile (to overstate the point) they aren't really offending Yahweh. They're hurting themselves.

JEREMIAH 7:21–8:9

The Misleading Scholars

[21]Yahweh Armies, Israel's God, has said this: Add your burnt offerings to your sacrifices, eat meat. [22]Because I didn't speak

46

with your ancestors or command them on the day I brought them out of the country of Egypt regarding matters concerning burnt offering and sacrifice. [23]Rather I commanded them this message: "Listen to my voice, and I'll be God for you and you'll be a people for me; walk in every way that I command you so that it may go well for you." [24]But they didn't listen, they didn't incline their ear, they walked by their counsels, by the determination of their evil mind. They went back, not forward, [25]from the day that I brought your ancestors out from the country of Egypt until this day. I sent them all my servants the prophets, sending daily and urgently, [26]but they didn't listen to me, they didn't incline their ear, they stiffened their neck; they acted more evilly than their ancestors.

[27]You're to speak to them all these things, but they won't listen to you. You're to summon them but they won't respond to you. [28]You're to say to them: This is the nation that hasn't listened to the voice of Yahweh its God. They haven't accepted discipline. Truthfulness has perished, cut itself off from their mouth.

[29] Shave your hair and throw it away,
       take up a lament on the bare places.
   Because Yahweh has rejected and discarded
       the generation with which he's furious.

[30]Because the Judahites have done evil in my eyes (Yahweh's declaration). They've set up their abominations in the house over which my name was proclaimed, so as to defile it. [31]They've built the shrines at Tophet, in the Ben-hinnom Canyon, to burn their sons and daughters in fire, which I didn't command; it didn't come into my mind. [32]Therefore, now, days are coming (Yahweh's declaration) when people will no longer talk about "Tophet and the Ben-hinnom Canyon" but rather "Slaughter Canyon." They'll bury in Tophet because there's no [other] place. [33]This people's carcasses will be food for the birds of the heavens and the animals of the land, with no one disturbing them. [34]I'll silence from Judah's cities and Jerusalem's streets the sound of rejoicing, of celebration, the voice of groom and bride. Because the country will become a desolation.

8:1At that time (Yahweh's declaration) people will take out the bones of Judah's kings, its officials, the priests, the prophets, and Jerusalem's residents from their graves, 2and expose them to the sun, the moon, and all the army of the heavens that they gave themselves to and served and followed and inquired of and bowed down to. They won't be gathered up and buried; they'll become dung on the surface of the ground. 3Death will be preferable to life for all the remains that remain of this evil family in all the remaining places where I'll drive them (a declaration of Yahweh Armies).

4   You're to say to them, Yahweh has said this:
     When people fall, do they not get up—
       if they turn, do they not turn [back]?
5   Why is this people turning,
       Jerusalem, with a permanent turning?
     They've held onto deceit,
       they've refused to turn [back].
6   I have paid heed and listened;
       they don't speak dependably.
     There's no one relenting of his evil,
       saying, "What have I done?"
     In its entirety it has turned, in their alacrity,
       like horses flooding into battle.
7   Even the stork in the heavens—
       it acknowledges its set times.
     The dove, the swift, and the crane—
       they keep the time for their coming.
     But my people—it doesn't acknowledge
       Yahweh's decision.
8   How can you say, "We are experts,
       Yahweh's teaching is with us"?
     Actually—there, the false pen of the scholars
       has made it into falsehood.
9   The experts have been shamed,
       they've shattered and been captured.
     There—they've rejected Yahweh's message;
       what expertise do they have?

Yesterday a student asked me whether a particular book would be taken seriously by the wide majority of Old Testament scholars. The response I forgot to make was that whatever is the consensus of scholars today won't be the consensus in a decade's time. Whatever is the latest theory today will be old hat in a decade. The idea that there's progress in our understanding is a myth. It's therefore unwise to base your thinking on the latest scholarship because you can be sure that the next decade's latest scholarship will be convinced that it was wrong. So writing scholarly books is a pointless exercise. Excuse me while I commit suicide.

At least it's not a new problem. In Jeremiah's day there were people who were experts in **Yahweh**'s **teaching**, in the **Torah**. We don't know what form the Torah would have had in Jeremiah's day, but the usual scholarly view is that the book of Deuteronomy is the part that especially links with his time. The usual scholarly view! There I go again! But let's suppose that this view is correct. Much or most of the rest of the material in the Torah would also be in existence. It wouldn't be surprising if there was also other teaching material in circulation, material that never made it into the Torah (as there were other Gospels in circulation in the early centuries of the church in addition to the four that came to be in the New Testament). Some of that material might be edifying and useful; it just never became part of the Torah. But some of it was misleading. Jeremiah's critique of the community and its leadership points to ways it was misleading. The ordinary people who accepted the religious practices that Jeremiah condemns were encouraged by experts. It's not impossible to provide semiplausible support for worshiping more than one god or seeking to make contact with your dead family members or offering human beings as a sacrifice. We scholars are experts at providing semiplausible rationales for things we want to support. Our false pen can turn Yahweh's teaching into falsehood. The moral is, never trust scholars just because they're scholars.

Don't trust priests either (as both priest and scholar, I'm in deep trouble in this section of Jeremiah). Priests oversee worship, and they encourage people to take worship seriously. They are of course right to do so. But the beginning of Jeremiah 7 has indicated how in **Israel** two things were wrong with people's worship. It wasn't that they were insincere in the sense that they didn't mean what they said and sang; their worship came from the heart. One problem lay in the nature of the worship, such as worshiping other gods and sacrificing people, the kind of practices referred to in connection with Tophet and the Ben-hinnom Canyon below Jerusalem. The priests must have facilitated the horrifying acts of worship in the temple to which Jeremiah refers. The other problem lay in the mismatch between worship and everyday life. People could combine sacrificial worship with taking advantage of people such as widows and orphans.

Jeremiah puts them in their place by referring them back to the Torah. When they arrived at Sinai after leaving Egypt, what did Yahweh first talk to them about? You can check out the answer in Exodus 19–20. It wasn't about offering sacrifices. Jeremiah refers to two main sacrifices: the whole burnt offering that all went up in smoke to Yahweh and the sacrifice that the people also ate part of so that it was an act of fellowship. Given your failure in those other aspects of a relationship with me, Yahweh says, you can eat the burnt offerings as well as those other sacrifices for all I care.

The consequence of their actions will be that Tophet will become a place resonant of death in a new sense—not the slaughter and consequent burning of people who are sacrificed but the slaughter and burial (or unburied exposure) of the countless Jerusalemites who'll lose their lives when Yahweh lets Jerusalem fall. Eventually people who recognize the wickedness of Jerusalem's worship will exhume the bodies of **Judah**'s leaders and people who meanwhile escaped this fate and thought they could rest in peace. Even death doesn't mean escaping exposure and shame. Likewise people who escape death by being taken off into **exile** will find it's only a living death.

Why, then, persist in turning away? Turn back!

JEREMIAH 8:10–9:6

Does God Really Punish?

¹⁰ Therefore I'll give their wives to other men,
  their fields to [different] possessors.
Because from small to great,
  every one of them is greedy for loot.
Prophet and priest alike,
  every one of them is acting falsely.
¹¹ They've healed my dear people's wound too easily,
  saying, "Things are well, they're well,"
  when they're not well.
¹² They've been shameful, because they've committed
    an outrage;
  they neither manifest any shame
  nor do they know how to be disgraced.
Therefore they'll fall among the people who fall;
  at the time when I deal with them, they'll collapse
  (Yahweh has said).
¹³ Gathering up—I'll destroy them (Yahweh's
    declaration):
  there'll be no grapes on the vine,
  no figs on the fig tree.
The leaves will wither,
  and what I have given them will pass away.

¹⁴ Why are we staying?—gather up,
  we'll come into the fortified cities and perish
    there.
Because Yahweh our God is letting us perish
  and drink poisoned water,
  because we've offended against Yahweh,

51

15   hoping for things to go well but there was nothing
        good,
        for a time of healing but there—terror.

16   From Dan its horses' snort has been heard:
        at the sound of its steeds' neighing
        the entire country has shaken.
    They came and devoured the country and what
        fills it,
        the city and the people who live in it.

17   "Because here I am, sending snakes against you,
        vipers that there's no charming, they'll bite you"
        (Yahweh's declaration).

18   My simper is on account of my groan,
        within me my spirit is sick.

19   There is the sound of my dear people's cry for help
        from the country far and wide:
    "Is Yahweh not in Zion,
        or is its King not in it?"
    "Why did they provoke me with their images,
        with empty foreign beings?"

20   Harvest has passed, summer is gone,
        but we ourselves haven't found deliverance.

21   Because of my dear people's wounding I'm broken,
        I mourn, devastation has taken hold of me.

22   Is there no ointment in Gilead,
        or is there no healer there?
    Because why has my dear people's restoration
        not developed?

9:1   If only my head were water,
        my eye a fountain of tears.
    I'd weep day and night
        for the slain among my poor people.

2   If only I could have a travelers' lodge in the
        wilderness,
        and abandon my people, go from them,
    because all of them are adulterers,
        a pack of people breaking faith.

³ They've bent their tongue, their bow has been
falsehood;
it's not in the cause of truthfulness that they've
been strong in the country.
Because they've proceeded from evil to evil,
and not acknowledged me (Yahweh's declaration).
⁴ Watch, each person, his neighbor;
don't trust any brother.
Because every brother is totally crooked,
and every neighbor goes about as a slanderer.
⁵ Each person cheats his neighbor;
they don't speak the truth.
They've taught their tongue false speech;
they've got tired being wayward.
⁶ You've dwelt in the midst of deceit;
in deceit they've refused to acknowledge me
(Yahweh's declaration).

At dinner last night, one of our friends was troubled by the way the Old Testament speaks of God's exercising violent judgment by means of **Israel**. I tried my usual ploy of asking whether she was as troubled by Jesus' speaking of millions of people being thrown into outer darkness where there'll be weeping and gnashing of teeth. She wondered if he meant that people would pay the price for their own decisions rather than God's actively sending them to hell. Her husband wondered if it was a strong way of urging people to repent. Someone else at the dinner party thought God was mainly concerned with purifying us.

I think Jeremiah would affirm all these four ways of seeing God's words. They're a warning of punishment, a warning of where people's acts may lead them, a warning designed to elicit change and a declaration about chastisement, and a warning that even God's acts to save us may be painful. One of Jeremiah's distinctive characteristics as a prophet is the way he identifies with God and with Israel. Indeed, it can be difficult to tell whether he's talking about his own feelings or about God's feelings. Jeremiah is filled with a sense of wrath at the way his people have broken faith with God; he and God both want that wrath to be poured out on the people. Yet Jeremiah is also filled with brokenness, desolation, and tears at what he sees in the people and what he knows is in store for them. Perhaps he's speaking of **Yahweh**'s weeping as well as his own. Whether or not this is so, his prophecies have made clear Yahweh's sorrow at the way his "wife" has abandoned him, the fountain of living water, and made herself rely on second-rate and uncertain water supplies.

The warnings Jeremiah issues on Yahweh's behalf are designed to break through people's stupidity to get them to turn back to Yahweh. The declaration that the men will see their wives taken by other men doesn't take into account what this action will mean for the wives. To Western readers it will seem less important that the men will also have their land taken over, but the Scriptures themselves would also see this event as horrifying because the gift of the land to Israel was key to the fulfillment of God's purpose for the world. The warnings are designed to avoid these predictable results of enemy invasion and victory, but warnings have teeth only if the person issuing them is prepared to implement the threats.

The attempt to break through continues in the imaginary conversation occupying the third paragraph. Reporting the conversation is another way of trying to get through to people (though in the context of the book, it explains why catastrophe became inevitable). Jeremiah's own spirit is sick. His people are distraught and crying out. Given that summer and harvest mark the end of the year, the saying about them resembles the gloomy comment we might make at the end of a year when nothing seems to have gone right or we have accomplished nothing. When people wonder why Yahweh doesn't rescue them, they speak as if he hasn't made the reason clear. He does so again in his question "Why?" The question about medicine has similar implications. It, too, may be a popular saying; it refers to a healing ointment from a tree in the area east of the Jordan. Its implication is that there's treatment available (that is, in Yahweh) but people won't avail themselves of it.

Jeremiah's anguish also reflects his awareness that the **Judahites** cannot be forced to turn back. They seem hell-bent on jumping over the cliff; he talks about their falling and collapsing, not just about being pushed. Their experience of catastrophe will be something they bring on themselves, yet it will also be something God brings on them. God plans to "send" them trouble, to "deal with" them. The Hebrew verb for "deal with" is traditionally translated "visit"; in effect it means "punish," so it has the chilling overtones of the idea that people will receive a "visit" from the mafia intent on dealing with a matter. But our use of words such as *punishment* or *judgment* in English easily gives a misleading impression of the significance of the Old Testament's words. In the Old Testament, *punish* relates more to the way a parent treats a child or a teacher treats a pupil than the way a court treats a criminal. It indeed suggests a discipline designed to reform and transform.

JEREMIAH 9:7–26

The Real Circumcision

> 7 Therefore Yahweh Armies has said this:
> Here am I; I'm going to smelt them, test them,
>   because how [else] can I act on account of my
>   dear people?
> 8 Their tongue is a sharpened arrow,
>   it has spoken deceit.
> With his mouth someone speaks with his neighbor
>   of how things will go well,
>   but in his inner self he lays his ambush.
> 9 For these things shall I not deal with them
>   (Yahweh's declaration)?

Or on a nation that's like this
    will I myself not take redress?
10 For the mountains I take up weeping and wailing,
    and for the wilderness pastures a lament.
Because they're laid waste, so that no one is passing
    through,
    and people don't hear the sound of cattle.
Both the birds of the heavens and the animals—
    they have fled; they've gone.
11 I shall make Jerusalem into heaps of rubble,
    the dwelling of jackals.
Judah's cities I'll make into a devastation,
    with no resident.

12 Who is the wise man who understands this,
    to whom has Yahweh's mouth spoken so that he
    can tell of it?
Why has the country perished,
    become wasted like a wilderness, with no one
    passing through?

13Yahweh said: Because they abandoned my teaching, which I put in front of them. They didn't listen to my voice, and they didn't walk by it. 14They followed the determination of their minds and followed the Masters, as their ancestors taught them. 15Therefore Yahweh Armies, Israel's God, has said this: Here am I; I'm going to feed this people bitter plants and make them drink poisoned water. 16I shall scatter them among the nations that they and their ancestors haven't known. I shall send off the sword after them until I have finished them off.

17 Yahweh Armies has said this:
Think, and summon the lamenting women so that
    they may come,
    send for the expert women so that they may come.
18 They must hurry and raise a wailing over us,
    so our eyes may run with tears,
    our pupils flow with water.

An odd news item of the past week has been a German court's decision that circumcision for religious reasons is illegal because it amounts to bodily injury, an assault on a boy's physical integrity. Protesters have asserted that banning circumcision amounts to an affront to basic religious and human rights. Controversy of this kind has erupted in several countries over the past decade. It sometimes surprises Christians to discover that circumcision wasn't a practice distinctive to **Israel**, but Israelites knew that other people observed the practice and sometimes speak with disdain of uncivilized people such as the **Philistines** who don't practice circumcision. It's a custom like sacrifice that **Yahweh** encourages Israel to continue observing, but with new meaning as a sign of belonging to Yahweh.

Circumcision also parallels sacrifice (and baptism) in having little significance if it is merely an outward rite. A major segment of the book of Jeremiah is coming to an end, and the last verses of the present section make this point as a kind of conclusion or reflection on what we've read so far. Circumcision is a vital sign of belonging to Israel (applied only to males, of course, though women were just as much a part of Israel). If males are not circumcised, they are cut off from the covenant people. When a non-Israelite family joins the people of Yahweh, its men have to be circumcised; men who are not circumcised cannot take part in the Passover festival. So it's a shock tactic for Jeremiah to lump his own people in with other peoples in his list of those who practice circumcision: Egypt, **Judah**, Edom, Ammon, Moab, and the desert peoples who have their own weird observances—weird to a Judahite, but is there an implication that shaving the forehead or temples is just another cutting rite like circumcision? One can hear the hiss of disgusted protest from people who hear the prophecy. There may be a political point behind the prophecy, if these are peoples united against the uncircumcised **Babylonians**. The sign of the covenant has become a mere political tag for Judah.

Jeremiah has another observation to make. These other peoples are circumcised but only outwardly, and the same applies to Judah. In making this point, Jeremiah moves from speaking of Judah, the nation's political designation in the context of that list, to its theological designation as Israel. Whereas the Israelite household was physically circumcised, it wasn't circumcised in spirit, in heart, in the inner person. Physical circumcision stands for the submission of one vital part of a man to God, the cutting down to size of a vital part of him. But the whole person of both men and women needs to be cut down to size and submitted to God (the image makes one wonder whether this inner circumcision is likely to be as painful and significant—as well as queasy making—as the physical act). That inner cutting down needs to happen so that it also happens in the people's life as a whole. It hasn't happened.

In substance this comment then links with the preceding paragraph. The natural human instinct is to be proud of one's expertise or insight, one's physical strength, or one's wealth and material resources. One could call this instinct "spiritual uncircumcision." Spiritual circumcision manifests itself in an acknowledgment of Yahweh, which means submitting to Yahweh, though the point that Jeremiah notes is that the God whom people acknowledge is the one characterized by commitment and the **faithful** exercise of **authority**. Those are characteristics you can trust, though also ones you have to emulate, so that failure to do so issues in the kind of judgment the rest of the section again envisages.

JEREMIAH 10:1–25

On Facing Reality

[1]Listen to the message that Yahweh has spoken to you, Israel's household. [2]Yahweh has said this:

> Don't learn the nations' way;
>   don't shatter at signs in the heavens.

Because the nations may shatter at those,

    because the nations' laws are emptiness.

Because someone cuts a tree from the forest,

    the work of a craftsman's hands, with an axe.

4 With silver and gold he beautifies it,

    with nails and hammers he strengthens it so it
      doesn't wobble.

5 They're like a scarecrow in a melon patch;

    they don't speak.

They're carried, carried, because they don't walk;

    don't be in awe of them.

Because they don't do evil,

    nor is doing good in them.

6 There is none like you, Yahweh;

    you are great and your name is great, with power.

7 Who would not be in awe of you, King of the
      nations,

    because it's appropriate to you.

Because among all the nations' experts

    and in all their dominion there's none like you.

8 As one, they're dense, stupid;

    the discipline of empty beings is wood.

9 Beaten silver is brought from Tarshish,

    gold from Uphaz,

a craftsman's work, a goldsmith's hands,

    their clothing blue and purple,

    the work of experts, all of them.

10 But Yahweh is the true God,

    the living God, the everlasting King.

At his wrath, earth shakes;

    nations cannot endure his rage.

11 [Yahweh says,] You're to speak in this way to them:

    The gods that didn't make the heavens and the
      earth

    will perish from the earth and from under the
      heavens.

¹² One who made the earth by his might,
    established the world by his expertise,
    by his understanding stretched out the heavens:
¹³ at his giving voice,
    there was a roaring of the waters in the heavens.
He brought up clouds from the end of the earth,
    he made lightning for the rain,
    he brought out wind from his storehouses.
¹⁴ Every human being proves dense, without
        knowledge;
    every goldsmith is put to shame by the image,
because his figure is a falsehood,
    and there's no breath in them.
¹⁵ They're emptiness, a work for mockery;
    at the time they're dealt with, they'll perish.
¹⁶ Not like these is the one who belongs to Jacob,
    because he's the former of everything.
Israel is the clan he possesses;
    Yahweh Armies is his name.

¹⁷Gather up your baggage from the country, [Jerusalem] you who dwell under siege. ¹⁸Because Yahweh has said this: Here am I; I'm going to fling away the people who dwell in the country at this moment. I'll pressure them so that they experience it.

¹⁹ Oh, alas for me, on account of my wound,
    my injury is sickening,
whereas myself I had said,
    "This is only an illness, and I shall bear it."
²⁰ My tent is destroyed,
    all my tent cords have broken.
My children have gone out from me, there are none
        of them,
    none to spread my tent again
    or hang out my tent cloths.
²¹ Because the shepherds are stupid,
    they haven't inquired of Yahweh.

Therefore they haven't succeeded,
    all their flock has scattered.
22 A sound, news—there, it's coming,
    a great commotion from a northern country,
to make Judah's cities a devastation,
    the dwelling of jackals.
23 I acknowledge, Yahweh,
    that an individual's road doesn't belong to him;
it doesn't belong to a person
    to direct his step as he walks.
24 Discipline me, Yahweh, only with judgment,
    not in your anger, so you don't make me small.
25 Pour your wrath
    on the nations that haven't acknowledged you,
    on the families that haven't proclaimed in
      your name.
Because they've devoured Jacob,
    devoured him and finished him off,
    and devastated his abode.

We were doing our monthly stint serving dinner at a homeless shelter last night, and I got to talk to one of the residents. She'd had a successful and lucrative career in the movie business and lived in a house in Malibu. Her husband had died, and she'd become lonely and married a man she met through work who had a vision for setting up a movie company, but the recession meant the business never took off. Indeed it soaked up all her assets as well as his; and as sometimes happens in such circumstances, tensions developed in the marriage, and eventually she felt she had no alternative but to drive away from their house with hardly anything more than she could put into her car. She feels so stupid for making the bad decisions that caused her life to fall apart.

It doesn't belong to an individual to direct his or her steps. It's a distressing admission, yet in another way a hopeful one. The woman I'd been talking to had been living in an unreal world. At one stage maybe she was pardonably deceived, but eventually she was naturally failing to face facts. To own that she wasn't in control of her life was a necessary stage to regaining some control, though paradoxically it also meant surrendering the claim to be in control or the aim of being in control. It meant admitting that God was in control and letting God be in control. In this passage it's a personified Jerusalem that Jeremiah speaks for. At this point Jerusalem is not actually making the admission; Jeremiah is putting the admission on its lips as the one it needs to make, the insight he wants it to reach. When you've acknowledged reality, you can make progress by opening yourself to help.

There's another form of stupidity that Jeremiah attributes to Jerusalem. Previous chapters have spoken much about the deities alongside **Yahweh** that people worshiped and the forms of worship in which they're involved that used images of the gods. In English we often speak of worshiping "idols," but there's an ambiguity to that word. It suggests both deities other than Yahweh and the statues that people made in order to represent these deities (or to represent Yahweh). Here Jeremiah focuses on the images.

In theory people didn't worship images. They knew that the deities that the images represented were much bigger and more transcendent than an image would suggest. But to the prophets, people who worship by means of images can't have it both ways. Either the image could represent the deity— in which case you can infer the nature of the deity from the nature of the image. Or the image couldn't represent the deity—in which case what is the point in having an image? Either way, the image's nature and the way it's made give the game away. It's made by a craftsman from wood and metal and given nice robes. Then the object the craftsman makes has to be propped up, can't speak or move, and has to be carried. There's no reason to be in awe of it or afraid of it (Jeremiah's verb could be read positively or negatively. It can't do anything, good or **evil**—it can't bring you blessing, and neither can it bring you trouble). "What do these facts tell you about the deity it represents?" Jeremiah asks.

Contrast these facts with the facts about Yahweh as the creator of the heavens and the earth. The person who worshiped by means of an image might believe that the deity it represented was the creator of the heavens and the earth, but that idea didn't makes sense. A creator can't be represented by an image. Yahweh can't be represented by an image, which gives you a clue regarding the identity of the real God, who had made himself known to **Israel**. *There* is a God to be in awe of.

So Jerusalem needs to take that reality seriously. Otherwise it will be compelled to heed the instructions Jeremiah gives: that it must pack its bags because Yahweh is throwing it out (that is, throwing its people out) of its homeland. The city had recognized (that is, its people had recognized) that it was in trouble, but it hadn't recognized how deep the trouble was. Jeremiah invites it to project itself forward to the time when it cannot avoid acknowledging it. For people reading Jeremiah in the **exile**, projection has become reality, but at least the recognition of reality provides a platform for moving forward. It's said that the first responsibility of a leader is to define reality.

The closing verses indicate how in your pain you don't have to censor your thinking and feeling before you say things to God. The verses are similar to part of Psalm 79. Maybe the preacher quotes the prayer book or hymnbook, or maybe the prayer book or hymnbook quotes the preacher.

JEREMIAH 11:1–17

No Shrugging of God's Shoulders

[1]The message that came to Jeremiah from Yahweh saying:
[2]Listen to the words in this covenant. So you're to speak them

to Judah's people and Jerusalem's residents, [3]and say to them, Yahweh, Israel's God, has said this: The person is cursed who doesn't listen to the words in this covenant [4]that I commanded your ancestors on the day I brought them out from the country of Egypt, from the iron smelter, saying, Listen to my voice and perform them in accordance with all that I command you, and you'll be a people for me and I'll be God for you, [5]to perform the oath that he swore to your ancestors to give them a country flowing with milk and honey this very day. I said, Yes, Yahweh.

[6]Yahweh said to me: Proclaim all these words in Judah's cities and Jerusalem's streets. Listen to the words in this covenant and perform them. [7]Because I testified and testified to your ancestors on the day I brought them out from the country of Egypt and until this day, testifying urgently, saying, Listen to my voice. [8]But they didn't listen or bend their ear but walked each person in the determination of their evil spirit. So I brought upon them all the words in this covenant that I commanded them to perform and they didn't perform.

[9]Yahweh said to me: A conspiracy has manifested itself among Judah's people and Jerusalem's residents. [10]They've turned to the wayward acts of their ancestors of old, who refused to listen to my words. As those people followed other gods, Israel's household and Judah's household have contravened my covenant that I sealed with their ancestors. [11]Therefore Yahweh has said this: Here am I; I'm going to bring upon them evil from which they won't be able to get away. They'll cry out to me but I won't listen to them. [12]Judah's cities and Jerusalem's residents will go and cry out to the gods to whom they've been burning sacrifices. But they won't deliver, they won't deliver them at the time when evil comes to them. [13]Because according to the number of your cities, Judah, have been your gods, and according to the number of your streets, Jerusalem, have you set up altars to shame, altars to burn sacrifices to the Master.

[14] You, don't plead on this city's behalf,
    don't raise a shout or plea on its behalf.

> Because I won't be listening at the time when they
>   call to me
>   on account of the evil that comes to them.
> 15 What business does my beloved have in my house,
>   as she performs her design?
> Many will take away the holy flesh from you,
>   because you do evil, then you exult.
> 16 "Flourishing olive, beautiful with shapely fruit,"
>   Yahweh called you.
> To a great roaring sound he's set fire to it,
>   and its branches have broken.
> 17 Yahweh Armies who planted you—
>   he's declared evil upon you:
> on account of the evil of Israel's household
>   and Judah's household,
> which they performed for themselves
>   to provoke me by burning sacrifices to the Master.

Christians sometimes think that Jews believe they're "justified by works." I just came across a quotation from a Jewish commentary on Exodus from a thousand years ago, which undermines that assumption. Why do the Ten Commandments not appear at the beginning of the **Torah**, it asks? It answers by means of a parable. A king tried to become ruler over a country, but its people wouldn't accept him because he'd done nothing for them. So he built them a wall, brought them water, and fought battles for them, then again said, "May I reign over you?" They responded, "Yes! Yes!" Likewise God expected **Israel** to accept his reign over them only after he'd redeemed them from Egypt, parted the sea for them, brought them manna, provided them with a well, sent them quail, and fought off the Amalekites for them. *Then* he said to them, "May I reign over you?" They replied, "Yes! Yes!"

The premise of Israel's relationship with God wasn't that they had taken an initiative in relation to God but that they had responded to what God had done for them. This was the nature of their covenant relationship with God. The trouble is, it wasn't working out that way. Although they had said at Sinai that they'd accept **Yahweh**'s **authority** over their lives, they failed to do so. The covenant meant Yahweh's saying, "I'll be your God" and Israel's saying, "We'll be your people." But they didn't keep their side of the commitment. They had broken the covenant, we might say. They haven't thereby destroyed the covenant—when we break a law, we don't thereby destroy the law. We don't even imperil it. We simply imperil ourselves. The people have flouted the covenant, and imperiled themselves.

The Hebrew word for a covenant is a political word—it also means a treaty. Jeremiah uses another political word in speaking of Israel's engaging in a conspiracy. **Judah** and other nations had joined together to resist **Assyrian** authority. The Judahites have also joined together to resist Yahweh's authority. They'll pay the penalty, as political rebels often do. Rebellion against an oppressive regime is one thing; rebelling against God is another. The terms of a treaty lay down the consequences for flouting it; the terms of the covenant do the same. Our committing ourselves to God isn't what brings about our relationship to God, but once God has reached out to us and we have responded, our committing ourselves to God is necessary to the relationship's working properly.

If the emperor discovers you have rebelled against him, you don't expect him to shrug his shoulders and not mind, and it's no use simply pleading for mercy or asking some other nation to plead with him on your behalf. So, if you rebel against God or ignore the demands of justice within the community to which he's committed, it's no good simply pleading for mercy or asking someone to pray for you or expecting him to shrug his shoulders. He's quite willing to deprive Jerusalem of the chance to share in the temple sacrifices. To put it metaphorically, he's quite willing to set fire to the tree he planted. Their only hope is to turn around.

JEREMIAH 11:18–12:17

Why Do the Faithless Do Well?

¹⁸ Yahweh has made it known to me so that I might
     know—
     then you let me see their deeds.
¹⁹ But I'd been like a docile lamb
     that's led to slaughter.
I didn't know that against me
     they had formulated their intentions:
"Let's destroy the tree with its sap,
     let's cut him off from the land of the living,
     so that his name isn't mentioned anymore."
²⁰ Yahweh Armies, who makes decisions with
     faithfulness,
     who tests the inner person and the spirit:
may I see your redress on them,
     because I have laid out my case to you.

²¹Therefore Yahweh has said this: About the people of Anatot who are seeking your life, saying, "You shall not prophesy in Yahweh's name, then you won't die by our hand"—²²therefore Yahweh Armies has said this:

Here am I; I'm going to deal with them;
     the young men will die by the sword.
Their sons and daughters will die by famine;
²³   there will be no remains of them.
Because I shall bring evil on the people of Anatot,
     the year when they're dealt with.
^{12:1} You'll be in the right, Yahweh, when I contend with
     you,
     yet in connection with your decisions I'll speak
     with you.
Why does the way of the faithless succeed,
     why are all the people who break faith secure?
² You plant them, yes they root;
     they go on, yes they produce fruit.

You're present in their mouth,
    but far from their inner person.
3 But you, Yahweh, have acknowledged me and seen me,
    you've tested my spirit in relation to you.
Drive them off like sheep to the slaughter,
    sanctify them for the killing day.
4 How long will the country mourn,
    the grass in all the fields wither?
Through the evil of the people who live in it,
    animals and birds come to an end,
because people say,
    "He doesn't look at our future."
5 If you [Jeremiah] have raced with runners and
      they've exhausted you,
    then how can you compete with horses?
If you're secure [only] in a country where things
      are well,
    then how will you do in the Jordan jungle?
6 Because yes, your brothers and your father's
      household—
    yes, they've broken faith with you;
    yes, they've called after you in full voice.
Don't put faith in them,
    when they speak good things to you.
7 I have discarded my household,
    I have deserted my own people.
I have given my dearly beloved
    into the hand of her enemies.
8 My own people have become to me
    like a lion in the forest.
She's given voice against me;
    therefore I have repudiated her.
9 My own people are a bird of prey, a hyena—
    the hyenas are against her, all around.
Go, gather up all the creatures of the wild,
    bring them to eat.
10 Many shepherds have destroyed my vineyard,
    trampled my share.

> They've made my lovely share
> > into a devastated wilderness.
> 11 Someone has made it a devastation;
> > it mourns before me, devastated.
> The entire country is devastated,
> > because there's no one taking it to mind.
> 12 Therefore destroyers have come
> > into all the bare places in the wilderness,
> > because Yahweh's sword devours.
> From one end of the country to the other end of
> > the country
> there's no well-being for all flesh.
> 13 They've sown wheat but reaped thorns,
> > they've wearied themselves but they don't achieve
> > anything.
> So be shamed by your harvest
> > because of Yahweh's angry blazing.

14Yahweh has said this: About all my evil neighbors who touch the possession that I gave to my people Israel. Here am I; I'm going to uproot them from on their land, and Judah's household I'll uproot from their midst. 15But after I have uprooted them I'll again show compassion to them and bring them back, each to his own possession, each to his country. 16If they really learn the ways of my people, swearing by my name "As Yahweh lives" as they taught my people to swear by the Master, they'll be built up in the midst of my people. 17But if they don't listen, I'll uproot that nation, uproot and destroy it (Yahweh's declaration).

In connection with Jeremiah's opening chapter, I mentioned a "How" question in connection with disability. There's also a "Why" question. My first wife was wheelchair-bound and unable to do anything for herself for the last twelve years of her life. In connection with such experiences, often people ask why God allows it. Conversely, why do people do well in life when they look like people who don't deserve it? (For some reason it wasn't a question I asked much, maybe partly because I could see God at work in bringing fruit out of Ann's disability, and partly because the people who "did well" even though they seemed not to deserve it didn't generally look any happier than we were.)

People whom Jeremiah knows are doing well when they don't deserve it; to make it worse, they're people who are attacking him. He'd been drafted as prophet by **Yahweh**, and he might have been tempted to assume that at least the ordinary people would listen to him even if the politicians didn't like it, or at least that the people from his own town would do so. But Yahweh opened his mind to something that maybe he should have been able to see but couldn't see. He was declaring that God was about to take action against **Judah**. It's a deep-seated human instinct to shoot the messenger when you don't like the news the messenger brings. Further, in Jeremiah's case the messenger is not only identified with the message but is the means of implementing the message. When God speaks, things happen, and Jeremiah is the one through whom God speaks (though the words of earthly kings aren't always effective, and maybe people are misinterpreting God's reluctance to implement his tougher threats and thinking that he cannot implement them). Jeremiah knows that God can test the inner person. God can test Jeremiah and test his attackers. Jeremiah is confident that he can appeal to God to take account of what he sees when he does this testing and to act accordingly. And God promises to do so.

The second paragraph takes up the question again. Maybe its implication is that Yahweh is slow about fulfilling that promise. All through the book we read of people's attacks on Jeremiah in one shape or another; it's a fair guess that the agonizing expressed in these protests to God also characterized his life all through. The elements of the agonizing are the same as in the previous paragraph. First there's a protest, which again refers to God's capacity to test and to know what

71

is inside people, to know about the contrast between the words and the inner attitude and intention. Then there's an appeal for God to act in judgment on Jeremiah's attackers. Third, there's a response from God, though one that's rather different from the previous response. We might expect God to tell Jeremiah he shouldn't pray that way and should be forgiving, but he doesn't do so—again the book shows how there are no constraints on the kind of thing we can say to God (as there are no constraints on the kind of thing God can say to us). God does confront Jeremiah, but in a different way. You think things are bad? God says. You'll have to get a grip, Jeremiah. They're going to get worse.

The line about people not believing that God looks to their future makes most explicit that the reason for including these protests and responses isn't what they reveal about Jeremiah's relationship with God. It's what they reveal about God's relationship with the people as a whole. Jeremiah is the one through whom God acts and speaks, so people's attitude to him is an expression of their attitude to God. Thus God's speaking about having abandoned Judah and about the reasons for this action follows directly on the account of exchanges between Jeremiah and God. People have rejected God's prophet and thus have rejected God; therefore God has abandoned them.

The references to their being God's own people and the country's being God's personal share underline the action's poignancy. Judah knows how precious its land is. Without land you have no life. The gift of this land is thus especially precious. Judah could thus hardly walk out on it. Yahweh uses this imagery to describe both his own relationship with the land and his relationship with the people. How extreme the situation must therefore be for him to abandon both. Yet these facts about Yahweh's relationship with the people and the land mean that abandonment needn't be the end of the story—if Judah is prepared to turn.

JEREMIAH 13:1–27

How Do You Get People to Change?

¹Yahweh said this to me: Go and get yourself a linen garment and put it around your waist, but don't let it come into water. ²So I got the garment in accordance with Yahweh's word and put it around my waist. ³Yahweh's word came to me a second time: ⁴Take the garment that you got, which is around your waist, and set off for Perat. Hide it there in a crevice of the cliff. ⁵So I went and hid it at Perat as Yahweh commanded me. ⁶After many days Yahweh said to me, Set off for Perat and take from there the garment that I commanded you to hide there. ⁷I went to Perat and dug and took the garment from the place where I'd hidden it, and there: the garment was destroyed; it would not be useful for anything.

⁸Yahweh's word came to me: ⁹Yahweh has said this: In this way I shall destroy Judah's majesty and Jerusalem's great majesty. ¹⁰This evil people who refuse to listen to my words, who walk by the determination of their mind, and follow other gods to serve them and bow down to them, will become like this garment, which isn't useful for anything. ¹¹Because as a garment sticks to someone's waist, so I made Israel's entire household and Judah's entire household stick to me (Yahweh's declaration) to be for me a people, a name, praise, and splendor. But they didn't listen.

¹²So you're to speak this message to them. Yahweh the God of Israel says this: Every bottle should be full of wine. They'll say to you, "Don't we know very well that every bottle should be full of wine?" ¹³You're to say to them, Yahweh has said this: Here am I; I'm going to fill all the residents of this country, the kings who sit on David's behalf on his throne, the priests, the prophets, and all Jerusalem's residents—with drunkenness. ¹⁴I'll smash them, one person against his brother, parents and children together (Yahweh's declaration). I shall not pity or spare or have compassion, so as to stop me destroying them.

¹⁵   Listen, give ear, don't be superior,
      because Yahweh has spoken.

73

16 Give honor to Yahweh your God
    before he brings darkness,
  before your feet stumble
    on the mountains in shadow,
  and you look for light but he turns it into deep
        darkness,
    makes it into dark gloom.
17 If you don't listen to this, my soul will weep inside,
    in the face of your majestic attitude.
  My eye will weep and weep, and run with weeping,
    because Yahweh's flock has gone into captivity.
18 Say to the king and the queen mother,
    "Get down, sit down.
  Because your headwear has come off,
    your splendid crown."
19 The Negev cities are closed,
    there's no one opening them.
  Judah is taken into exile, all of it,
    taken into exile, completely.

20 Raise your eyes [Jerusalem]
    and look at the people coming from the north.
  Where are the sheep that were given to you,
    your splendid flock?
21 What will you say when someone appoints over you
    ones whom you trained for yourself as allies—at
        the head?
  Won't contractions take hold of you,
    like a woman giving birth?
22 And when you say to yourself,
    "Why have these things happened to me?"—
  because of the magnitude of your waywardness
    your skirts have been stripped off and your body
        violated.
23 Does the Sudanese change his skin,
    the leopard his spots?
  You people too can do good,
    you who have been taught to do evil.

24 So I'll scatter them like chaff
    passing away in front of the wilderness wind.
25 This will be your fate,
    your lot measured out from me (Yahweh's
      declaration),
  because you disregarded me
    and trusted in falsehood.
26 Yes, I myself will lift up your skirts over your face,
    your humiliation will become visible,
27 your adulteries and your bellowings,
    your immoral scheming.
  On the hills, in the open country,
    I have seen your abominable deeds.
  Oh, alas for you, Jerusalem, you're not clean—
    how much longer will it be?

In the 1960s a man called Arthur Blessitt moved from Louisiana to Hollywood in order to preach to hippies, runaways, addicts, bikers, prostitutes, flower children, and would-be actors and rock stars; he became known as the minister of Sunset Strip. While he was there he made himself a twelve-foot-high wooden cross that he'd carry along Sunset Boulevard, sometimes getting in trouble with the authorities and being evicted from premises he used. In 1969 he began a walk with the cross that took him from Los Angeles to Washington. Then he took his cross around the world, starting in Northern Ireland; he made a point of visiting the most war-torn parts of the world. Something can happen when a message isn't only preached but also dramatized.

Jeremiah is bidden to act on the basis of that fact. The garment the story refers to is the equivalent of a pair of undershorts, the most basic piece of male clothing. It would be basic clothing a **Judahite** might be reduced to when Jerusalem is taken and its people forced to go into **exile** in **Babylon**. The place where Jeremiah takes the garment is just a few miles north of the city, near Anatot. It is called Perat, which in Hebrew is more or less the same as Euphrates, the area for which Judahite exiles are bound. The destruction of the garment speaks of the destruction coming on Judah and Jerusalem.

Presumably there were people who saw some aspect of the bizarre drama that Jeremiah enacts, but Jeremiah tells the story so as to make its point come home to people who didn't witness it. It appeals to the imagination, like Arthur Blessitt's 40,000-mile walk, which none of us witnessed. Imagine a pair of shorts covered in mold and unwearable. That's you, he says to the Judahites. He notes a further significance for the garment. Your undershorts are closer to you than anything, which is how close **Israel** was to **Yahweh**; but they didn't want to be so close.

Prophets use questions and conundrums as well as dramas. The comment about bottles looks like a popular saying, but Jeremiah's use of the saying turns its significance upside down. Yahweh has wine for Judah to drink, but it's a poisoned chalice, or wine that will simply make people drunk and lead to their getting involved in an enhanced version of the fighting that can be generated by drunkenness.

Prophets use violent and unpleasant language and imagery as well as questions and conundrums. The later paragraphs revert to addressing Jerusalem and take up the fact that a city can be personified as a woman. War takes a terrible toll on women, and Jeremiah uses the implications of that fact to describe what will happen to this "woman." It's as if she's someone who has willingly turned herself into a whore. Women are often driven into the sex trade by poverty and/or by the way they've been treated by men, but Jeremiah is more interested in using the common image of the loose woman or harlot, on whom men might sit in judgment (while perhaps being willing to take advantage of her services), in order to turn it back on such men. "You sit in judgment on an immoral woman, and you like the idea of her being exposed? Well, that's what you are, so how do you feel about being exposed?"

The question about a black person changing color or a leopard changing its spots opens up an agonizing question for a prophet. The presupposition of using these various devices (stories, drama, questions, conundrums, metaphors, similes) in a prophet's ministry is that it's possible to get people to change. Yet is it possible? Does Jeremiah mean, "A leopard can't change its spots, but you can change your ways" or "A leopard can't change its spots, and neither can you change your ways"? The audience has to decide which is true, and by their decision people will decide the outcome of their own lives.

JEREMIAH 14:1–22

The Prophet Who's Forbidden to Pray (2)

¹ What came as a message from Yahweh to Jeremiah
     concerning the matter of the drought:
² Judah mourns,
     its towns languish.
People look down to the ground,
     Jerusalem's crying goes up.
³ Their important people send their underlings for water;
     they come to the cisterns, they don't find water.
They return, their vessels empty;
     they're shamed, disgraced, they cover their head.
⁴ On account of the fact that the ground has
     shattered,
     because there hasn't been rain in the country,
the farmers are shamed,
     they cover their head.
⁵ When the hind in the open country, too, gives birth,
     it abandons, because there has been no grass.
⁶ When the donkeys stand in the bare places,
     they gasp for air like jackals.
Their eyes fail,
     because there's no vegetation.

7   Though our wayward acts testify against us, Yahweh,
      act for the sake of your name.
  Because our turnings away are many;
      we have offended against you.
8   Israel's hope,
      its deliverer in time of trouble,
  why should you become like an alien in the
        country,
      like a traveler who turns aside to stay the night?
9   Why should you become like someone bewildered,
      like a warrior who cannot deliver?
  But you're in our midst, Yahweh,
      your name has been proclaimed over us, don't
        let go of us.
10   Yahweh has said this to this people:
      Yes, they've given themselves to straying,
  they haven't restrained their feet.
      Given that Yahweh doesn't accept them,
      he'll now be mindful of their waywardness
      and will deal with their offenses.

[11]Yahweh said to me, Don't plead for good things on behalf of this people. [12]When they fast I won't be listening, when they make a burnt sacrifice or offering, I won't be accepting them, because by sword, famine, and epidemic I'm going to finish them off. [13]I said, "Oh! Lord Yahweh! There—the prophets are saying to them, 'You won't see the sword, famine won't happen to you, because I'll give you steadfast well-being in this place.'" [14]Yahweh said to me: It's falsehood that the prophets have prophesied in my name; I haven't sent them, not commanded them, not spoken to them. A false vision, divination and emptiness, their spirit's deceit, is what those people are prophesying to you. [15]Therefore Yahweh has said this to the prophets who prophesy in my name when I didn't send them and they're saying, "The sword and famine won't happen in this country": by sword and famine those prophets will come to an end. [16]And the people to whom they're prophesying will be thrown out into Jerusalem's streets because of famine and

sword. There'll be no one to bury them—them, their wives, their sons, and their daughters. I'll pour out on them their evil.

¹⁷ You're to speak this message to them:
   My eyes run down with weeping,
      night and day they won't stop.
   Because the dear daughter of my people has been
         broken,
      a great wounding, a very sickening injury.
¹⁸ If I go out into the open country—
      there, people slain by the sword.
   If I come into the city—
      there, sicknesses that come from famine.
   Because both prophet and priest go around the
         country
      but don't acknowledge it.
¹⁹ Have you totally rejected Judah,
      does your spirit loathe Zion?
   Why have you struck us
      and we have no one to heal us?—
   looking for things to go well, but there are no
         good things,
      for a time of healing, but there—terror.
²⁰ We acknowledge our faithlessness, Yahweh,
      our ancestors' waywardness.
   Because we have offended against you,
²¹   don't spurn us, for the sake of your name.
   Don't disgrace your honored throne;
      be mindful, don't contravene your covenant with us.
²² Are there any among the nations' empty beings who
         make it rain,
      or do the heavens give showers?
   Are you not the one, Yahweh our God?—
      so we look to you, because you made all these things.

My wife's daughter and her husband work on behalf of Darfuri refugees who long ago fled from Sudan to Chad, seeking to make their plight known in the United States. My wife often feels it's as if they're bashing their heads against a brick wall. Hundreds of thousands of Darfuri people have been living in camps for a decade, and the world takes little notice. Kathleen is inclined to wonder in her despondency whether for some reason God has said, "No, I'm leaving them as they are." Yet this doesn't stop us praying for them. Every evening when we are home for dinner, we pray a psalm on their behalf. When God doesn't answer your prayers or says no, you don't necessarily give up asking. Children don't necessarily take any notice when their parents say no to their requests or ignore them, and prayer is based on the assumption that we are the children of a heavenly father.

The **Judahites** have reason to turn to God, having been affected by a devastating drought. It may be hard for most Western people to picture the implications. You turn on the tap, and nothing comes out. If you have fruit and vegetables in your garden, you have no way of watering them, so they die. It's enough to drive you to prayer. The way Jeremiah describes the drought and its effects follows the way people would describe it in their prayers, as we see in the psalms. The description is designed to move **Yahweh** to action on people's behalf. It leads into an appeal to Yahweh not to continue behaving as if he has no obligation to help them (as if he's a visitor to the country) or has no ability to do so. It also implicitly grants that Yahweh has good reason not to help them—their wayward deeds and their offenses testify against them. In granting this fact, the prayer departs from the pattern of the psalms, which usually base their appeal on the fact that people haven't turned away from Yahweh. Unfortunately for these Judahites, it's those wayward deeds and offenses that preoccupy Yahweh. God has good reason to say no to Jeremiah's prayers, as isn't the case with our prayers for Darfur as far as we can see. The people talk about Yahweh's being their hope, but we know from preceding prophecies that this stance is precisely not the one that has characterized them. When children appeal to their parents for one more chance, sometimes the parents have to decide that it's time for discipline instead of leniency. For Yahweh, this is such a moment.

The second paragraph speaks about action worse than discipline, like throwing the children out of the family home. Judah's story as it will unfold in Jeremiah's day will indicate that something of this kind is indeed what Yahweh does. Meanwhile, however, it's still not over until it's over. When Jeremiah tells the people of an exchange like the one he's describing, it's yet another way of trying to break through their intransigence. They need to see Yahweh's response as a test of their seriousness. His account goes on to include his protest to Yahweh that this intransigence is at least partly attributable to their prophets' promises of a bright future. Yes, says Yahweh, the prophets whom I didn't send will deserve a punishment of their own, but this fact doesn't let Judah off the hook. People are expected to be discerning in evaluating their leaders, not simply to swallow what they say—especially when they're telling them things it would be nice to believe.

At least as frightening as Jeremiah's description of the worse fate that's coming is the fact that Jeremiah is indeed told not to pray for Judah anymore. Yet he and/or the people don't let that put them off from praying. It does no harm to take that bidding by Yahweh, too, as a kind of test. In addition to speaking of famine, in his lament Jeremiah now describes people being killed in battle, so maybe the situation has moved on. Once more he shows that he's capable of feeling a deep melancholy over his people's fate even while also sharing Yahweh's fierce anger at the waywardness that makes them deserve that fate. Once more he critiques the people's leaders who go around teaching but lack the moral and spiritual insight to be able to say what needs saying. The prayer comes to a climax with a more explicit acknowledgment than appeared in the first prayer that Yahweh is the people's only hope. Is this just Jeremiah's prayer, or one he prays on their

7 I'm winnowing them with a pitchfork
in the country's towns.
I'm bereaving, I'm destroying my people,
because of their ways from which they would not
turn.
8 Their widows will be more numerous
than the sand of the seas.
I shall bring to them (against mother, young man)
a destroyer at noon,
I shall let shock and terror
fall on them suddenly.
9 One who has borne seven languishes,
she's breathed out her life.
Her sun has set while it's still day;
she's shamed and disgraced.
Their remains I'll give to the sword
in front of their enemies (Yahweh's declaration).
10 Oh, alas for me,
my mother, that you bore me,
a contentious man and a disputatious man
for the entire country.
Whereas I haven't lent and they haven't lent to me,
everyone belittles me.
11 Yahweh said:
For sure I'm freeing you for good things,
for sure I'm intervening for you,
in the time of evil
and the time of distress.
The enemy—12can he break iron,
iron from the north or bronze?
13 Your wealth [Jerusalem] and your treasures I'll give
as plunder,
not for payment but for all your offenses,
yes through all your territory.
14 I shall make your enemies [Jeremiah] serve
in a country they haven't known.
Because fire is blazing in my anger;
it will blaze against you all.

15   You yourself know, Yahweh;
      be mindful of me, attend to me.
  Grant me redress from my persecutors;
      don't let me be taken because of your long-
         temperedness.
  Acknowledge my bearing insult because of you;
16   your words presented themselves and I ate them.
  Your message became joy to me,
      the delight of my heart.
  Because your name was proclaimed over me,
      Yahweh God of Armies.
17   I haven't sat in the company of revelers and exulted;
      because of your hand I've sat alone,
      because you'd filled me with wrath.
18   Why has my pain become endless,
      my injury grave, refusing to heal?
  You really have become to me like a deceiver,
      waters that are not reliable.

19   Therefore Yahweh has said this:
  If you turn back, I'll let you turn back;
      you can stand in front of me.
  If you express what is valuable rather than what is
        empty,
      you can be my very mouth.
  Those people will turn back to you,
      you won't turn back to them.
20   To this people I'll make you a bronze wall, fortified;
      they'll battle against you but not overcome you.
  Because I'll be with you
      to deliver you and rescue you (Yahweh's
        declaration).
21   I'll rescue you from the hand of evil people,
      redeem you from the clutch of the violent.

In the latter years of my first wife's life, from time to time I'd attempt to confront God about the way she was increasingly affected by her multiple sclerosis. God was inclined to be equally confrontational in his response (I could get away with a cry of pain to God, which was different and got a different response). Once I pressed God about whether it was possible for Ann to relate to him as her mind became more and more affected by the disease. God replied, "How I relate to Ann is between me and her, so shut up." On another occasion I said, "I'm not sure I trust you with Ann," to which God's smart reply was, "Would you trust you with Ann if you were me?" (My answer: "No.")

The great thing about a relationship with God is that it's real and the two parties can say anything to each other. Politeness is voluntary; no holds are barred. The resolution to the cliff-hanger at the end of the previous chapter, where Jeremiah has again told his readers about the prayer that he's praying or that they're praying or that they need to pray, comes with a snorting response to the effect that even if more impressive intercessors than Jeremiah were praying for this people, it would get them nowhere. Yahweh's response adds one new note to what we have read before, its reference to Manasseh. Manasseh was the grandfather of the reforming king Josiah, who reigned during Jeremiah's earlier years. It makes sense to assume that by now we are in the reign of Josiah's son Jehoiaqim, whose attitudes were more like Manasseh's than Josiah's. It's becoming clear that Josiah's reforms have had little permanent effect in Judah; it's as if Manasseh is still determining the dynamics of Judah's religious and political life. The sins of the parents are indeed visited on the children, grandchildren, and great-grandchildren, not because the children are punished for what their parents did even though the children are different, but because parents influence their children.

The dialogue between Jeremiah and Yahweh resumes in the second half of the section, taking a more personal form like my own exchange, though it relates to his ministry to Judah. The point about recording it in his prophetic scroll lies in what it says about Yahweh's relationship with Judah and what they need to learn about that relationship. "Neither a borrower nor a lender be," a Shakespeare character advised; Jeremiah has made neither mistake. On one hand, lending that involved charging interest contravened the **Torah**; on the other, trouble would obviously arise if a borrower couldn't pay back a loan. Jeremiah's concrete declaration stands for a generalization: "I have been an upstanding, reliable member of the community, yet everyone is against me." He's contentious and disputatious with the community in that he has to keep confronting it, and he's the victim of their contention and disputation as they react with affront to him. Yahweh's response is to reaffirm once more the promises he gave when commissioning Jeremiah as prophet. Yahweh will ensure he stands as firm as bronze or iron. For its attacks on Jeremiah, it's Jerusalem that will pay the price.

Jeremiah comes back to Yahweh again. Yahweh has recalled the terms of his relationship with Jeremiah that goes back to that commission, but Jeremiah can do such recalling, too. He accepted the words Yahweh gave him as enthusiastically as if it had been a tasty meal. He's demonstrated his trustworthiness, but Yahweh hasn't demonstrated the same trustworthiness. Like Jeremiah, Yahweh talks straight. There has been much talk of "turning" in Jeremiah's prophecies. He uses the same verb to mean "turn away" and "turn back." In the latter sense, English translations commonly use the verb "repent." Here Yahweh shifts the verb's application from Judah to Jeremiah himself. He's in danger of going the same way as his people. He too needs to turn again. Yahweh then adds another twist to the use of this versatile verb: if Jeremiah turns (back) to Yahweh, the Judahites will turn (back) to him, and he won't have to turn (back) to them. It's OK for Jeremiah to go through his spiritual crisis; he simply has to come out the other side of it. Yahweh doesn't promise that things will get better in the short term; he simply reaffirms once more those promises from his original commission.

JEREMIAH 16:1–21

Your Marriage Isn't Your Own

[1]Yahweh's message came to me: [2]You're not to get yourself a wife and you're not to have sons or daughters in this place. [3]Because Yahweh has said this about the sons and daughters that are born in this place, and about the mothers who bear them and the fathers who beget them in this country: [4]Gruesome deaths they'll die. They won't be lamented or buried. As dung on the surface of the ground they'll be. By sword and famine they'll come to an end. Their corpse will be food for the birds of the heavens and the animals of the earth. [5]Because Yahweh has said this:

> You're not to enter a house where there's a wake,
>   don't go to lament and grieve for them.
> Because I have gathered up my well-being from
>   this people
>   (Yahweh's declaration),
>   my commitment and compassion.
> [6] Great and small in this country will die;
>   they won't be buried.
> People won't lament for them,
>   gash themselves or shave their heads for
>   them.
> [7] People won't break bread for them in mourning,
>   to comfort someone over a death.
> They won't give them a cup of comfort to drink,
>   for his father or his mother.
> [8] You're not to enter a house where there is a party,
>   to sit with them to eat and drink.
> [9] Because Yahweh Armies, Israel's God,
>   has said this:
> Here am I—I'm going to bring to an end from
>   this place
>   in front of your eyes and in your days,
> the sound of joy and the sound of celebration,
>   the voice of groom and the voice of bride.

[10]When you tell this people all these things, and they say to you, "Why has Yahweh declared against us all this great evil, and what is our waywardness and our offense that we have committed against Yahweh our God?" [11]you're to say to them: Because your ancestors abandoned me (Yahweh's declaration) and followed other gods, served them, and bowed down to them. They abandoned me and didn't keep my teaching. [12]And you have acted more evilly than your ancestors. There you are, following each of you the determination of his evil mind, so as not to listen to me. [13]So I shall hurl you from upon this country to a country that you haven't known, you or your ancestors, and there you'll serve other gods, day and night, in that I won't show you grace.

[14]Therefore, now: days are coming (Yahweh's declaration) when it will no more be said, "As Yahweh lives, who brought up the Israelites from the country of Egypt," [15]but rather, "As Yahweh lives, who brought up the Israelites from the northern country and from all the countries where he'd driven them." I shall bring them back to their country, which I gave their ancestors.

[16] Here am I; I'm going to send for many fishers
        (Yahweh's declaration), and they'll fish for
           them.
     Afterwards I shall send
        for many hunters and they'll hunt for them,
     from upon every mountain and every hill
        and from the clefts in the cliffs.
[17] Because my eyes have been upon all their ways;
        they haven't hidden from my presence.
     Their waywardness hasn't stayed concealed
        from in front of my eyes.
[18] So I'll repay them first,
        double for their waywardness and their
           offenses,
     because of their profaning my country,
        with their abominable corpses;
        they filled my own land with their outrages.

¹⁹ Yahweh, my strength and stronghold,
    my refuge in the day of trouble,
to you the nations will come
    from earth's ends and say,
"Our ancestors possessed utter falsehood,
      emptiness,
    with nothing in them that would achieve
      anything.
²⁰ Can a human being make himself gods?—
    but they're not gods."
²¹ Therefore here am I, I'm going to make them
      acknowledge it
    with this stroke.
I'll make them acknowledge my hand and my
      might,
    and they will acknowledge that my name is
      Yahweh.

I've mentioned my first wife's illness, which was a dominant feature of our marriage for most of its forty-two years. If I'd wanted to separate Ann's illness from my work, I couldn't have done so. Being a pastor or seminary professor means you can't draw a sharp line between your work and the rest of your life; we lived on the job (in a house next to the church or on the seminary campus) for most of those years. But further, for my own sanity I needed to be able to make sense of the relationship between God and the life that Ann had to live and that I had to live, and as a theologian and pastor I could hardly avoid referencing that in my work, though maybe someone of another personality could have made more of a separation.

God wouldn't allow Jeremiah to make that separation. Traditional societies like **Israel** don't have much place for a loner; everyone belongs to a family. It would be odd not to get married. In Western society we are a bit schizophrenic about the matter. More people stay single, many from choice, yet psychologists say that on the whole married people are happier and healthier and live longer. I know people who are glad they're single (period), people who are glad they're single because they see too clearly the disadvantages of marriage (especially to anyone they know), and people who wish they were married, but it just hasn't happened.

The idea of deciding to stay single would hardly have occurred to Jeremiah unless God had given him an outlandish instruction about it. You can hypothesize that God's message gave him the excuse to do what he was already inclined to do (and/or that not many women would be interested in this odd guy with an odd vocation). Yet it makes little difference to the point this acted parable makes. One reason Jeremiah talks about the way people treat him is that it expresses the attitude they take to God. It's God they're ignoring, objecting to, or attacking. Jeremiah's life is part of his message. His staying single is part of that message.

Getting married is an extraordinary statement of hope—hope in your own future, in the other person, and in your joint future as well as hope that the world isn't going to end. (They say that getting married a second time involves a triumph of hope over experience.) The fate that hangs over Jerusalem makes this statement of hope inappropriate. Having children may be an even bigger statement of hope in the future of the world; many parents may be glad they won't have to face the future that their children will face. The fate that hangs over Jerusalem also makes this statement of hope inappropriate. Not having children implies Jerusalem has no future.

Yet the gloom with which the chapter starts, with the rationale **Yahweh** gives, is accompanied by a double statement of hope. The first statement declares that disaster won't be the end. "I won't show you mercy," Yahweh says. They'll be taken off into **exile**. But he goes on to speak of the day when people will be describing him not as the one who brought them out of Egypt but as the one who brought them back from this exile. Further, this promise is introduced by a "therefore." The theological logic is, "Of course taking them off into exile won't be the end of the story. I'll have to bring them back. And therefore . . ." Far from being an inexorably wrathful person, Yahweh is one in whom compassion is going to prevail over wrath in the end.

The second statement further envisages that the days to come will not only see Israel acknowledging Yahweh with new insight. The nations among whom they're exiled, who worship the gods that the exiles will be condemned to worship in fulfillment of their own misguided desires, will also come to recognize Yahweh. They'll come to see the truth about their humanly made religion that **Judah** itself needs to see. Which is at least part of the point in Jeremiah's inviting Judah to imagine their doing so. "If they're going to recognize it, can't you see you need to?" In addition, Jeremiah implies that Yahweh thus redeems the way he has to send the Israelites into exile by turning it into a means of reaching the other nations.

The context implies that it's Jeremiah who speaks of Yahweh as strength, stronghold, and refuge, which fits with his accounts of the pressure he's put under by his compatriots. But the jerky way whereby one paragraph follows another in most prophetic books reflects how the books were compiled by putting together shorter sayings that were separate and self-contained, deriving from different situations. Out of the context one can imagine the closing verses of the chapter as Israel's own testimony.

JEREMIAH 17:1–27

Who Am I?

¹   Judah's offense is written
      with an iron pen,

engraved with a diamond point
  on their mind's tablet,
and at the horns of their altars
²   in accordance with their children's being mindful
  of their altars and their columns,
by a flourishing tree and by high hills,
³   the mountains in the open country.
Your resources, all your treasures, I shall give as
    plunder,
  the shrines for your offenses in all your
    territory.
⁴ You'll forfeit hold, by your own act,
  of your own possession, which I gave you.
I'll make you serve your enemies
  in a country that you haven't known.
Because you have lit a fire by my anger
  that will burn forever.
⁵ Yahweh has said this:
Cursed is the man
  who trusts in human beings,
makes flesh his strength,
  and his mind turns aside from Yahweh.
⁶ He'll be like a shrub in the steppe;
  it cannot see that good will come.
It dwells in parched places in the wilderness,
  salty land where no one lives.
⁷ Blessed is the man who trusts in Yahweh,
  and Yahweh is his trust.
⁸ He'll be like a tree planted by water;
  it sends out its roots by a channel.
It isn't afraid that heat will come;
  its foliage will be flourishing.
In a year of drought it isn't anxious;
  it doesn't stop producing fruit.
⁹ The mind is more crooked than anything;
  it's wretched—who can know it?
¹⁰ "I am Yahweh, searching the mind,
  testing the inner person,

to give to a person in accordance with his ways,
    in accordance with the fruit proper to his deeds.
11 A partridge hatching when it didn't bring forth—
    someone who makes wealth but not by [right]
        exercise of authority.
In the midst of his days it will abandon him,
    and at his end he'll be [proved] a scoundrel."
12 Honorable throne, on high from of old,
    our holy place!
13 Israel's hope, Yahweh,
    all who abandon you will be shamed.
People who turn aside from me in the country will
        be written down,
    because they've abandoned
    the fountain of running water, Yahweh.
14 Heal me, Yahweh, so that I may find healing;
    deliver me, so that I may find deliverance,
    because you're my praise.
15 There are those people, saying to me,
    "Where is Yahweh's message?—
    yes, it should come."
16 I myself haven't hurried away from being a shepherd
        after you;
    I haven't longed for the wretched day.
You yourself know what has come out from my lips;
    it has been in front of your face.
17 Don't become a terror to me;
    you're my refuge on the evil day.
18 My persecutors must be shamed;
    I myself must not be shamed.
They're the one who must shatter;
    I myself must not shatter.
Bring upon them the evil day,
    break them with a double breaking.

19Yahweh said this to me: Go and stand in the ordinary people's gate by which Judah's kings come in and by which they go out, and in all Jerusalem's gates. 20Say to them: Listen to Yahweh's message, Judah's kings and all Judah and all Jerusalem's residents, who come in by these gates. [21]Yahweh has said this: Guard your lives, and don't carry a load on the Sabbath day or bring them through Jerusalem's gates. [22]Don't take out a load from your houses on the Sabbath day or do any work. Make the Sabbath day holy, as I commanded your ancestors—[23]but they didn't listen, they didn't bend their ear, but stiffened their neck so as not to listen and so as not to accept discipline. [24]But if you really listen to me (Yahweh's declaration) so as not to bring a load through the gates of this city on the Sabbath day but make the Sabbath day holy so as not to do any work on it, [25]then there will come through this city's gates kings and officials sitting on David's throne, riding on chariots and horses, they and their officials, Judah's people and Jerusalem's residents. This city will abide forever. [26]People will come from Judah's cities, from Jerusalem's environs, from Benjamin's country, from the Shephelah, from the mountains, and from the Negev, bringing burnt offering, sacrifice, grain offering, and incense, and bringing a thank offering to Yahweh's house. [27]But if you don't listen to me by making the Sabbath day holy and not carrying a load, and come through Jerusalem's gates on the Sabbath day, I'll set fire to its gates, and it will consume Jerusalem's fortresses and not go out.

In a poem he wrote in prison, on his way to being executed by the Nazis, Dietrich Bonhoeffer asked the question, "Who am I?" Am I one person today, and tomorrow, another? Do I look brave to other people, though before myself I'm "a contemptibly woebegone weakling"? In his book *Dementia* (Eerdmans, 2012), John Swinton glosses Bonhoeffer's question with further questions: Am I the same person I was twenty, thirty, forty years ago? How can I be the same person when almost all of the cells in my body have been replaced? I don't think in the same ways that I did when I was thirteen, and I don't have the same priorities. Who am I? Bonhoeffer's answer to the question is to remind himself that who he is is known by God. He lives in God's care.

His answer resonates with words from this chapter of Jeremiah, as Swinton goes on to comment. It means that trust is intrinsic to being human. By our nature, we are not designed to function independently of other human beings. Neither can we function without implicitly trusting in God to keep the world in being, to protect it. When **Judah** is expected to live by trust in God, this expectation implies Judah's modeling for the world what regular human life is designed to be.

Paradoxically, it seems hard to live on that basis. It's easier to think we can control our own destinies. So politically, Judah looks for support and protection sometimes to **Assyria**, sometimes to **Babylon**, sometimes to Egypt. Religiously, it looks to the **Masters** as well as to **Yahweh**. It's a fundamental denial of its vocation to be the people of Yahweh by modeling what humanity is supposed to be. It therefore earns a frightening condemnation. The curse and the blessing seek to drive Judah toward trusting Yahweh rather than trusting unreliable human resources or turning from Yahweh in other ways.

The curse and blessing are followed by a comment on how crooked and wretched is the human mind. What might we learn from this juxtaposition? One way our minds are crooked is that we have an infinite number of ways of justifying any action we'd like to take—for instance, action that avoids trusting in God and puts us in control of safeguarding our destinies. They're wretched insofar as there's no way we can cure our minds of their malaise. Further, because the only instrument we have for understanding our own minds is our own minds, we have no way out of the vicious circle. Even when we want to know the truth at one level, at another level we don't want to know, and we find ways of hiding the truth from ourselves. So is our situation hopeless?

The bad news and the good news is that what we don't know and can't get to know, God knows. Sometimes parents may understand their children better than they understand themselves; they may even be able to help the children understand themselves. It's what God is seeking to do for Judah through Jeremiah. Telling them they're crooked and wretched is a way of offering to straighten them out.

The paragraph about the Sabbath would have particular significance for Judahites living during and after the **exile**. From the exile onward, Judah was more involved with the other peoples around it; all were now provinces of the Babylonian and **Persian** empires. As is the case with Jewish people today, observing the Sabbath distinguished Judahites from other peoples. Thus Nehemiah has to deal with the problem of foreign merchants treating the Sabbath as an ideal day to get Judahites to buy their wares. So observing the Sabbath becomes a key marker of whether you take the covenant seriously, and it's thus the basis on which God's fulfilling the covenant promises depends. That later development points to factors that could make the Sabbath an issue in Jeremiah's own time. Stopping work for a day means forgoing the earnings you could gain on that day. It could make the difference between the family having food or going hungry. In fact, the Sabbath raises those questions about trust. If you're doing reasonably well, you have less excuse for working on the Sabbath, but that cleverness of the human mind to which Jeremiah referred then becomes a factor. What if the business goes less well next year? It would be as well to get some money in the bank this year.

The Sabbath commandment doesn't mention carrying loads; it presupposes the life of farmers rather than merchants. Jeremiah's exhortation illustrates how things God has said need to be updated as circumstances change. A prophet or preacher has to ask, "If God said such-and-such in that context, what would God say now?" Otherwise, we can be obeying the letter but not the spirit.

JEREMIAH 18:1–23
Clay in the Potter's Hand

¹The message that came to Jeremiah from Yahweh: ²Set off and go down to a potter's house, and there I'll let you hear my words. ³So I went down to a potter's house, and there he was doing work at the stones. ⁴If the object were to spoil that he was making with clay in the potter's hand, he'd remake it into another object as it was appropriate in the potter's eyes to do. ⁵Yahweh's message came to me: ⁶Like this potter can I not do to you, Israel's household (Yahweh's declaration)? There. Like clay in the potter's hand, so are you in my hand, Israel's household. ⁷Momentarily I may speak concerning a nation or kingdom about uprooting, demolishing, and destroying, ⁸but that nation concerning which I've spoken may turn back from its evil. I may then relent about the exile that I intended to do to it. ⁹But momentarily I may speak concerning a nation or kingdom about building and planting, ¹⁰and it may do what is evil in my eyes so as not to listen to my voice. I may then relent about the good that I said I'd do to it. ¹¹So now, will you say to Judah's people and Jerusalem's residents: Yahweh has said this: Right. I'm shaping evil concerning you. I'm formulating intentions concerning you. Do turn back, each person, from his evil way, and make your ways and your actions good. ¹²But they'll say, "It's desperate, because we'll follow our intentions, and we'll act, each person in the determination of his evil mind."

¹³   Therefore Yahweh has said this:
      Do ask among the nations,
          who has heard anything like this?
      She has done something very horrible,
          Ms. Israel.
¹⁴   Does Lebanon snow abandon
          the crags in the open country?
      Or do foreign waters,
          cool streams, uproot?
¹⁵   Because my people have disregarded me,
          so that they may burn sacrifices to something empty.

They've made them collapse on their ways,
    the age-old paths,
by walking on [other] tracks,
    a way not built up,
16 to make their country a devastation,
    something to whistle at forever.
Anyone who passes by it will be devastated
    and will shake his head.
17 Like the east wind
    I'll scatter them in front of the enemy.
At their back, not their face,
    I'll look at them, on their day of disaster.

18People said, "Come on, we'll formulate some intentions against Jeremiah, because teaching won't perish from the priest, planning from the expert, or message from the prophet. Come on, let's strike him down with the tongue, so we may not pay attention to any of his messages."

19 Pay heed to me, Yahweh,
    listen to the voice of the people who contend
        with me.
20 Is a person to repay evil for good?—
    because they've dug a pit for me.
Be mindful of my standing in front of you
    to speak good things concerning them,
    to turn away your wrath from them.
21 Therefore give their children to famine,
    tip them out to the edges of the sword.
Their women should be bereaved of children and
        widowed,
    their men should be struck down by death,
    their young men struck down by the sword in
        battle.
22 May an outcry make itself heard from their houses,
    when suddenly you bring a gang upon them.
Because they've dug a pit to capture me
    and laid snares for my feet.

23   Yahweh, you yourself know
      their entire plan against me, for my death.
   Don't expiate their waywardness,
      don't blot out their offenses from in front of you.
   They should become people who are made to
      collapse in front of you;
      in the time of your wrath, act against them.

There's a neat Christian song that expresses our commitment to being "clay in the potter's hand." It's a suggestive image. It means that we are malleable, open to being formed into what God wants us to be, so that we are more likely to live by the saying "Blessed are the flexible, for they shall not be broken." We trust God to mold us and direct us as he sees fit. The insight meshes with some scathing remarks in Isaiah 45 about people who resemble clay but who think they can talk back to the potter and ask whether he knows what he's doing.

One might see clay as simply malleable raw material that a potter can shape at will. Yet like wood or stone that a sculptor works, it can seem to have a mind of its own, so the potter may find himself having to be flexible as he does his work. Sometimes the clay won't turn into the shape he has in mind. He doesn't then throw it away, but he does roll it up and start again. Jeremiah goes down to the potter's workshop (in a lower part of the city, near the water supply) and observes this process. The insight that comes to him isn't so much that **Israel** *must* be clay in the potter's hand. It's that Israel *is* clay in the potter's hand, so it had better get used to the idea. Yes, there is indeed an interaction between potter and clay, and the clay can resist the potter's shaping, but the potter remains in control of what happens to the clay. The potter is sovereign but flexible.

It might seem that sovereignty would imply inflexibility, and political diatribe often pictures changing your mind as a weakness; it suggests you didn't foresee all the factors you should've taken into account in making your original decision. The Bible sees it a different way. It's happy with the idea that there's an interaction between divine sovereignty and human reaction. It implies that when you're confident about your ultimate sovereignty, you can afford to be flexible and to take the long view. That assumption makes sense of Israel's history and of the church's history, which don't look as if they're simply the outworking of an ideal divine plan. Translations sometimes speak of God's "repenting," which would be odd, for it would seem to imply that God had done something wrong, but "relenting" or "having a change of mind" better conveys the force of the Hebrew verb. Sometimes it can mean "regretting," though in the sense of being sorry that one had to do something, not in the sense of wishing one hadn't done it.

The "response" of the clay, then, can lead to the potter's relenting or having a change of mind about how to shape the clay. This change can be good news. Although Jeremiah keeps warning **Judah** that judgment is coming, God remains flexible. All Judah has to do is turn back. In two ways, however, Jeremiah's message makes a much more general point. On one hand, the principle of flexibility applies to promises as well as warnings. When Judahites in a few generations' time read the prophecies in this book, at a point when God is talking about restoring the community or is in the midst of doing so, they need to be aware of that fact. God could have a change of mind about restoring Judah if he doesn't get the right response. On the other hand, the double principle applies to nations in general, not just to Judah. Jonah applies it to Nineveh, and people in Jeremiah's day need to apply it to **Babylon** or to their own neighbors whose judgment Jeremiah will soon be declaring. The Old Testament assumes that God is involved in the destiny of all the nations and is interacting with them.

Even when Jeremiah reports the Judahites as saying that the situation is hopeless and that there's no way they're going to turn back to **Yahweh,** he's seeking to break through to get them to change their minds. The same significance attaches to the prayer he reports in the last paragraph. The priests, prophets, and experts (royal advisers) might want to get rid of Jeremiah because he was undermining their **authority.** Maybe another deeper yet more naive implication was that they were afraid his words might come true. He's reporting his prayer so that people may know how he's praying; and they know about the power of his words from God, so they know about the power of his words to God. Yesterday in church we happened to read Paul's account in Ephesians 3 of the way he was praying for the Ephesians; knowing about that prayer might have a galvanizing effect on them, arousing hope and openness. Knowing how Jeremiah was praying against you might have a parallel galvanizing effect, arousing fear and openness.

JEREMIAH 19:1–20:6

Pottery Smashed

[1]Yahweh said this: Go and get a potter's earthenware jug, and some of the elders of the people and some of the elders of the priests, [2]and go out into the Ben-hinnom Canyon, which is at the entrance of the Potsherd Gate, and proclaim there the words that I shall speak to you. [3]Say: Listen to Yahweh's message, Judah's kings and Jerusalem's residents. Yahweh Armies, Israel's God, has said this: Here am I; I'm going to bring evil on this place such that everyone who hears of it— his ears will ring, [4]since they've abandoned me, made this place alien, burned sacrifices in it to other gods that they hadn't acknowledged, they, their ancestors, and Judah's kings. They've filled this place with the blood of the innocent. [5]They've built shrines for the Master for burning their children in fire as burnt offerings to the Master, which I didn't command or speak of; it didn't come up into my mind. [6]Therefore days are coming (Yahweh's declaration) when this place will no longer

be called Tophet or Ben-hinnom Canyon but rather Slaughter Canyon. [7]I'll frustrate the plan of Judah and Jerusalem in this place. I'll make them fall by the sword in front of their enemies, by the hand of people who seek their lives, and give their corpse as food to the birds of the heavens and the animals of the earth. [8]I'll make this city into a devastation and something to whistle at; anyone who passes by it will be devastated and will whistle at all its injuries. [9]I'll cause them to eat the flesh of their sons and the flesh of their daughters, and they'll each eat the flesh of his neighbor in the siege and in the straits that their enemies, the people who seek their lives, impose on them.

[10]You're to break the jug in front of the eyes of the men who go with you, [11]and say to them, Yahweh Armies has said this: In this way I'll break this people and this city, as one breaks a potter's article, which cannot be mended again. In Tophet they'll bury, because there will be no place for burying. [12]Thus I'll do to this place (Yahweh's declaration) and to its residents, to make this city like Tophet. [13]Jerusalem's houses and the kings of Judah's houses will become like the place Tophet, defiled—that is, all the houses on whose roofs people have burned sacrifices to the entire heavenly army and poured libations to other gods.

[14]Jeremiah came from Tophet where Yahweh had sent him to prophesy, stood in the courtyard of Yahweh's house, and said to the entire people: [15]Yahweh Armies, Israel's God, has said this: Here am I; I'm going to bring upon this city and upon all its cities all the evil of which I've spoken concerning it, because they've stiffened their neck so as not to listen to my words.

[20:1]Pashhur son of Immer, the priest (he was the leading administrator in Yahweh's house), heard Jeremiah prophesying these things. [2]Pashhur struck the prophet Jeremiah down and put him in the stocks at the Upper Benjamin Gate that is in Yahweh's house. [3]Next day Pashhur let Jeremiah out from the stocks. Jeremiah said to him, "Yahweh has named you not Pashhur but rather Terror-is-all-around. [4]Because Yahweh has said this: Here am I; I'm going to give you to terror, you and all your friends. They'll fall by the sword of their enemies, with your eyes seeing it. I'll give all Judah into the hand of the king of Babylon. He'll exile them to Babylon and strike them down with the sword. ⁵I'll give this city's entire wealth—all its profit, all its valuables, and all the treasures of Judah's kings I'll give into their enemies' hand. They'll plunder them, take them, and carry them off to Babylon. ⁶You, Pashhur, and all the people who live in your house—you'll go into captivity. You'll come to Babylon, and there you'll die and there you'll be buried, you and all your friends to whom you've prophesied falsely."

In Hanoi there's an embassy that gives visas to people who want to find the bodies of relatives who died in Vietnam's wars. The family wants to be able to give them a proper burial to avoid their becoming angry ghosts rather than guardian spirits. Ideally the government would prefer to discourage such "superstitions," but it has launched a website called "Honoring Martyrs" to give people the opportunity to exchange information about the possible location of family members. Officials also work with spirit mediums to try to weed out fake mediums who are exploiting others' grief to make money.

The practices of traditional religion to which Jeremiah refers have a similar background in the conviction that when your relatives are dead, it doesn't mean they don't exist. They can continue to relate to you, maybe for good, maybe for **evil**. Like Vietnamese Communists, Western sociologists were convinced fifty years ago that religion was dying out but have more recently acknowledged that it's alive and well; the hysterical outbursts of atheist "evangelists" also witness to the fact. The Old Testament doesn't argue that ghosts or other gods don't exist. It grants their existence but expects **Israel** not to have anything to do with them. Israel's entire focus is to be given to **Yahweh**, the only supernatural being who has real power, the one to whom these other beings are subordinate. But traditional religion is a powerful thing, and through much of its history Israelites gave into its temptation. They thereby thumbed their noses at Yahweh.

Further, in the name of faith they sacrificed members of their family as a sign of their devotion to a deity who ruled death's realm. The practice horrifies Yahweh. It's not the kind of sacrifice he could ever have dreamed up. The point is made in another way by the story of Abraham's offering of Isaac, one of whose implications is that it's possible to imagine God's asking a father to sacrifice his son but not to imagine God's letting him go through with it.

The place where people make this most costly of sacrifices will become known not as a place of sacrifice but as a place of slaughter. There will be some poetic justice about this change. The so-called sacrifice is so abhorrent and unacceptable, place of slaughter is really what it already is. And when the large-scale slaughter comes, "Slaughter Canyon" will be an even more appropriate name. Indeed, Jerusalem itself will become a place characterized by slaughter.

Jeremiah has already offered a scathing critique of the religious observances that families undertook in the Ben-hinnom Canyon below Jerusalem. Here he adds another of his acted parables. They are more than mere illustrations. They resemble sacramental acts such as circumcision or baptism. They *do* something. It's God who commissions them, and they're the effective signs and means of God's putting into effect what they symbolize. Jeremiah is thus Yahweh's agent when he acts and speaks; it is part of the background to the **Judahite** leadership's desire to stop him acting or speaking. Halt and silence the one through whom God acts and speaks, and maybe you halt God's action. Here, there's another reason why this action is powerful. The previous chapter spoke of the potter reshaping the pot, which is an uncomfortable but ultimately positive act. At least in part, the pot stands for Israel. Here Yahweh doesn't merely reshape the pot but smashes it.

The traditional religion of Judah isn't merely popular religion, followed only by unsophisticated people who know no better. It's some of the elders and the senior priests that Jeremiah takes with him to witness his symbolic act. And it's a senior priest who subsequently has him arrested. The phrase "Terror is all around" recurs in Jeremiah; it was apparently a vivid tag line for warning people about the coming trouble. Here he sees Pashhur as someone who will have a personal experience of that terror. But when people are given new names, the new name often relates in some way to the old name. Pashhur and many of Jeremiah's readers would be able to work out that if you think of Pashhur's name as Aramaic (the international language of the day), it could mean "fruitful all around." His new name is a terrifying reversal.

JEREMIAH 20:7–21:10

Cursed Be the Day I Was Born

⁷ You've fooled me, Yahweh, I was foolish;
    you've taken hold of me and won.
I've become a laugh all the time,
    everyone makes fun of me.
⁸ Because every time I speak, I cry out,
    I proclaim violence and destruction.
Because Yahweh's message has become for me
    insult and derision all the time.
⁹ When I said, "I won't make mention of him,
    not speak in his name anymore,"
it became in my spirit like a raging fire,
    shut up in my bones,
    and I was weary of holding it in—I couldn't.
¹⁰ Because I heard the murmuring of many,
    "Terror is on every side—announce, let's
      announce it."
Every person who was my friend—
    they're watching my step:

"Perhaps he can be trapped and we can win
    against him,
    and take our redress from him."
11 But Yahweh—he's with me as a violent warrior;
    therefore my persecutors will collapse and
        not win.
  They're being utterly shamed because they
    aren't succeeding,
    a disgrace for all time that won't be
        forgotten.
12 Yahweh Armies, you who test the faithful,
    who see heart and mind,
  may I see your redress on them,
    because to you I've committed my cause.

13 Sing for Yahweh, praise Yahweh,
    because he's saved the life of the needy
    from the hand of evildoers.

14 Cursed be the day
    on which I was born.
  The day when my mother gave birth to me—
    may it not be praised.
15 Cursed be the man
    who brought the news to my father,
  "A male child has been born to you";
    he made him so joyful.
16 That man will become like the cities
    that Yahweh overthrew and didn't relent.
  He'll hear an outcry in the morning
    and a shout at noontime,
17 the one who didn't kill me before birth,
    so that my mother became my grave,
    her womb pregnant forever.
18 Why on earth did I come out from the womb
    to see trouble and sorrow
  and so that all my days might consume
    themselves in shame?

²¹:¹The message that came to Jeremiah from Yahweh when King Zedekiah sent to him Pashhur son of Malkiah and Zephaniah son of Ma'aseiah the priest to say, ²"Will you inquire on our behalf of Yahweh, because Nebuchadrezzar, king of Babylon, is doing battle against us. Perhaps Yahweh will act with us in accordance with his wonders, so that [Nebuchadrezzar] goes up from us." ³Jeremiah said to them: You're to say this to Zedekiah: ⁴Yahweh, Israel's God, has said this: Here am I; I'm going to turn back the battle implements that are in your hand, with which you're doing battle with the king of Babylon and the Kaldeans who are besieging you from outside the wall, and I'll gather them up into the midst of this city. ⁵I myself will do battle against you with an outstretched hand and a strong arm, with anger, rage, and great wrath. ⁶I'll strike down this city's residents, human beings and animals; they'll die in a great epidemic. ⁷After this (Yahweh's declaration) I'll give Zedekiah, king of Judah, and his staff and the people, those who remain in this city from epidemic, sword, and famine, into the hand of Nebuchadrezzar, king of Babylon, and into the hand of their enemies, into the hand of the people seeking their life. He'll strike them down with the mouth of the sword. He won't have pity for them. He won't have mercy. He won't have compassion. ⁸To this people you shall say, Yahweh has said this: Here am I, presenting before you the way of life and the way of death. ⁹The person who lives in this city will die by sword, famine, or epidemic. But the person who leaves and goes over to the Kaldeans who are besieging you will live. His life will be his as a trophy. ¹⁰Because I've set my face against this city for evil and not for good (Yahweh's declaration). Into the hand of the king of Babylon it will be given, and he'll burn it in fire.

When my first wife's multiple sclerosis starting taking more of an emotional and mental toll on her (though I don't think we recognized that this was what was happening), it began to take more of a toll on me, too. I felt she'd turned in on herself and could think only about the problems of her work as a psychiatrist and had no emotional space for me. This was when the Psalms began to be important to me. I had difficulty sleeping, and I would get up in the early hours and sit on the sofa crying out to God, and I realized that I was praying the way the Psalms do. I can't remember how far this helped during any given night; I do know that it didn't permanently solve the problem, as I'd be back there the next night or some subsequent night.

Jeremiah's problems are on a whole other level, but his report of his praying suggests parallel dynamics. One indication is that in this prayer he restates what he said to Yahweh in the prayer in chapter 15, though he formulates it in stronger terms. Yahweh had drafted him against his will to preach a message about violence and destruction coming from Yahweh's hand, putting him in a dangerous position in relation to people who didn't like his negative message, but also making him look totally stupid because his message failed to come true.

In bringing such experiences before God, however, the prayers that the Psalms invite people into make it possible to reframe one's understanding. Prayer is designed to change God, not you, but it can also change you. It's not that letting it all hang out makes you feel better (though that may be so). It's that bringing it before God can enable you to get a fresh angle on it or to regain the angle you had before your troubles knocked you off balance. God enables you to see things a different way. You see the implications of God's being part of the picture. Jeremiah realizes afresh what God had told him: that God is with him even when it doesn't look like it and that God will protect him. He can make the transition to praise that also appears at the end of psalms, on which he models his prayers. Sometimes they make that statement by faith, knowing God will make it true. Maybe Jeremiah also recognizes that it has in fact been true; he's still alive and praying, after all.

Whichever way he means it, however, the next paragraph places him back where he was, or rather places him in an even worse position. Through these chapters that incorporate his prayers, his anguish continues to deepen until it here reaches its lowest point. The chapter closes with no word from Yahweh and no statement of hope or faith. It thus follows the model of other psalms that make no transition to hope or praise, of which Psalm 88 is the most spectacular.

One can hardly fault Jeremiah. The features of his life that he describes persisted throughout his ministry. The placing of his account of his prayers in the first half of the book doesn't imply it belongs simply to the first half of his ministry. His book isn't arranged chronologically, and as a whole it makes clear that he was met with scorn, opposition, and hostility throughout, until the moment forty years after his commission by Yahweh and after Jerusalem's fall when some of his compatriots take him to Egypt by force, never to be heard of again.

The fact that the book isn't arranged chronologically is illustrated by the story about Zedekiah, which relates to the siege that eventually led to the city's fall and thus to the fulfillment of Jeremiah's warning. The **Judahite** leadership is trying to hold the city together and encourage it to stand firm and withstand the siege until the enemy get tired and go away, and Jeremiah is undermining their efforts by his treacherous encouragement to people to surrender one by one to the enemy on the basis that surrender rather than resistance is the way to life.

JEREMIAH 21:11–22:19

Criteria for Kingship

¹¹ And to the household of Judah's king:
    Listen to Yahweh's message.

¹² David's household,
   Yahweh has said this:
Exercise authority morning by morning,
   rescue the person who's been robbed from the
      hand of the oppressor,
lest my wrath go out like fire,
   and burns with no one quenching it,
   because of the evil of your deeds.
¹³ Here am I toward you [Jerusalem],
   you who dwell in the valley,
      a crag in the plain (Yahweh's declaration).
People who say, "Who can come down against us,
   who can come into our homes?"
¹⁴ I'll deal with you in accordance with the fruit of
      your deeds
   (Yahweh's declaration).
I'll set fire to its forest
   and consume all that's around it.

^{22:1}Yahweh said this: Go down to the house of Judah's king and speak there this message. ²Say: Listen to Yahweh's message, Judah's king, you who sit on David's throne, and your staff and your people who come through these gates. ³Yahweh has said this: Exercise authority and faithfulness, rescue the person who's been robbed from the hand of the oppressor, don't wrong alien, orphan, and widow, don't be violent, don't shed innocent blood in this place. ⁴Because if you really do implement this message, then through this house's gates will come David's kings sitting on his throne, riding chariot and horses, he and his staff and his people. ⁵But if you don't listen to these words, I swear by myself (Yahweh's declaration) that this house will become a desolation.

⁶ Because Yahweh has said this concerning the
      house of Judah's king:
You are Gilead to me,
   the summit of Lebanon.

If I don't make you a wilderness,
    cities that don't abide . . .
7   I'll sanctify destroyers against you,
        a man and his implements.
    They'll cut the choicest of your cedars
        and make them fall into the fire.

8Many nations will pass by this city and will say, each person to his neighbor, "Why did Yahweh act in this way to this great city?" 9And they'll say, "On account of the fact that they abandoned the covenant of Yahweh their God and bowed down to other gods and served them."

10 Don't weep for the one who's dead,
        don't lament for him.
    Weep and weep for the one who's going,
        because he won't return again
        and see the country of his birth.

11Because Yahweh has said this regarding Shallum son of Josiah, Judah's king, who was reigning in place of Josiah, his father, who has gone out from this place: He won't return here again, 12because in the place where they exiled him, there he'll die. This country he won't see again.

13 Hey! The one who builds his house without
            faithfulness,
        his lofts without the [right] exercise of
            authority!
    He makes his neighbor serve for nothing;
        he doesn't give him his earnings.
14 The one who says, "I'll build myself a vast house,
        spacious lofts."
    He cuts windows for it, paneled with cedar,
        painted with vermilion.
15 Are you a king
        because you're competing in cedar?
    Your father—didn't he eat and drink,

111

> and implement faithful exercise of authority—
> then things were good for him?
> [16] He made decisions for the week and needy—
> then things were good;
> isn't this to acknowledge me (Yahweh's
> declaration)?
> [17] Because you have no eye or mind
> except for loot,
> for shedding the blood of the innocent
> and for oppression and extortion.
> [18] Therefore Yahweh has said this
> concerning Jehoiaqim son of Josiah, Judah's king:
> They won't mourn for him,
> "Oh, my brother, oh, my sister."
> They won't mourn for him,
> "Oh my lord, oh, his majesty."
> [19] He'll be buried with a donkey's burial,
> dragged and dumped outside Jerusalem's gates.

We're in the midst of a U.S. presidential election, and the pollsters are reporting from day to day the electorate's views on the candidates. The sitting president is doing poorly, they say, on the basis of his handling of the economic situation and people's view of the difference his policies will make to their own financial situation, but they credit him with personal appeal and empathy. With regard to his rival, voters are preoccupied by his past focus on getting his private equity firm to make a profit and not on the kind of experience that would help create jobs. Some voters are relieved that both are men of faith while some declare themselves disillusioned with all politicians since Watergate.

What are the qualities a president or king needs? The opening two paragraphs provide the basic Old Testament answer. It's to exercise **authority** in a way that ensures the protection of people who might be taken advantage of by others. This is the responsibility of "David's household," of the person who "sits on David's throne." **Judah**'s kings have to keep remembering that their vocation is to fulfill the responsibility of the Davidic king to whom **Yahweh** made extraordinary commitments but of whom Yahweh has great expectations. To put it another way, it's to exercise authority in a way that expresses **faithfulness** to vulnerable people and thus to Yahweh.

The message follows straight on from words addressed to Zedekiah in the context of Jerusalem's siege, but the exhortation to rescue the oppressed doesn't have an obvious place in the context of a siege, and the message's opening words resemble challenges Jeremiah gave earlier in his ministry. Retrospectively, the message here functions to remind the king of the reason the city's fall is inevitable: because "David's household" in general (the succession of kings) had ignored obligations such as these. The people, in turn, had been convinced that their city's strong position made it invincible. When you have resources, you feel secure. They're having to face the fact that they were wrong.

Prospectively, the message provides the background to judgments on the other kings that follow, the kings who reigned during Jerusalem's closing decades. The one who's dead is Josiah, killed in battle in 609. The one whom people are encouraged to lament is his son Shallum, also known as Jehoahaz, who reigned for a few months in 609 but was deposed and exiled by the Egyptians. The one who built a big palace is his brother Eliaqim, also known as Jehoiaqim, who reigned from 609 until his death in 598. He was succeeded by his son Jehoiakin, who was deposed after a few months, exiled to **Babylon**, and replaced with another son of Josiah, Zedekiah. Jeremiah compares Jehoiaqim unfavorably with his father. Josiah reigned for thirty years, but it wasn't long enough to effect a lasting eradication of the traditional religious practices Jeremiah condemns. Neither would his pragmatic political policies have met with Jeremiah's approval, even if they hadn't led to his death. But Jeremiah can portray him as having lived up to the Davidic ideal. He ate and drank well, like David, but he implemented that commitment to the faithful exercise of authority.

JEREMIAH 22:20–23:8

The Wicked Play on Words in a King's Name

> ²⁰ Climb Lebanon and cry out [Jerusalem],
>   in Bashan lift your voice.
> Cry out from Abarim,
>   because all your friends are broken.
> ²¹ I spoke to you during your ease;
>   you said, "I won't listen."
> This was your way from your youth,
>   because you didn't listen to my voice.
> ²² All your shepherds—the wind will shepherd them;
>   your friends will go into captivity.
> Because then you'll be shamed and disgraced
>   because of all your evil.
> ²³ You who dwell on Lebanon, nesting among the cedars,
>   how needy of grace you'll be,
> when contractions come to you,
>   labor like someone giving birth.

²⁴As I live (Yahweh's declaration), if Koniah son of Jehoiaqim, Judah's king, were the ring on my right hand . . . Because from there I'd tear you off. ²⁵I'll give you into the hand of the people who seek your life, into the hand of the people whom you yourself dread, into the hand of Nebuchadrezzar, king of Babylon, into the hand of the Kaldeans. ²⁶I'll hurl you and your mother who bore you into another country where you were not born, and there you'll die. ²⁷Regarding the country where they'll be lifting up their longing to return: they won't return there.

²⁸ Is he a despised broken piece of pottery, this man
     Koniah,
        or an implement in which there's no delight?
     Why are they being hurled, he and his offspring,
        thrown to a country that they don't know?
²⁹ Country, country, country,
        listen to Yahweh's message.
³⁰ Yahweh has said this:
     Write down this person as childless,
        a man who won't succeed in his life,
     because no one of his offspring will succeed,
        sitting on David's throne
        and ruling again in Judah.

²³:¹Hey, shepherds who led astray and scattered my flock
(Yahweh's declaration). ²Therefore Yahweh, Israel's God, has
said this about the shepherds who shepherd my people: You—
you've let my flock scatter. You've driven them away and
not attended to them. Here am I; I'm going to attend to you,
to the evil of your deeds (Yahweh's declaration). ³I myself
will draw together the remains of my flock from all the
countries where I've driven them. I'll return them to their
abode, and they'll be fruitful and become many. ⁴I'll set up
shepherds over them and they'll shepherd them, and they
won't be afraid anymore or shatter or be missing (Yahweh's
declaration). ⁵Now. Days are coming (Yahweh's declaration)
when I'll set up for David a faithful branch. He'll reign as
king and show sense and exercise authority and faithfulness
in the country. ⁶In his days Judah will find deliverance and
Israel will dwell with assurance. This is the name by which
he'll be called: "Yahweh is our faithfulness." ⁷Therefore,
now: days are coming (Yahweh's declaration) when they'll
no longer say, "As Yahweh lives, who took up the Israelites
from the country of Egypt." ⁸Rather, "As Yahweh lives,
who took up and brought the offspring of Israel's household from the northern country" and from all the countries
where I will have driven them. And they'll live on their
land.

Names often matter. When we married eighteen months ago, I encouraged my wife to keep her name as it was so that in seminary and church circles it signaled that she continued to be a person in her own right and not simply my wife. When our new granddaughter was born a few weeks ago, her parents named her Leila Paz. Leila was a girl they got to know and care about in a refugee camp, but the name makes me think of Eric Clapton's Layla, a variant spelling of the same Arabic name. Paz is Spanish for "peace," about which Leila's parents are passionate. The name expresses a vision and a hope.

Zedekiah's name means "**Yahweh** is my **faithfulness**" (more strictly, "Yah is my faithfulness"—Yah is a shorter version of God's name). It suggests a conviction and a hope. It's thus typical of the names of kings and others in the Old Testament. Jeremiah's own name means "Yahweh exalts." Josiah means "Yahweh supports." Whereas Shallum was a common name related to the word *shalom*, meaning **well-being**, Jehoahaz means "Yahweh has grasped." The names Jekoniah (Koniah is an abbreviation) and Jehoiakin involve the same elements in two different orders, so that both mean "Yahweh establishes." Eliaqim means "God raises up," and Jehoiaqim means "Yahweh raises up" (I did once want to name our cat Jehoiaqim, but my first wife vetoed it on the grounds that she'd feel stupid standing at the front door calling out "Jehoiaqim," though she did settle for Tobias, aka Toby, even though he was apocryphal).

I imagine that from time to time people felt that Yahweh failed to live up to the statements of faith and hope expressed in their names (Jeremiah would've been among them) and that at least as often Yahweh felt that people also failed to live up to their names, which is the point Jeremiah implies about Zedekiah. If Yahweh were his faithfulness, that would imply some trust in Yahweh on his part. It would also imply some imitation on his part in the form of faithfulness to Yahweh and faithfulness to his people. None of that was forthcoming on the part of this king, whom subsequent stories will show to

116

be someone who lacks the personal resources for what was admittedly a monumentally demanding assignment as king. Somewhat pointedly Jeremiah declares that one day there'll be a king who will constitute a *faithful* branch for David, who will exercise *faithfulness* in the country, and whose name will be *Yahweh zidkenu*, "Yahweh our faithfulness."

The Old Testament never talks about a coming savior whom it calls the Messiah, but in passages such as this it does in effect talk about such a figure without using that word. The Old Testament hints at two considerations that led to that promise. Eventually there's the fact that **Judah** never has a king after the ones mentioned in this chapter, and God's promise to David would seem to mean that God had to put this situation right some day. When Jeremiah speaks about raising up a faithful *branch* for David, he implies that the Davidic "tree" has been cut down and declares that nevertheless a branch can grow out of its stump. But even before there ceased to be kings, they rarely lived up to the vision of one who'd exercise **authority** in faithfulness—hence the fact that the tree did get felled. This fact is the other background to Jeremiah's promise. God has a vision for a king who will reign in that way, and God promises to see it fulfilled. Even today we haven't seen that promise fulfilled, so it's important for us.

The other elements in that paragraph make the point more generally. Zedekiah isn't the only failed shepherd, but the sheep are ultimately Yahweh's. They've let themselves be led astray by these shepherds, and they're responsible for that failure. They can't make unreliable leadership an excuse, and they'll pay the penalty. Yet it's still the case that Yahweh is their chief shepherd, who therefore cannot but go looking for them to bring them home and also cannot but give them better shepherds than they had before. When you look at the later shepherds, people such as Sheshbazzar, Jeshua, Zerubbabel, Ezra, and Nehemiah, you can see that they served the flock better.

The opening invitation is to climb the mountains to the north, the east, and the south (there's only the sea to the west) in order to make loud lamentation for the defeat that will issue from the failure of Judah's leaders and its allies. The picture of Jerusalem living on Lebanon is a metaphor for city and temple being constructed with so much cedar.

JEREMIAH 23:9–40

Another Wicked Play on Words

9 Concerning the prophets:
My spirit has broken within me,
   all my bones have become weak.
I've become like someone drunk,
   like a man wine has overcome,
in the face of Yahweh and in the face of his holy words,
10   because the country is full of adulterers.
Because the country mourns in the face of a curse,
   the wilderness pastures have dried up.
Their running has become evil;
   their might, not right.
11 Because both prophet and priest are impious;
   even in my house I've found their evildoing
   (Yahweh's declaration).
12 Therefore their way will become for them like
      slippery slopes;
   they'll be driven into darkness and they'll fall
      there.
Because I shall bring evil upon them,
   the year when they're dealt with (Yahweh's
      declaration).
13 In Samaria's prophets I saw stupidity:
   they prophesied by the Master and led my
      people astray.
14 In Jerusalem's prophets I saw a horror:
   adultery, walking by falsehood,

and they strengthen the hands of evildoers,
  so that no one may turn from his evil.
They've become like Sodom to me, all of them,
  its residents like Gomorrah.

¹⁵ Therefore Yahweh Armies has said this concerning
      the prophets:
  Here am I; I'm going to feed this people bitter
      plants
  and make them drink poisoned water.
  Because from Jerusalem's prophets
      impiety has gone out to the whole country.

¹⁶ Yahweh Armies has said this:
  Don't listen to the words of the prophets
      who prophesy to you.
  They're giving you emptiness;
      they speak a vision from their mind,
      not from Yahweh's mouth.
¹⁷ They're saying to people who despise Yahweh's message,
      "It will go well for you."
  To everyone who's walking in the determination of
      his mind,
      they've said, "Evil won't come upon you."
¹⁸ Because who has stood in Yahweh's council,
      and seen and listened to his message,
      who has paid attention to his message and
      listened?
¹⁹ There—Yahweh's storm,
      fury has gone out.
  The storm is whirling,
      on the head of the faithless it will whirl.
²⁰ Yahweh's anger won't turn until he's acted,
      until he's performed the schemes in his mind.
  At the end of the time
      you'll understand it fully.
²¹ I didn't send the prophets, but those people ran;
      I didn't speak to them, but those people prophesied.

22 If they'd stood in my council,
    they'd have got my people to listen to my
        message.
    They'd have turned them from their evil way,
        from the evil of their deeds.
23 Am I a God nearby (Yahweh's declaration),
    and not a God far away?
24 If a man hides in a hiding place,
    will I not see him (Yahweh's declaration)?
    Don't I fill the heavens and the earth
        (Yahweh's declaration)?

25I have listened to what the prophets who prophesy false-hood in my name say: "I've dreamed, I've dreamed." 26How long? Is there in the mind of the prophets who prophesy falsehood, the prophets with deceit in their mind—27are they intending to get my people to disregard my name with their dreams that they recount, each to his neighbor, as their ancestors disregarded my name because of the Master? 28The prophet who has a dream with him should relate a dream, and the one who has my message with him should speak my message truthfully. What does straw have compared with grain (Yahweh's declaration)? 29Isn't my message like fire (Yahweh's declaration) and like a hammer that shatters rock? 30Therefore here am I, against the prophets (Yahweh's declaration), who steal my words each from his neighbor. 31Here am I, against the prophets (Yahweh's declaration), who take up their tongue and make a "declaration." 32Here am I, against the prophets of false dreams (Yahweh's declaration) who relate them and lead my people astray with their falsehoods and their recklessness, when I didn't send them, didn't command them. In no way will they achieve anything for this people (Yahweh's declaration).

33When this people or the prophet or priest ask you, "What is Yahweh's burden?" you're to say to them, "You're the burden and I'll discard you" (Yahweh's declaration). 34As for the prophet and the priest and the people that say, "Yahweh's burden," I'll deal with that person and his household. 35You're to say this, each to his neighbor, each to his brother: "What has Yahweh answered?" or "What has Yahweh spoken?" [36]But don't make mention of Yahweh's burden anymore, because the burden will belong to the person with his message, and you'll overturn the words of the living God, Yahweh Armies, our God. [37]You're to say this to the prophet: "What did Yahweh answer you?" or "What did Yahweh speak?" [38]If you say, "Yahweh's burden"—therefore Yahweh has said this: Since you said this thing, "Yahweh's burden," and I had said to you, don't say, "Yahweh's burden," [39]therefore here am I: I shall simply forget you and discard you, you and the city that I gave you and your ancestors, from in front of my face. [40]I shall put upon you insult in perpetuity, shame in perpetuity, which won't be forgotten.

For a while I was the faculty representative on the president's cabinet in our seminary, which means I had to get up early once a month for a meeting of people in the administration to discuss big policy questions (but not so much their ongoing implementation, which was the business of another body). I was expected to share the meetings' discussions with my faculty colleagues and thereby allay their fears or give them things to worry about and also discover their angle on issues under discussion so I could report back to the cabinet's next meeting. I knew that the faculty's perspectives, opinions, suggestions, or misgivings would not always win the day, but I knew they'd be listened to.

As a prophet, Jeremiah has an analogous position in Yahweh's cabinet, Yahweh's "council," hence his ability to tell Judah of Yahweh's intentions. His problem is that other prophets are giving the people very different versions of Yahweh's intentions. But Jeremiah knows they were not in the meeting. Their messages didn't come from overhearing the discussions there but from their own imaginations. One indication is that they talk about their dreams. Now, dreams can be a true means of God's speaking to people. There are many modern accounts of Christians going to tell people about Jesus and meeting the response "Yes, I had a dream of someone like this man." Both the Old and New Testament refer to God's speaking through dreams. Yet more often dreams simply reflect issues arising in our own spirits. They are generated from within us. So it is with the other prophets, Jeremiah says. If you've had a dream, tell us the dream, but don't confuse dreams with sitting in a cabinet meeting with God.

Jeremiah's further wicked play on words links with this insistence. One Hebrew word for a prophet's message is *massa'*, but there's another Hebrew word spelled the same way that refers to something you carry, a burden. So people could naturally ask Jeremiah whether he has a *massa'*, a message from Yahweh, and Jeremiah could respond by telling them that they themselves are Yahweh's *massa'*, a burden to Yahweh, though not a burden Yahweh intends to carry forever. Therefore, prophets, priests, or people who claim they know Yahweh's *massa'* (Yahweh's message) when actually it has been devised out of their own minds, should shut up. They shouldn't talk in terms of Yahweh's *massa'*. They don't know what they're talking about.

Jeremiah's problem is that his having attended a meeting of Yahweh's cabinet is as invisible as his fellow prophets' dreams. You can't prove anything by accounts of your religious experiences. He needs a more objective basis for critiquing the other prophets. His first argument is their impiety; there's something wrong with their spirituality, their religious observance. They can be deeply spiritual but wrong. Their leadership of worship in Yahweh's house shows it. Presumably he refers to the same forms of worship that he attacks elsewhere, such as the recognition of other deities as well as Yahweh and the offering of human sacrifice. His second criterion is a moral one. They're involved in adultery and deceit, and they collude with other people who are so involved instead of confronting them as prophets should. Indeed, they promise the people that things will go well in their lives despite the wrongdoing that they practice.

Jeremiah is mystified by the prophets and by their people. There's a mystery about human sin. The particular aspect of the enigma that preoccupies him here is their failure to take account of truths about God that in theory they surely acknowledge. They don't think they can escape God's awareness of their actions and God's reach to deal with them, do they? Doesn't he fill the entire cosmos?

JEREMIAH 24:1–25:11a

Lucky Figs and Unlucky Figs

[1]Yahweh showed me: there, two baskets of figs placed in front of Yahweh's palace (after Nebuchadrezzar, king of Babylon, exiled Jekoniah son of Jehoiaqim, king of Judah, Judah's officials, the craftsmen, and the smiths from Jerusalem and brought them to Babylon). [2]One basket was of very good figs, like early figs, one basket was of very bad figs that couldn't be eaten because of being bad. [3]Yahweh said to me, "What are you looking at, Jeremiah?" I said, "Figs—the good figs, very good; the bad, very bad, which couldn't be eaten because of being bad." [4]Yahweh's message came to me. [5]Yahweh, Israel's God, has said this: Like these good figs, so I'll mark down for good Judah's exilic community that I've sent off from this place to the Kaldeans' country. [6]I'll set my eye on them for good and bring them back to this country. I'll build them and not overthrow. I'll plant them and not uproot. [7]I'll give them a mind to acknowledge me, that I am Yahweh. They'll be a people for me and I'll be God for them, because they'll turn to me with their whole mind. [8]But like bad figs that can't be eaten because of being bad (because Yahweh has said this), so will I make Zedekiah, king of Judah, his officials, and the remains of Jerusalem that remain in this country and who are dwelling in the country of Egypt—[9]I'll make them a horror, an evil, to all earth's kingdoms, an insult and an example, a taunt and a

123

humiliation, in all the places where I drive them. [10]I'll send against them sword, famine, and epidemic until they come to an end from upon the land that I gave to them and their ancestors.

[25:1]The message that came to Jeremiah concerning all Judah's people in the fourth year of Jehoiaqim son of Josiah, king of Judah (it was the first year of Nebuchadrezzar, king of Babylon), [2]which Jeremiah the prophet spoke to all Judah's people and all Jerusalem's residents: [3]From the thirteenth year of Josiah son of Amon, king of Judah, to this day, twenty-three years, Yahweh's word has come to me, and I've spoken to you, speaking urgently, but you haven't listened. [4]Yahweh has been sending to you all his servants, sending urgently, but you haven't listened, you haven't bent your ear to listen: [5]"Will you turn, each one, from his evil way, from the evil of your acts, so that you may live on the land that Yahweh gave you and your ancestors, from earliest ages to furthest ages. [6]Don't follow other gods so as to serve them and bow down to them. Don't provoke me with the work of your hands, and I won't bring evil to you." [7]But you didn't listen to me (Yahweh's declaration), so as to provoke me with the work of your hands, to bring evil to you. [8]Therefore Yahweh Armies has said this: Since you haven't listened to my words, [9]here am I; I'm going to send and get all the northern families (Yahweh's declaration) and Nebuchadrezzar, king of Babylon, my servant, and bring them against this country and its residents, and all these nations around about. I'll devote them and make them a devastation, something to whistle at, desolation forever. [10]I'll eliminate from them the sound of rejoicing, of celebration, the voice of bride and groom, the sound of the mill and the light of the lamp. [11]This entire country will become a desolation, a devastation.

We walked past a supermarket last night and marveled at the size of the truck delivering produce, and we wondered how quickly the supermarket would empty if there were a big earthquake (answer: about two hours). Then we walked across a freeway bridge, and my wife reflected that this would be a bad moment for an earthquake, which corresponds to the thought I have when we cycle under another giant freeway bridge nearby. We'd then be unlucky; people who were not at the wrong place at the wrong moment would be lucky.

Jeremiah is talking about lucky figs and unlucky figs. That is, the good figs don't stand for faithful people, nor do the bad figs stand for the faithless. He has his vision at the moment when the **Babylonians** have removed Jehoiakin aka Jekoniah aka Koniah from the throne, taken him and other **Judahite** leaders off to Babylon, and put Zedekiah on the throne in his place. It's easy to imagine the PR exercise in Jerusalem that argued for seeing the people who escaped **exile** as the good figs—the people who didn't deserve to be taken to Babylon and the people with whom the future lies—and for seeing the people who were exiled as the bad figs who deserved what they got. We know from what Jeremiah has already said about both Jehoiakin and Zedekiah that he wouldn't view either of them or their company as good figs in the sense of faithful people. On the other hand, it would indeed seem that Zedekiah and company were lucky figs in the sense that they were the people who've escaped exile. Jeremiah's point is to turn that argument on its head. The future lies with the people who've been taken off into exile, even though they don't deserve it to be so; they'll need to be given a mind to acknowledge **Yahweh**. They don't have such a mind at the moment.

As usual, Jeremiah is trying to get through his audience's thick skulls to get them to come to their senses. Instead of congratulating themselves on their escape, they need to see the fate that also awaits them. If they'll do so, then all those threats about throwing away bad figs can be abandoned, in keeping with the lesson that emerged from watching the potter in Jeremiah 18.

The second paragraph takes us back half a decade again, back to a moment before the dividing of the figs. It's the year

125

Nebuchadnezzar came to the throne in Babylon (Jeremiah often spells his name Nebuchadrezzar—they're two different ways of turning the Babylonian name into Hebrew and then into English). Earlier that year, before his father's death, Nebuchadnezzar had led the Babylonian army to an epoch-making victory over the Egyptian army in a battle at Carchemish in northern Syria, which sealed Babylon's position as the controlling power in Judah's world. It means that Judah has had nearly a quarter of a century to respond to Jeremiah's preaching, but this time is coming to an end. It means Babylon will fulfill the role of the enemy from the north of which Jeremiah has spoken, and it means its fulfillment of that role will come soon. Yahweh is thus designating Nebuchadnezzar as "my servant." It's a term that has been applied previously to Abraham, Moses, Caleb, David, Job, Isaiah, and Eliaqim, but never to a foreigner or to someone whose purpose was destructive. Yahweh's designating the Babylonian king thus is a striking declaration of power in the political world; Nebuchadnezzar thought he was his own master, but unknowingly he's Yahweh's servant. It's also a frightening declaration of judgment in Judah's world.

JEREMIAH 25:11b–38

Bad News or Good News?

[11b]These nations will serve the king of Babylon for seventy years, [12]but when seventy years are complete, I shall deal with the king of Babylon and with that nation (Yahweh's declaration) for their waywardness, with the Kaldeans' country, and make it a devastation forever. [13]I'll bring upon that country all my words that I've spoken against it, all that's written in this book that Jeremiah prophesied against all the nations. [14]Because they, too, will serve many nations and great kings. I'll repay them according to their action and according to the work of their hands. [15]Because Yahweh, Israel's God, has said

this to me: Take this chalice of wine (wrath) from my hand and get all the nations to which I'm sending you to drink it. [16]They'll drink and throw up and go mad because of the sword that I'm sending among them.

[17]So I took the chalice from Yahweh's hand and got all the nations to which Yahweh sent me to drink: [18]Jerusalem and all Judah's cities, its kings and its officials, to make them a desolation, a devastation, something to whistle at, a humiliation, this very day; [19]Pharaoh, the king of Egypt, his staff, his officials, all his people, [20]and all the foreign group; all the kings of the country of Uz; all the kings of the country of the Philistines, Ashkelon, Gaza, Ekron, and the remains of Ashdod; [21]Edom, Moab, and Ammon; [22]all the kings of Tyre, all the kings of Sidon, and the kings of the shore that's across the sea; [23]Dedan, Tema, and Buz, and all the people shaved at the forehead; [24]all the kings of Arabia and all the kings of the foreign group who dwell in the wilderness; [25]all the kings of Zimri, all the kings of Elam, and all the kings of Media; [26]all the northern kings, whether near or far, each to his brother; all the kingdoms of the countries that are on the face of the land; and the king of Sheshak will drink, the last of them.

[27]You're to say to them: Yahweh Armies, Israel's God, has said this: Drink, get drunk, throw up, fall down, and don't get up again, because of the sword that I'm sending among you. [28]When they refuse to take the chalice from your hand to drink, you're to say to them, Yahweh Armies has said this, Drink, drink, [29]because here, in the city that's called by my name I'm beginning to bring evil, and shall you really be treated as innocent? You won't be treated as innocent, because I'm summoning a sword against all earth's inhabitants (a declaration of Yahweh Armies).

[30]   You're to prophesy all these things to them,
         and say to them:
      Yahweh roars from on high,
         from his holy dwelling he gives voice,
         he roars and roars against his abode.
      He chants a cry like grape treaders
         to all earth's inhabitants.

31 The noise has come to the end of the earth,
    because Yahweh has a contention against the
        nations.
  He's exercising authority toward all flesh;
    the faithless—he's giving them to the sword
    (Yahweh's declaration).
32 Yahweh Armies has said this:
  There is evil going out, from nation to nation;
    a great storm arises from earth's remotest parts.

33 People slain by Yahweh on that day will be from the end of the earth to the end of the earth. They won't be lamented or gathered up and buried; they'll become dung on the surface of the ground.

34 Howl, you shepherds, cry out,
    throw yourselves about, lords of the flock.
  Because the days of your slaughter are fully here;
    I'll scatter you, and you'll fall like a precious
        bowl.
35 Flight will perish from the shepherds,
    escape from the lords of the flock.
36 The sound of the shepherds' cry,
    the howls of the lords of the flock!
  Because Yahweh is destroying their pastures,
37   the meadows with their well-being will be ruined
    through the burning of Yahweh's anger.
38 He's abandoned his thicket like a lion
    because his country has become a devastation,
  because of the oppressor's blazing,
    because of his angry blazing.

It's possible to be pretty gloomy about the future. Today's news includes a white gunman killing six Sikh worshipers in a temple in Milwaukee, which other worshipers took as a hate crime reflecting the assumption that people dressed in Sikh fashion were Muslims and thus equated with the Taliban. The news also showed pictures of an exhausted and homeless family from Oklahoma, just one of many families that were the victims of wildfires over the weekend. Businesses are putting off investment and the hiring of new employees because they fear the continuing effects of recession. That's just the national news. In Syria there's civil war; in Mali something like it is threatened; and in Yemen forty-five people died in a suicide bombing. Will it go on forever?

Within Jeremiah's lifetime it was a reasonable question in **Judah** and elsewhere in the Middle East. Nebuchadnezzar has established **Babylon** in an apparently invincible position as heir to the **Assyrian** empire and is about to bring Judah and its neighbors firmly to heel, terminating Judah's earlier semi-independence. This chapter stands back from Judah's situation and looks at it in its broader international and chronological context, and thus brings the first half of the book of Jeremiah to a close.

It's both bad news and good news that Babylonian power will last seventy years. There's not much evidence that seventy years suggested an average lifetime (most people lived much shorter lives); more likely the figure relates to the use of seven to suggest completeness. It certainly denotes a long period, at the end of which virtually no one who was alive at the beginning will still be alive. In other words, hardly anyone who hears Jeremiah's message will see the end of Babylonian domination. But "seventy years" is not designed to suggest a precise period (the time from Jerusalem's fall to Babylon's fall was forty-eight years, though the time from the battle of Carchemish to Babylon's fall or from Jerusalem's fall to the temple rebuilding was closer to seventy years).

Therein lies the bad news. The good news is that at least Babylonian power won't last forever. Empires always think they'll do so. It's not simply for human reasons, such as the fact that empires get tired and new powers arise. It's for moral reasons; Babylon will need to be punished for its waywardness as Judah was. The poison chalice that **Yahweh** gives Judah and other nations will pass to Babylon, for which Sheshak is a cipher. We don't know why this name is used. It was hardly intended to conceal anything, since Babylon is named so often; maybe it was an insult.

It's chilling that Judah appears as just one recipient of the chalice—first, but first among equals. There's nothing special about Judah as Yahweh's chosen, because there's nothing special about its commitment to Yahweh. Jeremiah closes with another warning about the destiny of Judah's leaders, part of whose significance will be that it's never too late for them to start exercising a leadership that will hold back Yahweh's judgment rather than make it inevitable.

It would be nice to think that Jeremiah is exaggerating in his prognostications about world events, but he was pretty much right, which is one reason that Judah kept hold of his prophecies. One could say it's a matter of interpretation whether Yahweh was really involved in the war making and bloodshed of Jeremiah's day. Jeremiah might respond that the idea that world events unfold without God being involved is even more frightening than the idea that he *is* involved.

JEREMIAH 26:1–24

Not Always the Hollywood Ending

[1]At the beginning of the reign of Jehoiaqim son of Josiah, king of Judah, this message came from Yahweh: [2]Yahweh has said this: Stand in the courtyard of Yahweh's house and speak to all Judah's cities, the people coming to bow down in Yahweh's house, all the words that I'm commanding you to speak to them. Don't omit a thing. [3]Perhaps they'll listen and turn, each from his evil way, and I'll relent regarding the evil that I'm intending to do to them because of the evil of their deeds. [4]You're to say to them, Yahweh has said this: If you

don't listen to me by walking according to the teaching that I've set in front of you, [5]listening to the words of my servants the prophets whom I've been sending to you, sending them urgently (but you haven't listened), [6]I'll make this house like Shiloh, and make this city a humiliation to all the nations of the earth.

[7]The priests, prophets, and the entire people listened to Jeremiah speaking these words in Yahweh's house. [8]When Jeremiah finished speaking all that Yahweh had commanded him to speak to the entire people, the priests, prophets, and the entire people seized him: "You are definitely to die! [9]Why have you been prophesying in Yahweh's name, 'This house will become like Shiloh, and this city will be desolate, without resident'?" The entire people assembled against Jeremiah in Yahweh's house. [10]Judah's officials heard these things and went up from the king's house to Yahweh's house and sat in the entrance of Yahweh's New Gate. [11]The priests and the prophets said to the officials and the entire people, "A sentence of death is appropriate to this man, because he's prophesied against this city, as you've heard with your own ears." [12]Jeremiah said to all the officials and to the entire people, "It was Yahweh sent me to prophesy against this house and this city all the words that you heard. [13]So now make your ways and your deeds good and listen to the voice of Yahweh your God, so that Yahweh may relent of the evil that he's spoken against you. [14]And me—here am I in your hand. Do to me in accordance with what is good and right in your eyes. [15]Yet you must fully acknowledge that if you put me to death, you're putting the blood of someone who's innocent on yourselves. Because in truth Yahweh sent me to you to speak all these things in your ears."

[16]The officials and the entire people said to the priests and prophets, "The sentence of death isn't appropriate, because it was in the name of Yahweh our God that he spoke to us." [17]Some people from the country's elders got up and said to all the assembly of the people, [18]"Micah the Morashtite was prophesying in the days of Hezekiah, king of Judah. He said to Judah's entire people:

131

Yahweh Armies has said this:
  Zion will be plowed as open countryside.
Jerusalem will become heaps of rubble,
  the mountain of the house shrines in the forest.

[19]Did Hezekiah, king of Judah, and all Judah put him to death at all? Was he not in awe of Yahweh and did he not seek Yahweh's face, so that Yahweh relented of the evil that he spoke against them? We are going to do a great evil to ourselves."
[20]There was also a man prophesying in Yahweh's name, Uriah son of Shemaiah from Qiriat-jearim. He prophesied against this city and against this people in accordance with all Jeremiah's words. [21]King Jehoiaqim, all his warriors, and all the officials heard his words, and the king sent to put him to death, but Uriah heard and was afraid and fled, and came to Egypt. [22]But King Jehoiaqim sent men to Egypt, Elnathan son of Akbor and men with him, to Egypt. [23]They made Uriah leave Egypt and brought him to King Jehoiaqim, and he struck him down with the sword and threw his corpse into the common graves. [24]However, the hand of Ahiqam son of Shaphan was with Jeremiah so as not to give him into the people's hand to put him to death.

Last night we watched a French movie about a couple whose baby son developed a brain tumor. The movie focused on the way the couple coped, naturally with tensions and grief but also with determination and energy and more than a little therapeutic craziness. There were MRIs and surgeries, ups and downs, hopes and disappointments, and then rather a quick rush from when the boy is three or four to when he's eight and the neurosurgeon declares that he's totally free of the cancer and free to catch up on life and live normally. And I thought, "It's too neat a way for the movie to finish. Life so often isn't like that, but maybe even the French need a Hollywood ending."

The story about Jeremiah, Micah, and Uriah works the other way around. So far, nearly all the book has comprised messages Jeremiah gave, though sometimes these have been set in a story context. The book's second half takes the reverse approach. It's mostly stories (indeed, sometimes Jeremiah doesn't appear), though these do incorporate some messages from him. This first section neatly encapsulates the difference, because chapter 7 has already given us the text of his message about the threat that Jerusalem will end up like Shiloh; here we get the account of his delivering it and of people's reactions. The book of Jeremiah's focus on the man is unique among the Prophets. It brings out further a point that has been present in the first half, that people's attitude to God is expressed in their attitude to and their treatment of his representative.

We now discover that the time when Jeremiah delivered that Shiloh sermon was the beginning of the reign of Jehoiaqim, son of Josiah. Josiah was someone Jeremiah could be enthusiastic about, a king who at least tried to reform **Judah** religiously and socially. It wouldn't be surprising if Jeremiah was pretty angry at Josiah's getting himself killed in a military action that Jeremiah would hardly have enthused over—not because he was a pacifist but because Josiah was taking into his own hands matters that should be left to **Yahweh**. It wouldn't be surprising if Jeremiah was grieved, too. Certainly he opposed everything that Josiah's son Jehoiaqim stood for. While the son was very different from the father, they had in common an instinct to respect realpolitik, an instinct Jehoiaqim followed as unsuccessfully as his father; both were inclined to back the wrong horse politically.

To judge from the text of the sermon in chapter 7, however, it was the religious and social unfaithfulness that was the focus on this occasion; here the reference to heeding the teaching or **Torah** fits that theme. It fits the way Jeremiah antagonizes the priests, prophets, and people; the politicians come into the picture only later in the story. Jeremiah's boldness here and through the sequence of stories in the book's second half contrasts with the agonizing related in the first half.

We've noted that there's no implication that he went through his inner crisis during the first part of his ministry and stood with inner resolution through the second part. More likely the inner conflict and the outward boldness coexist, though one or the other will be more prevalent at any given moment. Someone at church on Sunday quoted to me the aphorism "Courage is fear that has said its prayers." That's Jeremiah.

Maybe it was also Micah. He was as straight as Jeremiah in his threats to Jerusalem, and the people's elders suggest that people's reaction to Micah models the appropriate reaction to Jeremiah. You can read Micah's prophecies in the book that bears his name, though the Old Testament doesn't tell of people's reaction to them. Maybe the elders are putting two and two together, given that they're right that Yahweh did spare Jerusalem in Hezekiah's day. (As an alternative to Micah, the Hebrew text also refers to Micaiah, whose story appears in 1 Kings 22. He can't be the sermon's original reference, however, for he lived in **Ephraim**, not in Judah, but he also embodies the point.)

There was no Hollywood ending for Uriah. Sometimes things do work out, as they did for Jeremiah. Sometimes they don't. Ahiqam had been a member of Josiah's staff who had supported Josiah's reformation, and he's evidently still able to exercise some influence. Uriah has no such luck.

JEREMIAH 27:1–22

Things Can Only Get Worse

[1] At the beginning of the reign of Jehoiaqim son of Josiah, king of Judah, this message came to Jeremiah from Yahweh: [2] Yahweh said this to me: Make yourself straps and bars and put them on your neck, [3] and send them to the king of Edom, the king of Moab, the king of the Ammonites, the king of Tyre, and the king of Sidon, by the hand of the aides who have come to Jerusalem to Zedekiah, king of Judah. [4] Command them

regarding their lords: Yahweh Armies, Israel's God, has said this: You're to say this to your lords: [5]I am the one who made the earth and the human beings and animals that are on the face of the earth, by my great power and my arm stretched out, and I give it to whoever is right in my eyes. [6]So now, I'm giving all these countries into the hand of Nebuchadnezzar, king of Babylon, my servant. Even the creatures of the wild I'm giving him to serve him. [7]All the nations will serve him, his son, and his grandson, until the time comes for his country, him too. Many nations and great kings will serve him; [8]the nation or kingdom that won't serve him (Nebuchadnezzar, king of Babylon), that won't give its neck to the yoke of the king of Babylon: I'll deal with that nation by sword, famine, and epidemic (Yahweh's declaration) until I have brought them to an end by his hand.

[9]So you, don't listen to your prophets, augurs, dreams, mediums, or diviners, who are saying to you, "Don't serve the king of Babylon." [10]Because they're speaking falsehood to you, so he may take you far from your country, and I drive you out and you perish. [11]But the nation that brings its neck to the yoke of the king of Babylon and serves him, I'll allow to stay on its land (Yahweh's declaration) and serve it and live on it.

[12]To Zedekiah, king of Judah, I spoke in accordance with these words: Bring your necks to the king of Babylon's yoke, serve him and his people, and live. [13]Why should you die, you and your people, by sword, famine, and epidemic, as Yahweh has said regarding the nation that doesn't serve the king of Babylon? [14]Don't listen to the words of the prophets who are saying to you, "Don't serve the king of Babylon," because they're prophesying falsehood to you. [15]Because I didn't send them (Yahweh's declaration) and they're prophesying falsely in my name, so that I'll drive you out and you'll perish, you and the prophets who are prophesying to you.

[16]And to the priests and to this entire people I spoke: Yahweh has said this: Don't listen to the words of the prophets who are prophesying to you, "Right: the things from Yahweh's house are going to be returned from Babylon now, very soon," because they're prophesying falsehood to you. [17]Don't listen to

them; serve the king of Babylon and live—why should this city become a desolation? [18]If they're prophets and Yahweh's message is with them, they should intercede with Yahweh Armies so that the rest of the things in Yahweh's house, in the house of the king of Judah, and in Jerusalem don't come to Babylon. [19]Because Yahweh Armies has said this about the pillars, the Sea, the stands, and the rest of the things that remain in this city, [20]which Nebuchadnezzar, king of Babylon, didn't take when he exiled Jekoniah son of Jehoiaqim, king of Judah, from Jerusalem to Babylon, and all the important people from Judah and Jerusalem—[21]because Yahweh Armies, Israel's God, has said about the things that remain in Yahweh's house, in the house of the king of Judah, and in Jerusalem: [22]To Babylon they'll be transported, and there they'll be, until the day when I deal with them (Yahweh's declaration) and bring them up and return them to this place.

As a newly ordained minister I was required to take part in "postordination training," irreverently known as "potty training." It's no criticism of it that decades later I remember little about it, but I do have one vivid memory. The third year of the program involved monthly meetings with a senior rector in the diocese, along with two of my peers. This rector told us that in the ten years he'd been in his parish (one of the flagship parishes in the diocese), he'd seen no growth, only decline. I guess he'd seen growth in individuals; he was referring to statistics such as the number of people attending services. What struck me wasn't so much the objective facts but the way this rector could own them, and do so in front of three young-sters like us.

Jeremiah has to try to get people to face tough facts, which include the fact that things are only going to get worse. Actually they've been doing so for three hundred years, and politically speaking they aren't going to get better for quite a few centuries. The main part of this chapter is dated in the reign of Zedekiah (the beginning also likely has that background—the opening reference to Jehoiaqim is odd in this context). Things have moved on since the story of Jeremiah's narrow escape from martyrdom. Jehoiaqim died young, like his father, and his own son Jehoiakin succeeded him. Unfortunately for him, a **Babylonian** invasion immediately followed; the Babylonians took Jerusalem, deposed Jehoiakin, took him and many other Jerusalemites to Babylon, and replaced the eighteen-year-old by his uncle, Zedekiah. These events fulfilled those warnings of Jeremiah that nearly led to his martyrdom.

Yet you don't have to reread those warnings very closely to see that the events of 597 left a lot unfulfilled. They were a shot across the bows. The city hasn't been destroyed; the temple is still functioning. But only if **Judah** heeds that shot does it evade a more comprehensive barrage, and there's no sign yet of any heeding. So boring old Jeremiah continues to play the same old tune. Actually he broadcasts it, playing it not only to Judah but to the other peoples around who are also going to pay the price for resisting **Yahweh**'s intention to let Nebuchadnezzar rule the area for a while (until his own time comes). Jeremiah plays further with the image of servanthood. When you're the servant of someone powerful, you have power yourself as you go about serving him. So as Yahweh's servant, other peoples must serve Nebuchadnezzar, and even the wild animals must do so. It's not clear what the practical implications would be for the animals; the point is metaphorical or rhetorical— it further underscores the mastery of Nebuchadnezzar that people must acknowledge. The nations must see themselves as like domesticated animals, and if even the wild animals must serve him, then at this moment of time mere domesticated animals must certainly submit willingly to his yoke, with its bars and straps, in order to play their role.

Jeremiah's broadcast to the other peoples is meant for Judah to overhear, but it has independent implications. One is that Yahweh is the lord and creator of the whole world. As creator, Yahweh is lord of political events all over the world. He can do as he likes in the world. It needn't mean that every political event, change of regime, or emergence of a new superpower has special significance; God may often just let things work themselves out. It does mean that he can be doing something deliberate through political events when he wishes. A second implication is that he's involved in the destiny of these other peoples and that they need to heed what he's doing. The principle of Yahweh's relationship with Judah applies to them, too. If they heed the way Yahweh is acting (and thus submit to Nebuchadnezzar), things will work out well for them; if they resist Yahweh, trouble will follow. Yahweh uses the same means (sword, famine, epidemic) to work with them as he does with Judah—and vice versa. A third is that their destiny is bound up with Judah's. It's for Judah's sake (in a negative way) that Yahweh is giving Nebuchadnezzar power in their area. The focus of Yahweh's action is Judah. The other peoples need to fit in with what Yahweh is doing with Judah (ultimately that will be for their salvation, and for the world's).

Though the city has been breached, it hasn't been destroyed. Though the temple has been pillaged, it still stands. Though some things from the temple have gone, many remain. Though a king has been transported, another king reigns in his place. Yet this means things can get much worse, and the Judahites mustn't believe the people who are saying they'll get better soon (because they were hired to say so). The people speaking thus should be praying rather than offering reassurances.

JEREMIAH 28:1–17

No T-shirts Saying "False Prophet"

¹That year, at the beginning of the reign of Zedekiah, king of Judah, in the fifth month of the fourth year, Hananiah son of Azzur, the prophet, who was from Gibeon, said to me in Yahweh's house in front of the priests and the entire people: ²"Yahweh Armies, Israel's God, has said this: I'm breaking the

king of Babylon's yoke. [3]In yet two years' time I'm going to return to this place all the things from Yahweh's house that Nebuchadnezzar, king of Babylon, took from this place and brought to Babylon. [4]And I'm going to return to this place Jekoniah son of Jehoiaqim, king of Judah, and all Judah's exilic community who came to Babylon (Yahweh's declaration), because I'm breaking the king of Babylon's yoke." [5]Jeremiah the prophet said to Hananiah the prophet in front of the priests and the entire people standing in Yahweh's house—[6]Jeremiah the prophet said, "Amen! So may Yahweh do. May Yahweh perform your words, which you've prophesied, returning the things from Yahweh's house and the entire exilic community from Babylon to this place. [7]Nevertheless do listen to this word that I'm speaking in your ears and the ears of the entire people. [8]The prophets who were before me and before you, from of old, prophesied concerning many countries and about great kingdoms, regarding battle, famine, and epidemic. [9]The prophet who prophesies of things going well—when the prophet's message comes about, he can be acknowledged as one whom Yahweh sent in truth." [10]But Hananiah the prophet took the bar from on Jeremiah the prophet's neck and broke it. [11]Hananiah said in front of the entire people: "Yahweh has said this: In this way I shall break the yoke of Nebuchadnezzar, king of Babylon, in yet two years from all the nations' necks."

Jeremiah the prophet went his way. [12]But Yahweh's message came to Jeremiah after Hananiah the prophet broke the bar from on Jeremiah the prophet's neck: [13]Go and say to Hananiah, Yahweh has said this: You broke bars of wood, but you're to make bars of iron. [14]Because Yahweh Armies, Israel's God, has said this: I'm putting an iron yoke on the neck of all these nations so that they serve Nebuchadnezzar, king of Babylon. They shall serve him; even the creatures of the wild I am giving him. [15]Jeremiah the prophet said to Hananiah the prophet, "Do listen, Hananiah. Yahweh hasn't sent you, and you're one who has made this people trust in falsehood. [16]Therefore Yahweh has said this: Here am I; I'm going to send you off from upon the face of the land. This year you're going to die, because you've spoken of turning aside in relation to Yahweh." [17]Hananiah the prophet died that year in the seventh month.

In a restaurant last night we sat near a man in a Union Jack t-shirt, and as we left I yielded to the temptation to ask him if he had the Queen's permission to wear it. He grinned and said something that indicated that he was indeed a Brit, and his wife assured me in a Scottish accent that this permission had been granted the previous week. Today I'm wearing a t-shirt bearing the word *Security* in Hebrew, but I'm not actually an Israeli security guard. I often wear t-shirts I've bought at concerts, but people's t-shirts are not reliable indicators of what concerts they went to; sometimes they find them in the thrift store.

Metaphorically speaking, both Jeremiah and Hananiah wore t-shirts that said "Prophet." The story keeps applying that word to both of them. If you had been in the temple, you wouldn't have been able to see any obvious difference between them. Both introduce their messages by saying, "**Yahweh** has said this." The form of words is the one a king's representative uses; prophets are people who relay messages from the heavenly king. Both Jeremiah and Hananiah acted as well as spoke. The yoke is a means of harnessing an animal for its tasks. It's not oppressive if one assumes that the animal can be domesticated, for the yoke carries with it an assurance of food and shelter. Jeremiah urges the people to accept that they have this kind of relationship with Nebuchadnezzar, and Hananiah uses the same symbolism to urge them not to accept it. Beyond bringing the point home to the people, because the prophet acts as the king's representative, the action implements what it pictures. That is true of Jeremiah's making a yoke and of Hananiah's breaking it.

So when this chapter introduces Hananiah, it simply calls him a prophet, like Jeremiah. When just before the time of

Christ Jewish scholars translated this chapter into **Greek** for the benefit of people who didn't know Hebrew, they called him a pseudo-prophet or false prophet, which helped their readers understand the text. But Hananiah didn't go around in a t-shirt saying "False Prophet" (I might wear such a t-shirt, however, just to make people think). His t-shirt said "Prophet," like Jeremiah's. Casting about for a way of articulating what makes him a false prophet, Jeremiah declares that Yahweh didn't send him. But his credentials look plausible. Jeremiah points out that prophets are usually people who bring bad news rather than good news. You don't usually need prophets to tell people that things are going to be OK. Until things are manifestly horrible, they're naturally inclined to assume that things will continue to be OK. Yet the promises Hananiah makes fit the promises Isaiah once invited Jerusalem to trust in.

Indeed, you might be tempted to think that Hananiah looks more like the real prophet. He's a more powerful personality than Jeremiah. When he breaks the yoke that Jeremiah's wearing, Jeremiah simply goes his way. You could get the impression that he slinks away defeated. He has nothing else to say. Evidently there are times for going your way and leaving God to sort things out, for resisting the temptation to say something when God hasn't given you something to say (come to think of it, there are no times for yielding to that temptation). Hananiah has the gift of the gab. Whether Jeremiah has it or not, he isn't exercising it. He waits until he has a sense of God's saying something and then watches for the frightening fulfillment. You could wonder if Hananiah's death is a coincidence. With the reserve the Old Testament often shows, the story doesn't actually say, "So, you see, Jeremiah's prophecy was fulfilled, and he was proved to be the true prophet." It leaves us to work it out. It also hints that we should work hard to avoid being commissioned as prophets or thinking we are so commissioned, in case we are fooling ourselves.

JEREMIAH 29:1–32

Settle Down

[1]These are the words in the document that Jeremiah the prophet sent from Jerusalem to the rest of the elders of the exilic community, the priests, the prophets, and the entire people that Nebuchadnezzar had taken into exile from Jerusalem to Babylon [2](after King Jeconiah, the queen mother, the eunuchs, the officials of Judah and Jerusalem, the craftsmen, and the smiths left Jerusalem), [3]by the hand of Elasah son of Shaphan and Gemariah son of Hilqiah, whom Zedekiah, king of Judah, sent to Babylon to Nebuchadnezzar, king of Babylon: [4]Yahweh Armies, Israel's God, has said this to the entire exilic community that I sent into exile from Jerusalem to Babylon: [5]Build houses and live [there], plant gardens and eat their fruit. [6]Take wives and have sons and daughters, take wives for your sons and give your daughters to husbands, so they may have sons and daughters. Become many there; don't become few. [7]Seek the well-being of the city where I've sent you into exile; plead on its behalf with Yahweh, because in its well-being there will be well-being for you.

[8]Because Yahweh Armies, Israel's God, has said this: Your prophets who are in your midst and your diviners must not deceive you. You must not listen to your dreams, which you're dreaming. [9]Because they're prophesying to you falsely in my name; I haven't sent them (Yahweh's declaration). [10]Because Yahweh has said this: At the completion for Babylon of seventy years I'll deal with you, and perform for you my message about good things, returning you to this place. [11]Because I myself acknowledge the intentions that I'm formulating for you (Yahweh's declaration), intentions for your well-being and not for evil, to give you a future, a hope. [12]You'll call me and come and plead with me and I'll listen to you. [13]You'll inquire of me and find me if you seek help from me with your entire spirit. [14]I'll be available to you (Yahweh's declaration) and I'll restore your fortunes. I'll draw you together from all the nations and from all the places where I've driven you (Yahweh's declaration). I'll return you to the place from where I've sent you into exile.

[15]Yet you've said, "Yahweh has set up prophets for us in Babylon." [16]Yet Yahweh has said this regarding the king who sits on David's throne and the entire people that lives in this city, your brothers who haven't gone out with you into exile— [17]Yahweh Armies has said this: Here am I; I'm going to send off against them sword, famine, and epidemic. I'll make them like horrible figs that may not be eaten because of being bad. [18]I'll pursue them with sword, famine, and epidemic and make them a horror to all the kingdoms of the earth, a curse, a devastation, something to whistle at, and an insult among all the nations where I drive them out, [19]on account of the fact that they didn't listen to my words (Yahweh's declaration), in that I sent them my servants the prophets, sending urgently. But you haven't listened (Yahweh's declaration). [20]So you people, the entire exilic community that I sent off from Jerusalem to Babylon, listen to Yahweh's word. [21]Yahweh Armies, Israel's God, has said this regarding Ahab son of Qolaiah and Zedekiah son of Ma'aseiah who are prophesying to you in my name: Here am I; I'm going to give them into the hand of Nebuchadrezzar, king of Babylon. He'll strike them down in front of your eyes. [22]A belittling will be derived from them for the entire exilic community of Judah in Babylon: "May Yahweh make you like Ahab and Zedekiah, whom the king of Babylon roasted in fire, [23]since they performed stupidity in Israel and committed adultery with the wives of their neighbors and spoke a message in my name that was false, which I hadn't commanded them." I am the one who knows and who testifies (Yahweh's declaration).

[24]And regarding Shemaiah the Nehelemite you're to say: [25]Yahweh Armies, Israel's God, has said this: Since you're the one who has sent documents in your name to the entire people in Jerusalem, to Zephaniah son of Ma'aseiah the priest, and to all the priests, saying, [26]Yahweh has made you priest instead of Jehoiada the priest, so that there are administrators over Yahweh's house for anyone who's mad and is prophesying, and you're to put him into the stocks and into the neck iron. [27]So now, why have you not stopped Jeremiah from Anatot who's prophesying to you? [28]Because

on account of this he's sent to us in Babylon, saying, "It will be a long time. Build houses and live [there], plant gardens and eat their fruit."

[29]Zephaniah the priest read this document out in the hearing of Jeremiah the prophet. [30]Yahweh's message came to Jeremiah: [31]Send to the entire exilic community, saying: Yahweh has said this regarding Shemaiah the Nehelemite: Since Shemaiah has prophesied to you and I myself hadn't sent him, and he's got you to trust in falsehood, [32]therefore Yahweh has said this: Here am I; I'm going to deal with Shemaiah the Nehelemite and with his offspring. He won't have anyone dwelling among this people and he won't see the good things that I'm going to do for this people (Yahweh's declaration), because he's spoken of turning away from Yahweh.

When I first moved to California, people would ask how long I'd be here, thinking it might be just for an academic quarter or year. They'd be a bit taken aback when I said, "I want to die here," so I would add, "but not too soon," yet they'd still be taken aback, so I stopped saying it. It was a kind of marker when I bought a three-hole-punch to replace my British two-hole one, bought a street atlas, and subscribed to the local newspaper. But I'm still a British citizen, because I could never *feel* American—I was British for too long. I still sound British to people in the United States, though in Britain I use expressions that give me away in the opposite direction. I sometimes say that my home is the middle of the Atlantic.

I'm not in forced exile. I can go back to Britain if I wish. The **Judahites** in **Babylon** think they're there for just a short while. Their prophets are telling them so. Jeremiah's job is to tell them to settle down. The exhortation to seek the **well-being** of their city could look like an encouragement to fight poverty, create jobs, and be good citizens. Such commitments have nothing to do with Jeremiah's point. People aren't being urged to seek the welfare of their own city but to commit themselves to a city where they don't belong and that they think they'll soon leave. They're to seek the welfare of the city where they're forced to live because their own welfare is tied up with that city, precisely because they're going to be stuck there for seventy years—in other words, forever as far as the present generation is concerned.

A parallel in the life of the Western church might be that if God has taken it into exile so that the church no longer counts in our culture, we need to settle down in that position until God wants to restore us, rather than trying to turn the church into something the culture wants. Maybe we have prophets who tell us we can return from this exile sooner rather than later, and maybe we have dreams of this kind, and the prophets might be right, and the dreams might be God given. In Jeremiah's day, however, such dreams came out of people's own heads. They hadn't taken seriously enough the reason that God had taken his people into **exile**. But the people also need to beware of becoming demoralized. When you've been taken off into exile, can you be bothered to build and plant? Do you want to bring children into this godforsaken world? Actually, the message says, your job is to flourish. The destiny of the people of God is to increase, not decrease.

Christians also "claim" the promise about God's having plans for the people to give them a future and a hope, and again we do so in ways that have nothing much to do with Jeremiah's point but more to do with the Western church's position in exile. Once again Jeremiah's words presuppose that there's no quick fix for the community's situation. This doesn't mean the situation is hopeless. It does mean people need to be prepared to take the long view. It will be a while before normal communication is restored between **Yahweh** and Judah, communication that involves the expected Old Testament pattern of their bringing their needs in prayer to Yahweh and of Yahweh's responding. At the moment, there's a time-out. We Westerners like to think of hope and a future as applying to us as individuals and as implying that things will soon change. Jeremiah's point is that hope and a future apply to the community and mean taking the long view. My individual hope comes from being a part of the project with God's people that God is committed to completing, even if I see little progress in my time.

The exilic community had prophets assuring it that Yahweh would soon restore it; its people were not so different from us with regard to looking for quick action. There was evidently reasonable communication between Judah and Babylon. Jeremiah could get his letters put into a diplomatic bag. Understandably, the Judahite prophets in Babylon who were false yet totally sincere became hopping mad at his writing to "their" people and contradicting them in a way that would further decrease the community's morale. So these prophets are taking advantage of the communication possibilities to write back and urge the religious authorities in Jerusalem to fulfill their responsibilities and shut Jeremiah up. When the priest reads the letter to him, Jeremiah doesn't tell us whether the priest implies that Jeremiah should indeed shut up, or whether (for instance) the priest just thinks Jeremiah needs to know what is going on. Certainly Jeremiah tells us of no word of judgment for the priest. The word of judgment goes to the prophet who tried to lean on him and to the people who listen to him, who have to decide whether to believe Jeremiah's exhortations about settling down or whether to believe that things are going to get worse in Jerusalem before they get better.

JEREMIAH 30:1–22

Compassion Has the Last Word

[1]The message that came to Jeremiah from Yahweh: [2]Yahweh, Israel's God, has said this: Write down for yourself all the words that I've spoken to you in a scroll. [3]Because there: days are coming (Yahweh's declaration) when I shall restore the fortunes of my people Israel and Judah, Yahweh has said. [4]So

these are the words that Yahweh had spoken concerning Israel and Judah.

⁵ Because Yahweh had said this:
We've heard the sound of fright, fear, and lack
of peace—
⁶ do ask and see if a male is giving birth.
Why have I seen every man with his hands on
his stomach
(like someone giving birth)
and why have all faces turned to paleness?

⁷ Oh, because that day is of great magnitude,
so that there has been none like it.
It's a time of trouble for Jacob,
but from it he'll find deliverance.

⁸ On that day (a declaration of Yahweh Armies)
I'll break its yoke from on your neck
and tear off your straps.
They won't serve foreigners anymore with it,
⁹ but will serve Yahweh their God,
and David their king,
whom I'll set up over them.
¹⁰ So now, don't be afraid, my servant Jacob
(Yahweh's declaration), don't shatter, Israel.
Because here am I; I'm going to deliver you from
far away,
and your offspring from the country of their captivity.
Jacob will return and be still,
be at calm with no one disturbing him,
¹¹ because I am with you
(Yahweh's declaration) to deliver you.
Because I'll make an end of all the nations
where I've scattered you.
Yet I won't make an end of you,
though I discipline you with judgment
and certainly don't treat you as innocent.

¹² Because Yahweh has said this:
Your wound is grave [Jerusalem],
   your injury sickening.
¹³ There's no one arguing your case for dressing,
   there's no healing, recovery, for you.
¹⁴ All your allies have disregarded you,
   they don't inquire of you.
Because I struck you down with an enemy's blow,
   the discipline of someone violent,
on account of the magnitude of your waywardness,
   the number of your offenses.
¹⁵ Why do you cry out because of your wound,
   that your injury is grave?
It was on account of the magnitude of your
      waywardness,
   the number of your offenses,
   that I did these things to you.

¹⁶ Therefore all the people who are consuming
      you will be consumed,
   and all your foes (all of them) will go into
      captivity.
Your plunderers will become plunder,
   and all who despoiled you I'll give as spoil.
¹⁷ Because I'll bring up healing for you
   and I'll cure you of your injuries (Yahweh's
      declaration).
Because they've called you "Outcast."
   "It's Zion; there's no one inquiring about it."

¹⁸ Yahweh has said this:
Here am I, intending to restore the fortunes of
      Jacob's tents,
   and on his dwellings I'll have compassion.
A city will be built on its tell;
   a fortification will sit on its authorized place.
¹⁹ Thanksgiving will go out from them
   and the sound of revelers.

> I'll make them many and they won't become few;
>> I'll make them honorable and they won't become
>>> insignificant.
> 20 His children will be as of old,
>> his community will stand secure before me,
>> and I'll deal with all his oppressors.
> 21 His leader will be from within him
>> and his ruler will come out from his midst.
> I'll draw him near and he'll approach me,
>> because who is the one who has set his own mind
>>> to approaching me
>> (Yahweh's declaration)?
> 22 You'll be a people for me,
>> and I'll be God for you.

A variant on whether you see the glass as half full or half empty is whether you look to the future with hope or anxiety. I'm a mildly anxious person myself—I don't worry much about particular threats or problems, but I'm susceptible to a vague unease. I therefore appreciate the way the form of prayer we use each morning acknowledges the reasons for anxiety (we pray not to be overcome by adversity) but puts more emphasis on hope (God has given us new birth to a living hope through Jesus' resurrection). And I like the saying that depression comes from living too much in the past and anxiety comes from living too much in the future. Only living in the present moment with God will relieve both.

For the next four chapters the book of Jeremiah reverts to Jeremiah's prophecies rather than stories about him, and it combines realism with promise. Like previous prophecies, this chapter speaks as if catastrophe is imminent. We can imagine Jeremiah's collecting his prophecies in this way when Jerusalem was about to fall to the **Babylonians** in 587. It's a prophet's regular vocation to disturb the comfortable and comfort the disturbed; Jeremiah has been focusing resolutely if distressingly on the first. Here he's making the kind of transition to the second that would be possible and necessary at such a moment. God's commissioning the writing down of his promises adds to the guarantee that they'll be fulfilled; writing things down has that effect. It gives the community something to hold onto, and in due course it makes the promises available to future generations. It wouldn't be surprising if the writing down of his prophecies here was a stage in the process whereby the book of Jeremiah came into being.

Jeremiah begins by referring twice to **Israel** and **Judah**—in other words, **Ephraim** and Judah—which together comprise Jacob, "my servant." As someone from Anatot, Jeremiah would be especially sensitive to Ephraim's future as well as Judah's. The fact that Ephraim had ceased to exist more than a century ago doesn't mean God is finished with it. God is committed to Israel as a whole, not just to Judah. Jacob is **Yahweh**'s servant, so Yahweh is committed to Jacob.

Typically, the promises received partial fulfillment over the next few decades but left much to be desired. "Restoring the fortunes" is a nicely ambiguous expression. Certainly the Judahites had a chance to go back to Judah, and some people seized it and did rebuild the temple. They stopped having to serve the Babylonians, but they had to serve the **Persians**. A descendant of David was something like governor of Jerusalem, but not king. The use of expressions such as "I'm with you to deliver you" is nice because they repeat the promise God made to Jeremiah back at the beginning (as well as to other people faced with demanding vocations, like Moses or Mary). They might remind us that Yahweh's commitment to Jeremiah is a personal application of his commitment to his entire people and that Yahweh's commitment to Jeremiah is one that can be claimed by the entire people.

Once again, however, there's some irony in the promise. We know from Jeremiah's story that Yahweh's presence and deliverance don't mean you have an easy time as Yahweh's servant. You experience what Yahweh slightly euphemistically calls discipline. At least you know that your deserved tough experiences aren't just punishment. They're part of a relationship like that of teachers and pupils or parents and children. Being taught a lesson may be hard, but at least it's not pointless.

Yahweh has said that Judah's attackers will have no compassion and that he himself will steel himself so as to have no compassion, but that declaration isn't his last word on this topic. It couldn't be. Compassion is one of the basic characteristics at the center of Yahweh's person, so compassion won't stay submerged forever. Likewise the suspension of celebration that Yahweh announced in bidding Jeremiah not marry will come to an end, and the city will have reason for thanksgiving in connection with the restoration Yahweh has brought about. In the previous chapter Yahweh urged the community not to hold back from having children and thus become few; in this chapter he promises that he'll make sure they grow rather than shrink in this way.

Best of all is the last line of this section. "I'll be God for you, and you'll be a people for me" is the basic covenantal commitment to which Jeremiah has often drawn people's attention, usually with the implication that they haven't kept their side of the commitment and have therefore imperiled the relationship (at God's expense as well as their own). Jeremiah declares that God's purpose will have the last word in this connection, too.

JEREMIAH 30:23–31:20

Rachel Weeps for Her Children

23 There is Yahweh's storm, wrath has gone out,
    a storm is raging, on the head of the faithless it whirls!
24 Yahweh's angry blazing won't turn back until he's acted,
    until he's performed the schemes in his mind;
    at the end of the time you'll understand it.

^{31:1} At that time (Yahweh's declaration)
    I shall be God for all Israel's families
    and they'll be a people for me.
 ² Yahweh said this:
The people found grace in the wilderness,
    those who had escaped the sword.
As Israel went to find its rest:
 ³   "from afar Yahweh appeared to me."
With lasting love I loved you;
    therefore I've continued commitment.
 ⁴ I'll build you up again
    so that you are built up, Ms. Israel.
You'll again deck yourself with your tambourine
    and go out in the revelers' dance.
 ⁵ You'll again plant vineyards on Samaria's
        mountains;
    planters will have planted and will begin to have
        the use of them.
 ⁶ Because there will be a day
    when lookouts call out on Ephraim's mountains,
"Come on, let's go up to Zion,
    to Yahweh our God."

 ⁷ Because Yahweh has said this:
Resound with joy for Jacob,
    bellow at the nations' crossroads.
Let them hear, exult, and say,
    "Yahweh, deliver your people,
    the remains of Israel!"
 ⁸ Here am I; I'm going to bring them from the
        northern country,
    I'll draw them together from the furthest reaches
        of the earth,
among them the blind and lame,
    the pregnant and giving birth, together;
    a great congregation will return here.
 ⁹ With weeping they'll come,
    and with prayers for grace I'll bring them.

I'll lead them to streams of water by a straight way
    on which they won't fall down.
Because I've been a father to Israel;
    Ephraim is my firstborn.

10   Listen to Yahweh's message, you nations,
    announce it on shores far away.
Say, "The one who scattered Israel will draw it together,
    and keep it like a shepherd his flock.
11   Because Yahweh is redeeming Jacob,
    restoring him from a hand that's too strong for
       him."
12   They'll come and resound on Zion's height
    and shine because of Yahweh's good things,
over the grain and new wine and fresh oil,
    over the newborn of the flock and the cattle.
Their spirit will become like a watered garden;
    they won't sorrow ever again.
13   Then a girl will rejoice with dancing,
    young men and old together.
I'll turn their mourning into celebration,
    comfort them and make them rejoice after their
       grief.
14   I'll saturate the priests' appetite with fat,
    and my people will be full of my good things
    (Yahweh's declaration).
15   Yahweh has said this:
A voice makes itself heard in Ramah,
    lamentation, anguished weeping,
Rachel is weeping for her children;
    she's refused to find comfort over her children,
    because they're not there.
16   Yahweh has said this:
Restrain your voice from weeping
    and your eyes from tears.
Because there will be a remuneration for your work
    (Yahweh's declaration);
    they'll return from the enemy's country.

¹⁷ There's hope for your future (Yahweh's declaration);
    your children will return to their territory.
¹⁸ I've heard, I've heard Ephraim lamenting,
    "You've disciplined me and I've accepted discipline
    like a calf that hadn't been trained.
Have me back and I'll turn back,
    because you are Yahweh my God.
¹⁹ Because after I turned back I repented;
    after I came to acknowledge it I struck my thigh.
I was shamed, yes disgraced,
    because I bore the insult of my youth."
²⁰ Is Ephraim not a dear son to me
    or a delightful child,
that every time I speak against him,
    I'm so mindful of him again?
Therefore my insides moan for him,
    I have deep compassion for him (Yahweh's
    declaration).

North of Bethlehem on the Jerusalem road is the traditional site of the tomb of Rachel, the great love of Jacob's life and the mother of Joseph (and thus grandmother of **Ephraim** and Manasseh); she died in giving birth to **Benjamin**. The tomb's location is the background to the image of her weeping when all the baby boys of Bethlehem were killed by Herod after Jesus' birth in Bethlehem; she's weeping over these children of hers. Maybe it's just an image, or maybe it's an indication that people who've died can know about things that happen in their family and can be affected by them. Either way, it's a reminder of links between the generations.

Jeremiah's prophecy presupposes that link when it speaks of this previous occasion when Rachel wept. The Ramah to which he refers would presumably be the town of that name in Benjamin, not far from Jeremiah's own home. It would be a natural place from which to imagine her watching her "children" trudge off into **exile**. In this context the children are people from Ephraim who were transported more than a century previously. Once again Jeremiah is indicating that **Yahweh** isn't only concerned for the **Judahites** to whom Jeremiah directly preaches. Yahweh hasn't forgotten the exiles of a century ago (nor—he also makes clear—has he forgotten the other nations). Yahweh can still hear Rachel weeping about them, and he responds to her weeping. She's been unwilling to be consoled, but he now provides her with a reason for consolation. They're not gone forever. Somehow, some of them, at least, will return. There's a lot of work involved in parenting; a mother knows that fact especially well. Rachel's story shows how it may cost a mother her life. But her hard work won't be fruitless. She'll get paid, even if it's after she's fallen asleep. It won't be as if she'd died in childbirth and her children had died without giving birth to the next generation. Exile won't mean the eradication of the family. The family line will continue.

This section again makes creative use of the verb that can mean "turn," "turn away," "turn back," and "bring back." The turning story is as follows: First, people turned away from Yahweh in order to turn to other deities or other political resources. Therefore Yahweh let them go: "See how that will work out, then." But as someone with the instincts of a Rachel, Yahweh can't finally let them go, so Yahweh will bring them back to their own country. The expression for "restoring the fortunes" is also significant here, because it uses Hebrew words that would remind people of that word for "turn," something like "turn back the fortunes." And further, Yahweh will look for them to turn back to him. It's from this idea that we get the idea of "conversion," though we are inclined to use it only of people's turning from one faith to another. Jeremiah invites us to see conversion or turning as something the people of God do. The church is often in need of conversion, and during our lives as individuals we may several times be in need of conversion. And the nature of "turning" is that it's visible. It's not something that just happens in the heart.

155

The great thing is that we can be sure of being received back. Once again Jeremiah repeats that commitment of Yahweh that **Israel** will be a people for God and he'll be God for all Israel's families. The reference to families makes it more personal. The relationship with God doesn't apply just to the nation as a whole, but neither does it just apply to individuals so that it can be something inside our heads. It applies to each extended family. Then he recalls the story that lies behind this commitment. Yahweh had ensured that they escaped Pharaoh's sword, cared for them in the wilderness, appeared to them and gave them their rule of life. Ms. Israel was like Yahweh's daughter, or as Jeremiah puts it later, Ephraim was like Yahweh's firstborn son. How could he give up on this people? His relationship with his children isn't only like a father's. It's like a mother's, like Rachel's own. "I have deep compassion for him," Yahweh says, or "I have only compassion for him." More literally, "With compassion I have compassion." In speaking of compassion Yahweh uses the word for a mother's womb. God has the feelings of a mother, Rachel-like feelings, for us.

JEREMIAH 31:21–40

The Power of Being Forgiven

> 21 Set up markers for yourself,
>   put up signposts for yourself.
>   Apply your mind to the highway,
>   the way you went.
>   Turn back, Ms. Israel,
>   turn back to these cities of yours.
> 22 How long will you waver,
>   daughter who's turned away?
>   Because Yahweh has created something new in
>   the country:
>   a woman surrounds a man.

156

23   Yahweh Armies, Israel's God,
       has said this:
     They'll again say this thing
       in the country of Judah and its cities,
       when I restore their fortunes:
     "May Yahweh bless you,
       faithful abode, holy mountain."
24   Judah and all its cities together will dwell in it as
         farmers,
       and people will go about with the flock.
25   Because I'm saturating the weary person
       and filling everyone who languishes.
26   Upon this I woke up and looked,
       and my sleep had been nice for me.

27There: days are coming (Yahweh's declaration) when I'll sow Israel's house and Judah's house with human seed and animal seed. 28As I was watchful over them to uproot and pull down, to destroy and overthrow, so I'll watch over them to build and plant (Yahweh's declaration). 29In those days they'll no longer say, "The parents ate sour grapes but the children's teeth feel rough." 30Rather, each person will die for his waywardness. Everyone who eats sours grapes, his teeth will feel rough. 31There: days are coming (Yahweh's declaration) when I'll seal with Israel's household and Judah's household a new covenant, 32not like the covenant that I sealed with your ancestors on the day I took hold of them by the hand to bring them out of the country of Egypt, my covenant which they contravened, though I was master over them (Yahweh's declaration). 33Because this is the covenant that I'll seal with Israel's household after those days (Yahweh's declaration). I'm putting my teaching inside them and I'll write it on their mind; and I'll be God for them and they'll be a people for me. 34They'll no longer teach each person his neighbor and each his brother, saying, "Acknowledge Yahweh," because all of them will acknowledge me from the least of them to the greatest of them (Yahweh's declaration), because I'll pardon their waywardness, and their offenses I won't keep in mind anymore.

157

³⁵ Yahweh has said this
    (the one who gives the sun as light by day,
    the laws of the moon and stars as light by night,
  who stirs up the sea so that its waves roar—
    Yahweh Armies is his name):
³⁶ If these laws disappear from before me
    (Yahweh's declaration),
  Israel's offspring may also cease from being a nation,
    for all time.

³⁷ Yahweh has said this:
  If the heavens above may be measured
    and earth's foundations below be explored,
  also I may reject the entire offspring of Israel
    for what they've done (Yahweh's declaration).

³⁸There, days are coming (Yahweh's declaration) when the city will be built up for Yahweh from the Hananel Tower to the Corner Gate, ³⁹and the measuring line will go out again straight to Gareb Hill and turn to Goah. ⁴⁰The entire valley (corpses and ashes) and all the open country as far as the Qidron Wash and as far as the Horses Gate on the east will be holy for Yahweh. It won't be uprooted or destroyed again ever.

Last night we listened to one of our favorite singer-songwriters performing an upbeat song with a downbeat account of her life (well, a downbeat account of a life—one mustn't imagine that every song is autobiographical). It tells of a father's leaving and never returning, which meant she spent her time "waiting for love to come back." Both mother and father remarried and she got muddled in the middle and caught the blues and herself never really married well. She's spent her life waiting for love to come back, but she knows that life is booby-trapped. "My hands are tied and my heart is chained, waiting for love to come back."

There's no doubt that parents eat sour grapes and their children's teeth get set on edge, like that weird feeling around your gums when you eat something tart. The sins of parents get visited on the children all right. It's not that the children are punished for their parents' offenses, but they do pay a price for them. It's therefore strange that Jeremiah should say it won't happen anymore. It's built into human experience.

Maybe there are two reasons for Jeremiah's statement. One is that his contemporaries did experience a particularly spectacular example of the principle. There had been a pattern to the sins of the ancestors that had persisted over generations, even centuries—an inclination to follow the patterns of the traditional religion of Canaan and an inclination to rely on alliances with other peoples to safeguard their political position. And many generations had gotten away with it. God had been long-tempered, had kept giving the people more time, more chances to turn back. In Jeremiah's day, God says, "That's it; no more second chances." They couldn't claim they didn't deserve it, but they could claim they were unlucky. Jeremiah's promise is that Jerusalem's fall in 587 doesn't set a pattern.

The other reason is that it's possible to make the shortcomings of one's parents or of one's parents' generation an excuse. Some gang members do it in a song in the musical *West Side Story* where they comment that their mothers are all junkies and their fathers are all drunks. "Golly, Moses, naturally we're punks!" Notwithstanding the effect of parents on children, Jeremiah declares that every generation stands before God responsible for its destiny in the sense that if it turns back to God, God responds. No, God doesn't punish the children for their parents' sins irrespective of their own responses to God.

Alongside that promise is the promise of the new covenant. It's a mystery to God and to Jeremiah how **Israel** could possibly have decided to disregard God's expectations of its life by worshiping other gods, making images to aid them in worship, attaching God's name to things to which it didn't belong (like those political policies), ignoring the Sabbath, and so on. Evidently something more radical needs to be done for Israel. How will God achieve that inner change to which he refers? Maybe the answer lies in the closing line of the promise, in the statement about God's pardoning their wrongdoing. Being forgiven by someone is a powerful thing. God intends to pardon the people's waywardness and restore them to their country. Maybe that has the power to change them. The woman surrounding the man is presumably Ms. Israel clinging to Yahweh.

It looks as if things worked out that way. After the exile, people did give up worshiping other deities, making images, misusing God's name, and ignoring the Sabbath. God kept this covenant promise. In Jeremiah's day the promise is part of what can motivate people to believe in the possibility of the exiles returning. The references to Israel (that is, Ephraim) and Judah again make explicit that God hasn't forgotten the people who belonged to the old Northern Kingdom that went out of existence a century before. That fact has important implications for Judah, too. If God could totally abandon Ephraim, then maybe God could totally abandon Judah. But if God cannot do the first, it would imply that God cannot do the second. It points Christians to a selfish reason for recognizing that God hasn't abandoned the Jewish people. If God could do so, he could also abandon us.

That fulfillment didn't mean everything was simply hunky dory. People continued to need to teach and exhort one another to acknowledge God. Similarly when in Jesus' dying and rising God gave an even more spectacular expression of his willingness to pardon waywardness, that act hasn't meant that people stopped needing to teach and exhort (otherwise I wouldn't be writing this book, and you wouldn't be reading it). So the new covenant promise was fulfilled soon after Jeremiah's day and fulfilled again in Jesus, but it still awaits fulfillment. In

Romans 11, indeed, Paul sees this promise about forgiveness as due to be fulfilled in the future after "the full number of the Gentiles has been gathered in"—in other words, it still lies in the future.

The line about sleep suggests that the preceding promises were received in a dream. They really came from God, which again indicates that we should not take too absolutely the comments about dreams in Jeremiah 23. Not all dreams are manufactured by the dreamers.

JEREMIAH 32:1–25

On Putting Your Money Where Your Mouth Is

[1]The message that came to Jeremiah from Yahweh in the tenth year of Zedekiah, king of Judah (it was the eighteenth year of Nebuchadrezzar). [2]The king of Babylon's forces were then besieging Jerusalem, while Jeremiah the prophet was confined in the prison courtyard at the king of Judah's house, [3]where Zedekiah, the king of Judah, had confined him, saying, "Why are you prophesying, 'Yahweh has said this: Here am I; I'm going to give this city into the hand of the king of Babylon, and he'll capture it, [4]and Zedekiah, the king of Judah, won't escape from the Kaldeans' hand because he'll definitely be given into the hand of the king of Babylon (his mouth will speak to his mouth, his eyes will see his eyes), [5]and he'll be transported to Babylon (that is, Zedekiah) and will be there until I deal with him (Yahweh's declaration); when you do battle with the Kaldeans, you won't succeed'?"

[6]Jeremiah said, Yahweh's message came to me: [7]Now, Hanamel son of Shallum, your uncle, is going to come to you, saying, "Acquire for yourself my field in Anatot, because the right of restoration belongs to you, to acquire it." [8]Hanamel, my uncle's son, did come to me, in accordance with Yahweh's message, to the prison courtyard, and said to me, "Will you acquire my field in Anatot in the country of Benjamin, because the right of possession is yours and the restoration is

yours; acquire it for yourself." So I knew that it was Yahweh's message. [9]I acquired the field from Hanamel, my uncle's son, in Anatot, and weighed out the silver to him, seventeen shekels of silver. [10]I wrote in a document, sealed it, got witnesses, and weighed the silver on scales. [11]I took the acquisition document, the sealed one (the commandment and the laws) and the open one, [12]and I gave the acquisition document to Baruk son of Neraiah son of Mahseiah in the sight of Hanamel my cousin and of the witnesses inscribed in the acquisition document and of all the Judahites sitting in the prison court-yard. [13]I ordered Baruk in their sight: [14]Yahweh Armies, Israel's God, has said this: Take these documents, this acquisition document (both the sealed one and this open document), and put them in an earthen container so that they may last for many days. [15]Because Yahweh Armies, Israel's God, has said this: Houses, fields, and vineyards will again be acquired in this country.

[16]I pleaded with Yahweh after giving the acquisition document to Baruk son of Neraiah: [17]Oh, Lord Yahweh! There— you made the heavens and the earth by your great strength and your outstretched arm. Nothing is too wonderful for you, [18]one who keeps commitment with thousands but repays the waywardness of parents into the lap of their children after them, great warrior God (Yahweh is his name), [19]great in planning and mighty in deed, you whose eyes are open to all the ways of human beings to give to each person in accordance with his ways and in accordance with the fruit of his deeds, [20]who put down signs and portents in the country of Egypt to this day, and in Israel and among humanity, and made a name for yourself this very day. [21]You brought your people Israel out of the country of Egypt with signs and portents and with a strong hand and an outstretched arm and with great fearfulness. [22]You gave them this country that you swore to their ancestors to give them, a country flowing with milk and honey. [23]They came and possessed it, but they didn't listen to your voice or walk by your teaching. All that you commanded them to do, they didn't do. So you've made all this evil happen to them. [24]There—ramps have come to the city to capture it,

and the city is given into the hand of the Kaldeans who are doing battle against it, because of sword, famine, and epidemic. What you said has happened. There you are, looking at it. [25]And now you've said to me, Lord Yahweh, "Acquire the field for yourself with silver and get witnesses," and this city is given into the Kaldeans' hand!

When we came to California, we were buying a house for the first time—we had always lived in church or seminary housing. It felt as if we were growing up. Two or three years ago, a friend of mine was wondering about buying a house, but prices had been going down, and it wasn't clear whether they might continue to do so. Eventually, however, she took the plunge. Last year my younger son and his wife did the same. Last week, my stepdaughter and her husband thought they were going to take the plunge when they found a house that would be ideal for their needs, but someone beat them to it, so they're having to look again. There might not necessarily be as much financial security in buying a house as once seemed to be the case—it may not be a wise investment. But there's another kind of security. You have a roof over your head.

Maybe for people in the West, owning your own house has a similar importance to owning your land in a traditional society. The analogy is incomplete, however, because owning your land means being in a position to grow your crops (and build your house in your spare time). Land means security in a more profound sense. As we see in Genesis, **Israel**'s ancestors lived without that security, but they could manage because they were shepherds rather than farmers. But the very first words that God addressed to Abraham included a promise that his family would eventually have their own land (and, conversely, I'm told that one of the first ways English colonists gained control of native Americans was by taking away their land, not allowing them to own it or work it or be on it, which eventually forced them to work for the colonists). When God brought the Israelites out of Egypt, that was a step in a right direction in that it rescued them from subservience, but that deliverance wasn't going to get them far until they had land. Being able to take over land in Canaan (mostly land the Canaanites weren't very interested in) was as important as being able to escape from Egypt.

The Old Testament calls it land flowing with milk and honey; it must have seemed wonderful compared with either confinement in Egypt or vulnerability in the wilderness. There were hills on which sheep and goats could graze (so there's milk), and you can grow date trees and fig trees there (so you can make fruit honey, the major source of sweetness in Israel). But there was a reason that the Canaanites weren't very interested in the areas where Israel originally settled. Compared with the fertile plains, it was tough land. Many of those hills were covered by forest, and you could never be sure there'd be enough rain when you needed it.

But you had land. It was distributed randomly among the twelve clans and then distributed within the clans to their families, who possessed the land but didn't exactly own it. How could you own land, which you didn't create (it was God who created it and to whom it belonged)? So you couldn't sell it. But when you got into trouble—suppose you were not able to produce enough food for the next year (or you were disorganized or lazy), and you needed to borrow food—you could use the land you possessed as surety for the loan. The risk was that you'd lose the right to keep control of the land—it might technically remain yours, but your creditor would take it over.

Something of this kind has happened to part of Jeremiah's family's land in Anatot, and Jeremiah is next in line within the extended family to use his own assets to "redeem" the land by settling the debt and thus "restoring" the situation to what it should be and restoring the members of his family who are in trouble. Although he's confined at the palace guardhouse to stop him going to the temple and preaching his subversive message there, he's evidently accessible to visitors.

It's an extraordinary act of faith on Jeremiah's part. The **Babylonians** have overrun the country, for goodness' sake! They're about to take Jerusalem! And Jeremiah is investing in real estate! But he's not simply buying when the market is down. **Yahweh** has promised that there will again be trade in houses, vineyards, and fields in the country. In other words, normal life will return. It's all very well to say that you believe in Yahweh's promises. It's something else to put your money where your mouth is. In a sense he had no option; God first told him what would happen, and then it happened, so how could he resist? Yet, he ends up saying to Yahweh, "You've asked of me something crazy!" It was like a buying a house when everyone knew that prices were likely to continue their downward spiral.

JEREMIAH 32:26–44

Is Anything Too Extraordinary for Yahweh?

[26]Yahweh's message came to Jeremiah: [27]Here am I, Yahweh, the God of all flesh. Is anything too extraordinary for me? [28]Therefore Yahweh has said this: Here am I; I'm going to give this city into the hand of the Kaldeans and into the hand of Nebuchadrezzar, king of Babylon, and he'll capture it. [29]The Kaldeans who are doing battle against this city will come and set this city on fire and burn it, and the houses where people burned sacrifices on the roofs to the Master and poured drink offerings to other gods, so as to provoke me. [30]Because the Israelites and the Judahites have been doing only what is evil in my eyes from their youth, because the Israelites have only been provoking me by the work of their hands (Yahweh's declaration). [31]Because to me this city became directed toward my anger and wrath from the day when they built it until this day, to remove it from in front of me [32]on account of all the evil of the Israelites and the Judahites that they did to provoke

165

me, they, their kings, their officials, their priests, their prophets, Judah's people, and Jerusalem's residents. [33]They turned their back and not their face to me; I taught them, teaching them urgently, but there were none of them listening so as to receive discipline. [34]They put their abominations in the house over which my name was proclaimed, to defile it, [35]and they built up the shrines of the Master in the Ben-hinnom Canyon to make their sons and their daughters pass through the fire to Molek, which I didn't command them, and it didn't come into my mind, to do this outrage, so as to make Judah offend.

[36]So now therefore Yahweh, Israel's God, says this concerning this city of which you're saying, "It's given into the hand of the king of Babylon by sword, famine, and epidemic": [37]Here am I; I'm going to draw them together from all the countries where I've driven them in my anger and wrath and great fury, and return them to this place and let them dwell with assurance. [38]They'll be a people for me, and I'll be God for them. [39]I'll give them a single mind and a single way, to be in awe of me all the days, so that things will be good for them and for their children after them. [40]I'll seal for them a lasting covenant that I won't turn from them, and I'll do good to them. I'll put awe for me in their minds so that they don't turn away from me. [41]I'll have delight toward them, in doing good to them. I'll plant them in this country in truth, with all my mind and soul. [42]Because Yahweh has said this: As I have brought to this people all this great evil, so I'm going to bring on them all the good things that I'm speaking about. [43]A field will be acquired in this country of which you're saying, "It's a devastation, without human being or animal; it's given into the Kaldeans' hand." [44]People will acquire fields for money and write it in a document and seal it and get witnesses, in Benjamin's country, Jerusalem's environs, Judah's cities, the cities in the mountains, the cities in the Shephelah, and the cities in the Negev. Because I'll restore their fortunes (Yahweh's declaration).

I have to preside over a funeral today and then over a memorial next week for someone who has already been cremated.

Whether your body dissolves gradually in the ground or burns up quickly in the fire, the idea that we are all going to be raised to new life at the end of all things takes some believing—or rather it takes some imagining. When God told Abraham and Sarah they were going to have a baby when they seemed too old (and when Sarah had anyway never been able to conceive when she was young), he commented, "Is anything too extraordinary, too supernatural, too awe-inspiring, too hard for **Yahweh**?" In a sense it's now easy to believe that God will raise us from death at the end, because he's given evidence of his ability to do the impossible in raising Jesus already. And anyway, he's the creator, and re-creating from nothing shouldn't be any more difficult than creating from nothing.

This chapter in Jeremiah is the other occasion when God challenges someone with the question "Is anything too extraordinary for me?" It's a situation rather like the one Abraham and Sarah faced. Isaiah 51 draws attention to the analogy. A few decades after Jeremiah's day, when **Judahites** in Jerusalem and **Babylon** seem demoralized, that prophecy reminds them of the rock or quarry from which they were originally dug (that is, Sarah's infertile womb) and reminds them that Abraham was only one man (yet all of later **Israel** descended from him).

I don't know whether people in Jeremiah's own day were inclined to be more or less demoralized than their descendants will be when the **exile** has gone on for a few decades. It's possible that the story of Jeremiah's going through the process of buying the land indicates that the Babylonians have lifted Jerusalem's siege while they dealt with another challenge, but if so, everyone knows they'll be back. The city is going to fall. It's just a matter of time. And so it turned out—the date at the beginning of the story indicates that the events took place just a few months before the city fell. Zedekiah is certainly formulating his exit strategy, though it will turn out to do him no good. How crazy is Jeremiah, acquiring land at a time like this? Did Hanamel laugh all the way back to Anatot with Jeremiah's shekels, planning his own exit strategy (move his family across the Jordan for a few years until things quiet down) and wondering at his cousin's naiveté? What use was land going to be to anyone in the foreseeable future?

It would be of no use if you leave God out of the picture. But nothing is too extraordinary for the God who is God of all flesh. The Israelites knew that Yahweh wasn't just their little local tribal deity but the creator and lord of the whole world and of all humanity and all life—at least, on a good day they knew it was so. So it was entirely possible to believe that God could bring about the time when leases on land would again be negotiated anywhere in the country. To underline the point, Jeremiah gives a list of all the areas in Judah. It covers Jerusalem and its environs, the area farther south on the mountain ridge and even farther south in the Negev, and the cities in the foothills nearer the Mediterranean. Not least it includes **Benjamin**, technically a separate clan area, where Jeremiah's own land is located.

In once again describing the abhorrent practices of Judah's religion, Jeremiah adds a reference to Molek, the deity who was the king of Sheol, the abode of the dead, according to the religious ideas people were following.

JEREMIAH 33:1–26

Expect Great Things

¹Yahweh's message came to Jeremiah a second time, while he was still detained in the prison courtyard: ²Yahweh has said this (Yahweh is going to do it, he's going to form it, he is going to make sure of it—Yahweh is his name): ³Call to me and I shall answer, and tell you great things, secret things that you haven't known. ⁴Because Yahweh, Israel's God, has said this about the houses in this city and about the houses of Judah's

kings that were torn down in connection with the ramps and the sword: [5]People are coming to do battle with the Kaldeans—and to fill them with the corpses of the people that I will have struck down in my anger and my wrath, when I've hidden my face from this city because of all their evil. [6]Here am I, I'm going to make recovery and healing grow up for it. I'll heal and reveal to them abundance of well-being and truth. [7]I'll restore Judah's fortunes and Israel's fortunes and build them up as before. [8]I'll purify them from all their waywardness with which they offended against me, and I'll pardon all their wayward acts with which they offended against me and rebelled against me. [9]For me it will mean a name to celebrate, and praise and splendor, for all the nations of the earth that hear of all the good things that I'm going to do with them, and they will be in awe and will shiver because of all the good things and all the well-being that I'm going to do for [Jerusalem]. [10]Yahweh has said this: A voice will make itself heard in this place, of which you are saying, "It's desolate, without human being, without animal, in Judah's cities and Jerusalem's devastated courtyards, without human being, without animal," [11]the voice of joy and of celebration, the voice of groom and of bride, the voice of people saying, "Confess Yahweh Armies, because Yahweh is good, because his commitment lasts forever," bringing a thank offering to Yahweh's house, because I'll restore the country's fortunes as before (Yahweh has said).

[12]Yahweh Armies has said this: In this place, desolate, without human being or animal, and in all its cities, there will again be an abode for shepherds resting a flock. [13]In the mountain cities, the lowland cities, the Negev cities, Benjamin's country, Jerusalem's environs, and Judah's cities, sheep will again pass under the hands of the one counting (Yahweh has said). [14]There, days are coming (Yahweh's declaration) when I'll perform the good word that I spoke concerning Israel's household and Judah's household.

[15]In those days and at that time I'll grow for David a faithful branch, and he'll implement authority and faithfulness in the country. [16]In those days Judah will find deliverance and Jerusalem will dwell with assurance. This is what it will be

called: "Yahweh is our faithfulness." [17]Because Yahweh has said this: There won't be cut off from David someone sitting on the throne of Israel's household. [18]And from the priests, the Levites, there will not be cut off someone before me offering up the whole offering and burning the grain offering and performing the sacrifice, for all time. [19]Yahweh's word came to Jeremiah: [20]Yahweh has said this: If you people can contravene my covenant about the day and my covenant about the night so that there's no day and night at their time, [21]also my covenant with David my servant may be contravened so that there's no son for him reigning on his throne, and with the Levites, the priests, ministering to me. [22]As the heavens' army cannot be counted and the sea's sand cannot be measured, so I'll multiply the offspring of David my servant and the Levites who minister to me.

[23]Yahweh's message came to Jeremiah: [24]Have you not seen what this people have spoken, "The two families that Yahweh chose—he's rejected them"? They've despised my people so that they are no longer a nation in front of them. [25]Yahweh has said this: If it's the case that I haven't laid down my covenant about day and night, the laws about the heavens and the earth, [26]then it's also the case that the offspring of Jacob and the offspring of David my servant may be rejected so as not to take from its offspring rulers for the offspring of Abraham, Isaac, and Jacob. Because I shall restore their fortunes and have compassion on them.

In the 1780s a shoemaker and part-time Baptist preacher near Northampton in England named William Carey used to do his work with a world map on the wall in front of him, and while he worked he'd pray for the nations of the world, many of whom knew little or nothing about Jesus Christ. He was convinced that the church should be doing something about that ignorance. It was a strange idea to his contemporaries; it was surely God's job to convert the heathen, not ours. Eventually Carey produced a pamphlet arguing his conviction about the question, *An Enquiry into the Obligations of Christians to Use*

Means for the Conversion of the Heathens. In 1792 in a sermon he argued, "Expect great things; attempt great things," and next year set off for India to put his life where his mouth was.

A Baptist Old Testament scholar friend of mine traces Carey's stress on expecting great things to Jeremiah's promise about the "great things" God here makes a commitment to doing. It's significant that the "expecting" comes before the "attempting." It's when you have promises from God to hold onto that you can act on the assumption that they'll come true—rather than going out on a limb and daring God not to keep up.

With this section the four chapters dominated by **Yahweh**'s promises to **Judah** come to an end. Here the promises become very broad. Oddly, it might seem, the context is still Jerusalem's imminent fall and its aftermath. The promises give people no chance to escape the horror of what is going to happen (if we assume the perspective of Jeremiah's listeners) or of what has happened (if we assume the perspective of his later readers). But they do pile up images for the work of restoration that Yahweh will do—recovery, healing, **well-being**, truth, building, purification, pardon, joy, celebration, confession of what God has done, commitment, deliverance, security, **faithfulness**.

The promises do go on to become concrete. **Israel** had two forms of regular leadership, kings and priests. Both kings and priests were under God's judgment along with the people as a whole, and it could look as if Yahweh was abandoning his undertaking to David's line as the royal family and to Levi as the priestly clan. In the **exile** there are no kings reigning and there's no regular ministry to be exercised in the temple. Yahweh promises this won't be the end of the story for the priesthood or for the line of David, any more than for the people as a whole (the two families of **Ephraim** and Judah, the descendants of Abraham, Isaac, and Jacob). God's promises to David and to Levi will stand forever. A few decades later, you could say that these promises have seen some fulfillment. Not only are people free to return to Judah. People from David's family (Zerubbabel) and from the priestly clan (Jeshua) are exercising **authority** in Jerusalem. Yet no one from David's line ever reigned as king, and in this sense it doesn't seem that God kept his promise to David. Then with the further destruction of the temple in AD 70 it doesn't seem that God kept his promise to Levi.

There are people today who expect to see a Davidic monarchy reestablished, and a new temple built with Levi offering its sacrifices. The more usual Christian view is that Jesus' coming was a fulfillment of God's promise to David, though this approach doesn't help much with the promise to Levi, because Jesus was a Judahite, not a Levite. Maybe Jeremiah would point out that we need to read these promises in light of what he said about promises and warnings in his chapter about the potter. Circumstances, too, sometimes mean we have to renegotiate promises. What we can't do (or what God doesn't do) is renege on promises arbitrarily—that's a major emphasis in this chapter. If God reworks promises, it's in order to make the fulfillment better than the original formulation, not to abandon them. God's original vision was for Israel as a whole to be a kingly nation and a priestly people, and when that kingly nation and priestly people becomes one whose membership comes from all the nations, you could say it is indeed a super-fulfillment.

JEREMIAH 34:1–22

A Dangerous Prayer

[1]The message that came to Jeremiah from Yahweh (when Nebuchadrezzar, king of Babylon, and all his forces and all the kingdoms of the earth ruled by his hand and all the peoples were doing battle against Jerusalem and all its cities): [2]Yahweh, Israel's God, has said this: Go and say to Zedekiah, king of Judah: Yahweh has said this: Here am I, I'm going to give this

city into the hand of the king of Babylon, and he'll burn it in fire. [3]You yourself won't escape from his hand, because you'll definitely be seized and be given into his hand. Your eyes will see the eyes of the king of Babylon. Your mouth will speak to his mouth. You'll come to Babylon. [4]Yet listen to Yahweh's message, Zedekiah, king of Judah. Yahweh has said this to you: You won't die by the sword. [5]You'll die in peace. Like the burning [of incense] for your ancestors, the earlier kings who were before you, so people will burn it for you. "Oh, my lord," they'll lament for you, because I myself have spoken the message (Yahweh's declaration). [6]Jeremiah the prophet spoke all these words in Jerusalem to Zedekiah, king of Judah. [7]The king of Babylon's forces were doing battle against Jerusalem and against all Judah's remaining cities—with Lachish and Azekah, because these remained among Judah's cities as fortified cities.

[8]The message that came to Jeremiah from Yahweh after King Zedekiah "cut" a covenant with the entire people in Jerusalem to proclaim a release to them, [9]each person to send off his male Hebrew servant and his female Hebrew servant as free persons (an individual Judahite his brother), so that they wouldn't serve them. [10]All the officials and the entire people that entered the covenant obeyed by sending off each person, his male and female servant as free persons so that they wouldn't serve them anymore. So they obeyed and sent them off, [11]but later they turned back and brought back the male and female servants whom they had sent off as free persons, and subjected them as male and female servants. [12]Yahweh's message came to Jeremiah from Yahweh: [13]Yahweh, Israel's God, has said this: I myself "cut" a covenant with your ancestors on the day I brought them out of the country of Egypt, out of a household of servants, saying, [14]At the end of seven years you're to send off, each person, his Hebrew brother who has sold himself to you and served you for six years; you're to send him off as a free man from being with you. Your ancestors didn't listen to me; they didn't bend their ear. [15]Just now you yourselves turned back and did what was right in my eyes by proclaiming a release, each person to his neighbor, and

you "cut" a covenant in front of me in the house over which my name was proclaimed. [16]But you've turned back and profaned my name; you've brought back, each person, his male and female servant whom you sent off as free persons to live their life, and you've subjected them as male and female servants to you. [17]Therefore Yahweh has said this: You haven't listened to me by proclaiming a release, each person to his brother, each to his neighbor. Here am I, I'm going to proclaim to you a release (Yahweh's declaration)—to sword, epidemic, famine. I'm going to make you a horror to all earth's kingdoms. [18]I'm going to make the people who are passing over my covenant, who haven't performed the words in the covenant that they "cut" in front of me, the calf that they cut into two and passed between its parts: [19]Judah's officials and Jerusalem's officials, the overseers, the priests, and the entire people of the country who passed between the parts of the calf. [20]I shall give them into the hand of their enemies, into the hand of those who seek their life. Their corpse will be food for the birds of the heavens and the animals of the earth. [21]Zedekiah, king of Judah, and his officials I'll give into the hand of their enemies, into the hand of those who seek their life, into the hand of the king of Babylon's forces who are pulling back from you. [22]Here am I, I'm going to give a command (Yahweh's declaration) and I'll bring them back to this city and they'll do battle against it and capture it and burn it with fire, and Judah's cities I'll make a devastation without resident.

Someone was talking to me today about some issues concerning sexual propriety and the importance of not giving the wrong message to a person of the opposite sex. He'd hurt his wife by giving the impression that he was flirting with a woman when he wasn't intentionally doing so, though the woman and other people might've interpreted his behavior as flirting. Well, at least (he said), it occurred in church, so it wasn't likely that she would be open to a relationship with a married man. Well (I said), maybe it's less likely than is the case with people outside church, but lots of men and women in church have affairs, so we can't afford to take anything for granted. In many aspects of life, you might think that it's obvious what the people of God should and would naturally do, but it ain't necessarily so.

In Jeremiah's context, the point applied to the way they treated their bond servants. Many English translations use the word "slave," but that word is misleading. **Israel** and other Middle Eastern peoples hardly had slavery in the sense of people "owning" other people, able to do what they liked to them. The word that's used is the ordinary word for a servant, the word used for God's servants. It could apply to people who were like employees, who were at least in theory free to leave whenever they liked (though in practice they might have nowhere else to go and no other way of having shelter or livelihood). Here, it applies to bond servants, who are like the people who had their passage paid to come to the Americas and had to commit themselves to work for a set period in return. In Israel's case, people might become bond servants because the family fell into hopeless debt; it was the way they paid off the debt and got a new start. It provided people with a safety net. But there was a term limit to their service. At the end of a seven-year period, they were to go free.

That was the theory as laid down in the **Torah**. But Jeremiah notes that the present generation's ancestors hadn't been in the habit of observing the term limit; indeed, the Old Testament includes no reports of occasions when it happened. Evidently it hadn't been observed in Jerusalem in Jeremiah's day. Instead of letting servants go after six years, their masters were somehow able to hold onto them, maybe because they had nowhere else to go unless the masters also gave them the wherewithal for a new start (as again the Torah lays down).

We are once more in the context of Jerusalem's siege. We don't know why people suddenly agreed to do what the Torah said; the cynic wonders whether providing for servants had become more of a problem during the siege than the benefit they brought. Nevertheless, maybe their doing the right thing was the background to the relatively positive statement to Zedekiah that Jeremiah makes in the first paragraph. But then the siege got lifted temporarily, so letting the servants go didn't look like such a good idea. The disgusting nature of the masters' behavior is underlined by Jeremiah's referring to the servants as brothers and neighbors. In the way they treated people who belonged to their community, which was their family, the Jerusalemites had been ignoring considerations that should be obvious. And now they had made the situation worse. They had entered into a covenant in front of **Yahweh**, using Yahweh's name. So in abandoning it, they were now profaning Yahweh's name, treating it as something that didn't matter. One could see it as an example of taking Yahweh's name in vain.

Sealing a covenant is often described as "cutting" a covenant; the background to that expression lies in the ceremony to which Jeremiah's last paragraph refers (Genesis 15 gives more information). The ceremony for making a covenant could involve cutting up an animal or bird and walking between the parts while saying a prayer to be dismembered like the creature if one fails to keep the covenant. Even God prays that prayer. Jeremiah promises that Zedekiah and company will have their prayer answered. With one of his trademark plays on words, he declares that they're going to be on the receiving end of a different kind of "release" from the one they owe their servants. Yahweh will remove the forces that hold back sword, epidemic, and famine (the implication is that only because of God's holding them back are they protected).

Jeremiah assumes that it should indeed have been easy for people to accept the obligation to free their bond servants after the set period. One reason is that the idea of freeing servants was built into their own origins. Yahweh had freed them from a situation where they were servants in Egypt. How could they possibly keep other people in permanent or semi-permanent servitude? But they couldn't see it.

JEREMIAH 35:1–19

On Witnessing by Your Obedience to Your Special Vocation

[1]The message that came to Jeremiah from Yahweh in the days of Jehoiaqim son of Josiah, king of Judah: [2]Go to the Rekabites' house and speak with them, and bring them to Yahweh's house to one of the chambers and get them to drink wine. [3]So I got Ja'azaniah son of Jeremiah son of Habassiniah and his brothers and all his sons and the entire household of the Rekabites [4]and brought them to Yahweh's house to the chamber of the sons of Hanan son of Jigdaliah, the man of God, which was near the officials' chamber, which was above the chamber of Ma'aseiah son of Shallum, the guard of the threshold. [5]I put in front of the members of the Rekabites' household bowls full of wine and cups, and said to them, "Drink wine." [6]They said, "We won't drink wine, because Jonadab son of Rekab our ancestor commanded us, 'You're not to drink wine, you and your descendants forever. [7]You're not to build a house, you're not to sow seed, you're not to plant a vineyard. They're not to be yours. Rather, live in tents all your days, so you may live for many days on the surface of the ground where you're sojourning.' [8]We have obeyed the voice of Jehonadab son of Rekab our ancestor regarding all he commanded us so as not to drink wine all our days, we, our wives, our sons, and our daughters, [9]and not to build houses for us to live in; and we don't have vineyard or field or seed, [10]but we've lived in tents and obeyed and acted in accordance with all that Jonadab our ancestor commanded us. [11]But when Nebuchadrezzar, king of Babylon, came up against the country we said, 'Come on, we'll come into Jerusalem in face of the Kaldeans' forces and in face of Syria's forces.' So we've lived in Jerusalem."

[12]Yahweh's message came to Jeremiah: [13]Yahweh Armies, Israel's God, has said this: Go and say to Judah's people and Jerusalem's residents: Will you not accept discipline by listening to my words (Yahweh's declaration)? [14]It has been performed, the words of Jehonadab son of Rekab which he commanded his descendants not to drink wine. They haven't drunk up till this day because they've obeyed the command of their

ancestor. But I myself have spoken to you, speaking urgently, but you haven't obeyed me. [15]I've sent to you all my servants the prophets, sending them urgently, saying, Will you turn, each one, from his evil way and make your deeds good, and not follow other gods so as to serve them, and you'll live on the land that I gave to you and your ancestors, but you haven't bent your ear, you haven't obeyed me. [16]Because the descendants of Jehonadab son of Rekab have performed the command of their ancestor which he gave them, but this people—they haven't obeyed me.

[17]Therefore Yahweh, God of Armies, Israel's God, has said this: Here am I, I'm going to bring to Judah and to all Jerusalem's residents all the evil that I spoke against them, since I spoke to them and they haven't listened, I called to them and they haven't answered. [18]But to the household of the Rekabites Jeremiah said, "Yahweh Armies, Israel's God, has said this: Since you obeyed the command of Jehonadab your ancestor and kept all his commands and acted in accordance with all that he commanded you, [19]therefore Yahweh Armies, Israel's God, has said this: There shall not be cut off for Jonadab son of Rekab someone standing in front of me for all time."

Fortuitously, I completed the translation of Jeremiah 35:1–19 just as the moment arrived when we often have a glass of wine before dinner. The instant transition from translation to imbibing is possible only because I'm working at home. Our seminary campus is dry, so students and faculty often meet across the street for happy hour at a restaurant. I have no problem with the oddness of this apparently inconsistent arrangement. Alcohol's place in our communities' lives is complicated, and nowhere more complicated than in the United States. So it's appropriate that we should distance ourselves from alcohol a bit and let the campus focus on a different form of happiness but also feel free to imbibe in moderation.

The Rekabites' vocation reminded **Israel** of that same ambiguity. The Old Testament elsewhere makes clear that wine is a great gift, with a proper place in celebrating what God had done for his people (though Israel's wine probably had a lower alcohol content than wine in the Western world), but that drunkenness can also become a problem. The Rekabites' lifestyle demonstrated that they didn't need alcohol to live a satisfactory life although it may have been so by accident as their abstinence was part of a bigger picture. They also didn't build proper houses but lived in tents outside the city, and they didn't grow crops but (presumably) pastured sheep. They thereby continued to live the kind of life that Israel had lived before it became a settled people, the kind of life presupposed by the account of the people's time in the wilderness at the beginning, between Egypt and Canaan.

Jeremiah alone mentions the Israelite group called the Rekabites, and he doesn't tell us why their ancestor Jonadab committed them to this lifestyle. Jonadab or Jehonadab (Jeremiah alternates between the two forms of the name) may not have been an immediate son of Rekab; he lived only two centuries before Jeremiah's day (2 Kings 10 recounts how he supported reformist action in **Ephraim**). It's a plausible guess that the Rekabites saw the ways in which settled life could make Israel go soft and could encourage them to become too much like the Canaanites, even though settling in the land was God's gift and the fulfillment of God's promise.

So they fulfilled a role like that of people in the West who commit themselves to being teetotal and remind the rest of us that alcohol isn't a necessity and can be a problem. There are other examples of such commitments. Pacifists and conscientious objectors remind the rest of us that taking part in war may be a necessary **evil**, but it's still an evil. Vegetarians remind us that God did concede to humanity the right to eat meat, but it wasn't why animals were created. Maybe the fact that the Rekabites are currently living in the city as result of the **Babylonian** invasion illustrates how even people with a particular vocation don't have to be legalistic about it.

Jeremiah's omitting to clarify why the Rekabites adopted their lifestyle reflects the fact that his interest in them lies elsewhere. They had been faithful to the charge that Jonadab laid on them, but Jeremiah gives no indication that they had their vocation from God; Jonadab dreamed it up. They did what he said. How much greater is the contrast, then, with the **Judahites,** who didn't even do what God said. In the present section of Jeremiah, we've moved back a decade into Jehoiaqim's day, the eve of Jerusalem's earlier fall in 597, but there's a link of substance with the story of Zedekiah and the release of bond servants. It was a clear requirement from God that people should release people in the seventh year of their service, but the Judahites simply ignored that requirement. They had something to learn from the Rekabites, all right. And whereas Judah as a whole is destined for destruction, the Rekabites will continue to exist.

JEREMIAH 36:1–32

The Bold Miscalculation

[1]In the fourth year of Jehoiaqim son of Josiah, king of Judah, this message came to Jeremiah from Yahweh: [2]Get yourself a document scroll and write in it all the messages that I've spoken to you about Israel and Judah and all the nations from the day I spoke to you (from the days of Josiah) until this day. [3]Perhaps Judah's household will listen to all the evil that I'm intending to do to them, so that they may turn back each person from his evil way and I may pardon their waywardness and their offenses. [4]So Jeremiah summoned Baruk son of Neraiah, and Baruk wrote from Jeremiah's mouth all Yahweh's messages that he'd spoken to him, on a document scroll. [5]Jeremiah commanded Baruk, "I'm under constraint; I can't come to Yahweh's house. [6]You're to come and read the scroll that you've written from my mouth, the messages from Yahweh, in the ears of the people at Yahweh's house on a fast day, and you're also to read them in the ears of all Judah who come

from their cities. [7]Perhaps their prayer for grace will reach Yahweh and they'll turn back each person from his evil way, because Yahweh's anger and wrath are great, of which he's spoken concerning this people." [8]Baruk son of Neraiah did in accordance with all that Jeremiah the prophet commanded him by reading in the scroll Yahweh's messages at Yahweh's house. [9]In the fifth year of Jehoiaqim son of Josiah, king of Judah, in the ninth month, they proclaimed a fast before Yahweh, the entire people in Jerusalem and the entire people coming from Judah's cities into Jerusalem. [10]Baruk read in the scroll Jeremiah's messages at Yahweh's house in the chamber of Gemariah son of Shaphan, the scribe, in the upper courtyard at the entrance of the New Gate at Yahweh's house, in the ears of the entire people.

[11]Micaiah son of Gemariah son of Shaphan listened to all Yahweh's messages from the scroll. [12]He went down to the king's house to the scribe's chamber. There: all the officials were sitting there, Elishama, the scribe, Delaiah son of Shemaiah, Elnathan son of Akbor, Gemariah son of Shaphan, Zedekiah son of Hananiah, and all the officials. [13]Micaiah told them all the messages that he'd heard when Baruk read in the scroll in the people's ears. [14]All the officials sent Jehudi son of Netaniah son of Shelemiah son of Cushi to Baruk, saying, "The scroll in which you read in the people's ears—will you take it in your hand and go." So Baruk son of Neraiah took the scroll in his hand and came to them. [15]They said to him, "Will you sit down and read it in our ears." Baruk read it in their ears. [16]When they heard all the messages, they were afraid, each toward his neighbor. They said to Baruk, "We must definitely tell the king all these messages." [17]They asked Baruk, "Will you tell us how you wrote all these messages from his mouth." [18]Baruk said to them, "From his mouth he proclaimed to me all these messages and I would write them on the scroll in ink." [19]The officials said to Baruk, "Go hide, you and Jeremiah. No one is to know where you are." [20]They came to the king in the courtyard; the scroll they deposited in Elishama the scribe's chamber, but they told in the king's ears all the messages. [21]The king sent Jehudi to get the scroll, and he got it from Elishama

the scribe's chamber. Jehudi read it in the king's ears and in the ears of all the officials standing in attendance on the king. [22]The king was sitting in the winter house (in the ninth month) with the firepot in front of him, burning. [23]As Jehudi read three or four columns, [the king] would cut it with a scribe's knife and throw it into the fire in the firepot until the entire scroll was consumed by the fire in the firepot. [24]They weren't afraid and they didn't tear their clothes, the king and all his staff who heard all these messages, [25]even though Elnathan, Delaiah, and Gemariah entreated the king not to burn the scroll. He didn't listen to them. [26]The king commanded Jerahmeel, the king's son, and Seraiah son of Azriel, and Shelemiah son of Abde'el, to capture Baruk the scribe and Jeremiah the prophet, but Yahweh hid them.

[27]Yahweh's message came to Jeremiah after the king burned the scroll and the messages that Baruk wrote from Jeremiah's mouth: [28]Go back, get yourself another scroll, and write on it all the earlier messages that were on the earlier scroll that Jehoiaqim, king of Judah, burned, [29]and against Jehoiaqim, king of Judah, you're to say, Yahweh has said this: You're the one who burned this scroll, saying, "Why've you written on it, 'The king of Babylon will definitely come and destroy this country and eliminate from it human beings and animals'?" [30]Therefore Yahweh has said this against Jehoiaqim, king of Judah: There will not be for him someone sitting on David's throne, and his corpse will be thrown out into the heat by day and to the cold by night. [31]I'll deal with their waywardness, for him, for his offspring, and for his staff, and bring on them and on Jerusalem's residents and Judah's people all the evil that I spoke about them, but they didn't listen. [32]So Jeremiah got another scroll and gave it to Baruk son of Neraiah the scribe, and he wrote on it from the mouth of Jeremiah all the messages on the scroll that Jehoiaqim, king of Judah, burned in the fire. He also added to them many messages like them.

In church this Sunday morning, the first of our three passages from Scripture was the story of God's asking Solomon what he wanted, that most testing of questions, a test that Solomon passed magnificently. Like Saul and David, he has his best moments early in his story. Then we read the exhortation in Ephesians to be thankful at all times and for everything, and we read part of John's chapter about Jesus being the living bread, with John's chilling warning that people who don't eat Jesus' flesh don't have life in them. The passages were a test, a challenge, and a warning with monumental implications. Yet usually by the time we leave church, we've forgotten the Scripture passages. They go in one ear and out the other.

So we're not much better or much better off than Jehoiaqim. Once again we're back in the fourth year of his reign, the fateful year when Nebuchadnezzar became king of **Babylon**. I don't know that an astute political observer would've been able to speculate that it was a fateful year. While Nebuchadnezzar will turn out to be a man of huge achievements, his father Nabopolassar had been no nonentity. But **Yahweh** knows that Nebuchadnezzar's accession will be a turning point in **Judah**'s history. Jeremiah describes Nebuchadnezzar as Yahweh's servant, but not in a good way. Twice he'll besiege and capture Jerusalem and **exile** many of its people. Paradoxically, Yahweh evidently knows that these events are in the offing, yet they're not fixed and inevitable. That's the point of giving Jehoiaqim another warning. "Maybe they'll turn from their **evil** way," thinks Yahweh, "and I can pardon them. Maybe they'll start praying."

Having Jeremiah write down the messages of the past twenty-three years presupposes that the moment is at last arriving when they'll come true. It's been two decades' frustration and embarrassment for Jeremiah that he's been required to continue preaching a message that never came about as well as do strange things that embodied this message. If you feel there's a sameness about many of his messages, you're right. He's like the modern preacher who when asked why he kept preaching essentially the same sermon replied, "When they've taken note of that one, I'll preach another."

Until the invention of the computer, a hack typist like me would get someone else to type out anything that needed to be reasonably presentable, and while it's unlikely that Jeremiah couldn't write at all, in a similar way he would get a professional writer to write down something that was important and designed to be taken seriously. Maybe the constraint imposed on him was a ban on his going to the temple because he was known to be a troublemaker. He could get around the ban by sending Baruk.

The occasion they wanted for reading the scroll was a day of fasting, when many people were present, were in a solemn and repentant mood, and might be open to hearing Jeremiah's message. The fast day that arrived may have been linked to the Babylonian sack of Ashqelon that happened in late 604 and is reported in Nebuchadnezzar's records. That might indeed have frightened Judah into prayer and fasting.

The officials who first hear about the scroll feel caught. They know they have to take this event and these prophecies seriously. They also know that they have to tell their boss, and they can guess what his response will be and the response of his other officials. So they advise Jeremiah and Baruk to disappear while they go and tell Jehoiaqim what is happening. It's December, and winter can be cold as well as wet in Jerusalem; it snows some years. Unlike the average citizen one might assume that the king has a fire to keep him warm. As someone reads the scroll out, Jehoiaqim cuts it to pieces and burns it. It's a magnificent, stupid act of defiance. He's showing his staff that a king worth his salt doesn't have to take too much notice of a two-bit prophet. They're only words. He can burn them. They then cease to exist.

But you can't destroy God's words as easily as Jehoiaqim thinks or pretends that he thinks. And you can't silence the prophet and stop his scribe as easily as Jehoiaqim assumes. The king has to overcome not only their capacity to hide but also God's capacity to protect them, and he can't do so. Thus the words can be rewritten. Indeed, in a magnificently scary final line, the story tells us that the second scroll is much longer than the first.

It wouldn't be surprising if the writing of this scroll was an important stage in the genesis of the book of Jeremiah that we're reading. His words were meant for us, too.

JEREMIAH 37:1–21

The King Who Vacillates

[1]King Zedekiah son of Josiah became king in place of Koniah son of Jehoiaqim; Nebuchadrezzar, king of Babylon, made him king over the country of Judah. [2]He didn't listen, he or his staff or the people of the country, to the messages from Yahweh that he spoke by the hand of Jeremiah the prophet. [3]King Zedekiah sent Jehokal son of Shelemiah and Zephaniah son of Ma'aseiah, the priest, to Jeremiah the prophet to say, "Will you plead on our behalf with Yahweh our God?" ([4]when Jeremiah was coming in and going out in the midst of the people and they hadn't put him into confinement, [5]and when Pharaoh's forces had come out from Egypt, and the Kaldeans who were besieging Jerusalem had heard the news about them and had gone up from Jerusalem). [6]Yahweh's message came to Jeremiah the prophet: [7]Yahweh, Israel's God, has said this: This is what you people should say to the king of Judah who's sending you to me to inquire of me: "There, Pharaoh's forces that are coming out to you to help you will go back to their country, to Egypt. [8]The Kaldeans will come back and will do battle against this city, capture it, and burn it in fire." [9]Yahweh has said this: Don't deceive yourselves by saying, "The Kaldeans will certainly go from us," because they won't go. [10]If you struck down all the Kaldeans' forces who are doing battle with you, and people who were wounded remained, each in his tent, they'd get up and burn this city in fire.

[11]When the Kaldeans' forces went from Jerusalem in the face of Pharaoh's forces, [12]Jeremiah went out from Jerusalem to go to Benjamin's country to divide a share there in the

midst of the people. [13]He was at the Benjamin Gate, and a master of the guard was there whose name was Jiriyyah son of Shelemiah son of Hananiah. He seized Jeremiah the prophet, saying, "You're going over to the Kaldeans." [14]Jeremiah said, "It's a lie. I'm not going over to the Kaldeans." But he didn't listen to him. So Jiriyyah seized Jeremiah and brought him to the officials. [15]The officials were incensed at Jeremiah. They beat him and put him in the prison house, the house of Jonathan the scribe, because they had made it into the prison house.

[16]When Jeremiah came to the cistern house and the cells, and Jeremiah had lived there for many days, [17]King Zedekiah sent and got him, and the king questioned him in his house in secret. He said, "Is there a message from Yahweh?" Jeremiah said, "There is"; and said, "You'll be given into the hand of the king of Babylon." [18]Jeremiah said to King Zedekiah, "How have I committed an offense against you and your staff and this people, that you have put me into the prison house? [19]And where are your prophets who prophesied to you, 'The king of Babylon won't come against you and against this country'? [20]Now will you listen, my lord king; may my plea for grace reach you. Don't return me to the house of Jonathan the scribe, so that I don't die there." [21]So King Zedekiah gave a command, and they placed Jeremiah in the prison courtyard and gave him a loaf of bread per day from the bakers' street until all the bread came to an end from the city. So Jeremiah lived in the prison courtyard.

Three friends of mine live and seek to minister in Christ's name in a beautiful and peaceful-looking area of India, but they risk their lives in doing so. The appearance of the country is deceptive because the area is affected by Maoist terrorism. The land, they say, has drunk the innocent blood of countless ordinary people, the victims of a long-standing tug-of-war between government and Maoist forces. The forces of law and order victimize innocent villagers in seeking to collect information about Maoist movements while the Maoists kill people they suspect of being police informers as well as the parents of young people who find jobs in the police force. So my friends risk their lives every day, not knowing whether they may be taken for traitors by either side in this conflict.

The desperate situation in Jerusalem as the **Babylonians** besiege it means Jeremiah risks his life every day in being a prophet. Once again we've moved on nearly twenty years, from 604 to 587, from the reign of Jehoiaqim (the scene in chapter 36) through the brief reign of Koniah (aka Jekoniah or Jehoiakin), who was deposed by Nebuchadnezzar, and through most of the reign of his successor Zedekiah, to the months when the city's final fall is imminent. So the time changes, but the problem stays the same. The leadership in Jerusalem won't take any notice of **Yahweh**'s message. This particular moment is one when the Babylonian siege has been lifted because the Egyptians are coming to take on the Babylonians and thus seem to be justifying the **Judahites**' looking to them as a resource—but Jeremiah knows it will be only a temporary relief. But the relief of the siege gives Jeremiah a chance to go to Anatot, perhaps to complete the business relating to family land that we read about in chapter 32. The **Benjamin** Gate is the gate of Jerusalem that leads toward Anatot. Unfortunately an astute guard is suspicious about his real motives in leaving the city, and it turns into a moment when Jeremiah ends up in detention.

Once again, Zedekiah shows himself not to be up to the job. If at least he'd take a definite stance, even the wrong one, like his great-grandfather Manasseh, then in a strange way one would have more admiration for him. It was Nebuchadnezzar who had put him on the throne, but he can't make up his mind whether to be subservient to Nebuchadnezzar. He believes in Yahweh, but he can't make up his mind whether to live as if he trusts in Yahweh. He's capable of treating Jeremiah as a true prophet, so he asks Jeremiah to pray for the people and asks if there's a message from Yahweh, so he recognizes the two sides to Jeremiah's significance as a prophet—representing the people to God and representing God to the people. But he doesn't want people in general to know he's consulting Jeremiah. Is it so that he can decide not to follow Jeremiah if he doesn't like Yahweh's answer? Whatever his reason might be, he doesn't take any notice of the message. He lets Jeremiah be put under house arrest and then apparently be put into a more unpleasant form of imprisonment in a place where he might indeed die, but he then releases him from there and provides him with basic rations for as long as food is available.

The point of telling these stories about Jeremiah is again what they tell us about people's attitude toward God. It's frightening to be identified with God's message. More than once it almost cost Jeremiah his life. Back at the beginning, God had told him he'd be protected, and perhaps at one level he believes that promise, but it doesn't stop him from being understandably afraid.

JEREMIAH 38:1–28a

Truth to Power

[1]Shephatiah son of Mattan, Gedaliah son of Pashhur, Jukal son of Shelemiah, and Pashhur son of Malkiah heard the words that Jeremiah was speaking to the entire people: [2]Yahweh has said this: The person who lives in this city will die by sword, famine, or epidemic, but the person who goes out to the Kaldeans will live. His life will be his as a trophy. He'll live. [3]Yahweh has said this: This city will certainly be given into the hand of the king of Babylon's forces and they'll capture it. [4]The officials said to the king, "This man should surely be put to death, because by this means he's weakening the hands of the fighting men who remain in this city, and the hands of the entire people, by speaking to them in accordance with these words, because this man isn't seeking the well-being of this people, but evil." [5]King Zedekiah said, "There, he's in your

hand, because the king can't win against you in a matter." [6]So they got Jeremiah and put him into the cistern of Malkiah, the king's son, in the prison courtyard. They put Jeremiah [there] with ropes. There was no water in the cistern, but only mud. So Jeremiah sank into the mud.

[7]Ebed-melek the Sudanese, a eunuch, who was in the king's house, heard that they had put Jeremiah in the cistern. The king was sitting at the Benjamin Gate, [8]so Ebed-melek went out from the king's house and spoke to the king: [9]"My lord king, these men have done evil in all they've done to Jeremiah the prophet, whom they've thrown into the pit. He'll die in that place from hunger, because there's no more bread in the city." [10]So the king commanded Ebed-melek the Sudanese, "Get thirty people from here with you and get Jeremiah the prophet up from the cistern before he dies." [11]Ebed-melek got the men with him and came to the king's house to below the treasury. He got from there old rags and old clothes and threw them down to Jeremiah into the pit by the ropes. [12]Ebed-melek the Sudanese said to Jeremiah, "Will you put the old rags and clothes under your armpits, under the ropes." Jeremiah did so. [13]They pulled Jeremiah up by the ropes and got him up from the cistern.

So Jeremiah lived in the prison courtyard. [14]King Zedekiah sent and brought Jeremiah the prophet to him at the third entrance in Yahweh's house. The king said to Jeremiah, "I'm going to ask you for a message; don't hide anything from me." [15]Jeremiah said to Zedekiah, "When I tell you, will you not surely put me to death? And when I make a plan for you, you won't listen to me." [16]King Zedekiah swore to Jeremiah in secret, "As Yahweh lives, who made this life for us, if I put you to death or if I give you into the hand of these people who are seeking your life . . ."

[17]Jeremiah said to Zedekiah, "Yahweh, God of Armies, Israel's God, has said this: If you do go out to the king of Babylon's officers, you yourself will live, and this city won't be burned with fire. You and your household will live. [18]But if you don't go out to the king of Babylon's officers, this city will be given into the Kaldeans' hand and burned with fire. You won't

escape from their hand." [19]King Zedekiah said to Jeremiah, "I'm afraid of the Judahites who've gone over to the Kaldeans, in case [the Kaldeans] give me over into their hand and they attack me." [20]Jeremiah said, "[The Kaldeans] won't give you over. Do listen to Yahweh's voice, to what I'm speaking to you, so that he may do good things to you and you yourself may live. [21]But if you refuse to go out, this is the message that Yahweh has shown me. [22]There—all the women who remain in the king of Judah's household are going out to the officers of the king of Babylon. There—they're going to say, 'The men who were in alliance with you [Zedekiah] have deceived you and won against you. Your feet are stuck in the mire; they've turned their backs.' [23]They're going to bring out all your women and children to the Kaldeans, and you won't escape from their hand, because you'll be seized by the king of Babylon's hand, and you'll burn this city in fire."

[24]Zedekiah said to Jeremiah, "No one is to know of these words, and you won't die. [25]But if the officials hear that I've spoken with you, and they come to you and say to you, 'Will you tell us what you stated to the king? Don't hide it from us, and we won't put you to death. And what did the king state to you?' [26]you're to say to them, 'I was presenting my plea for grace before the king not to return me to the house of Jonathan to die there.'" [27]All the officials came to Jeremiah and asked him, and he told them in accordance with all these words that the king had commanded him. So they left off from speaking with him, because the thing hadn't become audible.

[28]Jeremiah lived in the prison courtyard until the day when Jerusalem was captured.

As I write, the Australian founder of Wikileaks is effectively a prisoner in the Ecuadorean embassy in London. If he leaves the embassy, Britain will arrest him and hand him over to authorities in Sweden that have sought his extradition. A number of countries, such as the United States, are infuriated at his organization's systematic release of secret documents that could be useful to the countries' enemies. To complicate matters, the basis for his extradition is allegations of rape and molestation in Sweden, but whether or not those charges are justified, one can see that he has reason for fearing that once he's extradited, he may end up on trial in the United States or elsewhere for his whistle-blowing activities. Is he a traitor or a friend of democracy in the West?

Is Jeremiah a traitor or a friend of **Judah**? He's a **Benja-minite**, not a Judahite, a prophet from the north causing trouble in the south (the reverse of the relationship that got Amos into trouble as a southerner preaching in the north). Benjamin's relationship with Judah was always ambiguous—technically it had been part of **Ephraim**, and it may have already come to terms with the **Babylonian** invaders. The demoralizing effect of Jerusalem's siege is apparent from the note indicating that many Jerusalemites had faced facts and gone over to the Babylonians. Zedekiah is having a hard time holding together the vestiges of his little kingdom. Jeremiah is making it harder. And Jeremiah tells the king that he should simply surrender to the Babylonians, which Jeremiah knows is the only way forward. Zedekiah can picture the treatment he'll get from his own citizens, who've seen the light before him and won't be so impressed when he eventually joins them.

Jeremiah is also providing Zedekiah with more opportunity to show that he isn't the man to rise to the occasion; you have to sympathize with Zedekiah, as with the Wikileaks founder. In a way, his staff have more of what it takes, and they're prepared to be pretty ruthless with Jeremiah. They urge the king to put him to death, and he knows he can't resist them and their arguments. But they don't simply kill Jeremiah but put him in a cistern where he's bound to die. While Jerusalem has a spring and thus a water supply, like other cities it also has a reserve water system in the form of a complex of cisterns attached to people's houses to collect water in the rainy season, but they'd be empty by the end of the summer, with just a layer of mud in the bottom. They'd be bottle-shaped, with a narrow opening at the top and thus little light.

Ironically, Jeremiah's rescuer is a foreigner, an African who has somehow come to be working in the palace. The irony is underscored by the comment that he's a eunuch, which means that even though he's presumably a resident alien and worshiper of **Yahweh**, he wouldn't be much use as a full **Israelite** because he couldn't contribute to the people's future (men were castrated in connection with service in a palace to stop them from getting involved with any of the palace women). The city gate is where a king would sit for judicial proceedings—citizens could come there to appeal to him. With yet more irony, Ebed-melek (the name means "king's servant") brings a case that concerns the king himself.

What's the point of bringing Yahweh's message to a man who won't take any notice and will probably put you to death for your trouble? There's poetic justice in the fact that the man who let Jeremiah be thrown into a pit full of mud will find himself stuck in mire (it's an image from the Psalms, for trouble you can't get out of). It will be the Babylonians who literally set fire to the city, but Zedekiah will have to carry responsibility for their doing so. In this sense he'll set fire to the city.

You could say that Jeremiah is economical with the truth in his closing exchange with the officials, if by such economy you mean he doesn't tell them everything—he doesn't actually tell them lies. But the Old Testament wouldn't worry too much if he did tell them a lie; it tells a number of stories about people who are not in power telling lies to oppressive people who are in power. It assumes that powerful people must tell the truth to powerless people but not that powerless people must tell the truth to oppressors. The latter expectation also means that the voices of the powerless don't participate in corrupt power.

JEREMIAH 38:28b–40:6

The Grimmest Scene in the Old Testament?

[28b]When Jerusalem was captured, [39:1]in the ninth year of Zedekiah, king of Judah, in the tenth month, Nebuchadrezzar, king of Babylon, and all his forces came to Jerusalem and besieged it. [2]In the eleventh year of Zedekiah, in the fourth month, on the ninth of the month, the city was breached. [3]All the officers of the king of Babylon came and sat in the Middle Gate— Nergal-sar-ezer, Samgar-nebu, Sar-sekim the head eunuch, Nergal-sar-ezer the head official, and all the rest of the king of Babylon's officers.

[4]When Zedekiah, king of Judah, and all the fighting men saw them, they fled. They went out by night from the city by way of the king's garden through the gate between the double wall. He went out by way of the steppe, [5]but the Kaldeans' forces pursued him and overtook Zedekiah in the Jericho steppes. They captured him and took him up to Nebuchadrezzar, king of Babylon, at Riblah in the country of Hamat, and he announced decisions about him. [6]The king of Babylon executed Zedekiah's sons at Riblah before his eyes, and the king of Babylon executed all the important people in Judah. [7]He blinded Zedekiah's eyes and shackled him in bronze chains to bring him to Babylon.

[8]The Kaldeans burned in fire the king's house and the people's housing, and Jerusalem's walls they demolished. [9]The rest of the people remaining in the city and the people who had gone over to him and the rest of the people remaining, Nebuzaradan the head of the guards took into exile to Babylon. [10]Some of the people who were poor, who had nothing, Nebuzaradan the head of the guards left in the country of Judah and gave them vineyards and fields on that day.

[11]Nebuchadrezzar, king of Babylon, commanded regarding Jeremiah by the hand of Nebuzaradan the head of the guards: [12]"Take him and keep your eyes on him and don't do any evil to him. Rather, as he speaks to you, do so with him." [13]Then sent Nebuzaradan the head of the guards, Nebushazban the head eunuch, Nergal-sar-ezer, head officer, and all the heads

of the king of Babylon—[14]they sent and got Jeremiah from the prison courtyard and gave him over to Gedaliah son of Ahiqam son of Shaphan to let him go out to a house. So he lived among the people.

[15]A message from Yahweh had come to Jeremiah while he was confined in the prison courtyard: [16]Go and say to Ebed-melek the Sudanese: Yahweh Armies, Israel's God, has said this: Here am I, I'm going to bring about my words regarding this city for evil and not for good. They'll happen in front of you on that day. [17]But I'll save you on that day (Yahweh's declaration), and you won't be given into the hands of the people that you're afraid of. [18]Because I'll definitely rescue you. You won't fall by the sword. Your life will be yours as a trophy, because you've trusted in me (Yahweh's declaration).

[40:1]The message that came to Jeremiah from Yahweh after Nebuzaradan the head of the guards sent him off from Ramah, where he'd taken him (he was shackled in chains) among the exiled community from Jerusalem and Judah, who were being exiled to Babylon. [2]The head of the guards took Jeremiah and said to him, "It was Yahweh your God who spoke of this evil for this place, [3]and he's brought it about. Yahweh has done as he spoke, because you people offended against Yahweh and didn't listen to his voice. So this thing has happened to you. [4]But now, here: I'm releasing you yourself today from the chains that are upon your hand. If it's good in your eyes to come with me to Babylon, come, and I'll have my eye on you. But if it's evil in your eyes to come with me to Babylon, don't. Look, all the country is in front of you. Regarding what is good and what is evil in your eyes to go, go there." [5]Still he would not go back. "Or go back to Gedaliah son of Ahiqam son of Shaphan whom the king of Babylon has appointed over Judah's cities and dwell with him in the midst of the people, or go to any place that's right in your eyes to go." The head of the guards gave him provisions and goods and sent him off. [6]So Jeremiah came to Gedaliah son of Ahiqam at Mizpah and dwelt with him in the midst of the people who remained in the country.

I hate this story about Jerusalem's fall and its aftermath, and I hate the fact that it comes more than once in the Old Testament (indeed, more than once in Jeremiah alone, for goodness' sake). I hate the picture of Zedekiah's having to watch his sons' execution. When I was in my twenties, my father would call us from a gas-station pay phone (my parents had no phone of their own) each Sunday at about 12:45 and ask, "You OK?" I'd say, "Yes, we're fine." He'd reply, "That's OK, then, I just wanted to check," and he'd put the phone down. Last week one of my sons celebrated his fifteenth wedding anniversary; this morning I mailed a forty-fourth birthday card to my other son. I often reflect on how you can't appreciate your own parents' feelings about you until you have children of your own. You just want to know that they're OK.

The stupid, incompetent, unlucky, vacillating Zedekiah fails even to run fast enough to get away from the **Babylonians** as he flees down the mountains from Jericho, through land that he knows so much better than his pursuers. So they force-march him a couple of hundred miles to Nebuchadnezzar's headquarters at Riblah in Syria, and there Nebuchadnezzar kills Zedekiah's sons in front of his eyes and then blinds him, probably by searing his eyes with hot iron. So the last sight his eyes ever see surely is the deaths of his sons. Zedekiah is about thirty years old; his sons will be mere boys. Part of the point about the blinding and killing will be punishment for Zedekiah's resisting the king who put him on the throne and with whom he was therefore expected to comply. Part will be to make it impossible for Zedekiah to exercise future leadership and to make it impossible for those sons to grow up to be kings in his place.

The paragraph abut **Yahweh**'s message to Ebed-melek is out of chronological order, but we've seen that the book of Jeremiah isn't very interested in chronological order. The promise to Ebed-melek forms a foil for the horrifying story about Zedekiah and also neatly accompanies the story of

Jeremiah's escape. A foreigner—an African, not an **Israelite**—and a **Benjaminite**, not a **Judahite**, both know better than the king.

Ebed-melek's name means "king's servant." The king might be the human king, but names combined with *melek* usually refer to God as King. With further irony, there were two occurrences of another name incorporating the word for king, Malkiah, in the previous chapter, where Ebed-melek was introduced. They seem to refer to two different people: one's a party to Jeremiah's being put into the cistern from which Ebed-melek rescued him; the other is the owner of the cistern and one of the sons of Zedekiah who loses his life.

Like Jeremiah, Ebed-melek has had the courage to confront the king, though this doesn't mean he lacked fear in doing so. His action implies some trust in the God who is his master, and God's promise to him recognizes both the fear and the trust. Zedekiah didn't know how to trust Yahweh and instead put his trust in political wisdom, thus showing it to be a lack of true wisdom. Ebed-melek knew where real wisdom lay. Yes, "courage is fear that has said its prayers."

The story portrays even the Babylonian administrator as recognizing what Zedekiah and his staff couldn't see. Following on Jerusalem's destruction, the Babylonians located their administrative center at Mizpah, five miles north of Jerusalem. One reason will be Jerusalem's devastated state, but another is that the Babylonians had likely already taken control of that area and already had a base there. The country's devastated state might be one reason for Nebuzaradan to think that moving to Babylon was more attractive than the prospect of staying here. He'd also know that Jeremiah was the prophet who had declared that message about Yahweh's intentions for the city. He might further suspect that there could be plenty of people who'd have it in for Jeremiah the traitor; having been right would be no excuse. But we know that Jeremiah is committed to the future of Yahweh's purpose in the country and trusts in it; he's invested in the family land there. Further, the man the Babylonians have appointed as governor is the son of Ahiqam, who had once saved Jeremiah's life (see chapter 26). This might promise the opening up of a future.

JEREMIAH 40:7–41:18

Things Can't Get Worse (Can They?) (1)

[7]All the officers in the forces in the open country, they and their men, heard that the king of Babylon had appointed Gedaliah son of Ahiqam over the country and that he'd appointed him for the men and women and children and those of the poor people of the country who hadn't been exiled to Babylon. [8]They came to Gedaliah at Mizpah—Ishmael son of Netaniah, Johanan and Jonathan the sons of Qareah, Seraiah son of Tanhumet, the sons of Ephai the Netophatite, and Jezaniah son of the Ma'akatite, they and their men. [9]Gedaliah son of Ahiqam son of Shaphan let it be heard by them and their men, "Don't be afraid to serve the Kaldeans. Go back to the country and serve the king of Babylon and it will go well for you. [10]Here am I, I'm going to live in Mizpah to serve before the Kaldeans who come to us. You, gather up wine, summer fruit, and oil, put them in your containers, and live in the cities that you'll have seized."

[11]All the Judahites in Moab, among the Ammonites, in Edom, and in all the countries heard that the king of Babylon had allowed remains to Judah and that he'd appointed over them Gedaliah son of Ahiqam son of Shaphan. [12]All the Judahites came back from all the places where they had been driven and came to the country of Judah to Gedaliah at Mizpah and gathered up wine and summer fruit, very much. [13]But Johanan son of Qareah and all the officers in the forces in the open country came to Gedaliah at Mizpah. [14]They said to him, "Do you actually know that Ba'alis, king of the Ammonites, sent Ishmael son of Netaniah to strike down your life?" But Gedaliah son of Ahiqam didn't believe them. [15]Johanan son of Qareah said to Gedaliah in secret at Mizpah,

"Let me go and strike down Ishmael son of Netaniah, and no one will know. Why should he strike down [your] life and scatter all Judah who've drawn together to you, and the remains of Judah perish?" [16]But Gedaliah son of Ahiqam said to Johanan son of Qareah, "Don't do this thing, because you're speaking falsehood about Ishmael."

[41:1]But in the seventh month Ishmael son of Netaniah son of Elishama, of the royal line, the king's commanders, and ten men came to Gedaliah son of Ahiqam at Mizpah. They ate bread there together at Mizpah. [2]And Ishmael son of Netaniah and the ten men who were with him got up and struck down Gedaliah son of Ahiqam son of Shaphan with the sword and killed him, the man the king of Babylon had appointed over the country. [3]And all the Judahites who were with him (with Gedaliah at Mizpah) and the Kaldeans who were present there, the fighting men, Ishmael struck down.

[4]On the second day after the killing of Gedaliah, when no one knew, [5]some people came from Shechem, Shiloh, and Samaria, eighty people, shaved bare, clothes torn, bodies gashed, grain offering and incense in their hand to bring to Yahweh's house. [6]Ishmael son of Netaniah went out from Mizpah to meet them, weeping as he went. When he reached them, he said to them, "Come to Gedaliah son of Ahiqam." [7]When they came inside the city Ishmael son of Netaniah slew them [and threw them] into the cistern, he and the men with him. [8]But ten men present among them said to Ishmael, "Don't kill us, because we have stores in the countryside, grain, barley, oil, and honey." So he held back and didn't kill them along with their brothers. [9]The cistern where Ishmael threw all the corpses of the men he struck down by means of Gedaliah, it was the one that King Asa made on account of Ba'asha, king of Israel; Ishmael son of Netaniah filled it with slaughtered bodies.

[10]Ishmael took captive all the remains of the people who were at Mizpah, the king's daughters and all the people who remained at Mizpah over whom Nebuzaradan the head of the guards had appointed Gedaliah son of Ahiqam. Ishmael son of Netaniah took them captive and went to cross over [the

Jordan] to the Ammonites. [11]But Johanan son of Qareah and all the officers in the forces with him heard all the evil that Ishmael son of Netaniah had done, [12]and they took all the people and went to do battle with Ishmael son of Netaniah. They found him by the great pool at Gibeon. [13]When all the company with Ishmael saw Johanan son of Qareah and all the officers in the forces who were with him, they were glad. [14]All the company that Ishmael had taken captive from Mizpah turned around and went back and joined Johanan son of Qareah. [15]But Ishmael son of Netaniah escaped, with eight men, from Johanan and went to the Ammonites. [16]Johanan son of Qareah and all the officers in the forces that were with him took all the remains of the company that he brought back from being with Ishmael son of Netaniah from Mizpah, after he struck down Gedaliah son of Ahiqam (men, fighters, women, children, and eunuchs, whom [Johanan] had brought back from Gibeon). [17]They went and stayed at Gerut-kimham near Bethlehem, in going to reach Egypt [18]on account of the Kaldeans, because they were afraid of them because Ishmael son of Netaniah had struck down Gedaliah son of Ahiqam whom the king of Babylon had appointed over the country.

News reports as I write (and over the past year or two) manifest a strange kind of naiveté about changes of government. A series of Middle Eastern countries have seen civil conflict and the overthrow of totalitarian regimes. What the revolutionary forces have in common is their commitment to overthrowing the regime, but they may have no common view on what should happen next and no way of coming to a common mind about the question. The first person I know of to use the expression "Arab spring" in describing these developments was a Western commentator, but he went on to express the suspicion that the process was likely to be more messy and drawn out than such a phrase implies.

You might have thought that Jerusalem's fall would simplify some things in Judah; actually things there get messier. Zedekiah had no monopoly on stupidity, self-serving behavior, incompetence, and bad luck. One could get the impression that Jerusalem's fall and "the **exile**" meant that the **Babylonians** transported Judah's entire population and that the end of the exile fifty years later meant that the entire people came back. Neither impression is correct. This story indicates that the Babylonians do transport the important people from Jerusalem, such as members of the administration, priests, and prophets (Jeremiah will later give figures, and they're numbers in the low thousands). It also notes that they didn't take the poor people, so in a strange sense the exile may have been good news for them. The prophets make clear that they've been the victims of land accumulation by their more powerful, astute, and wily (not to say unprincipled) compatriots. Many such people will have been among those taken into exile. Some of the people who had lost their land can now reclaim it as well as live for the first year on the fruit of abandoned olives and vines.

Other astute and wily people were among those who had seen the way the wind was blowing, got out of Jerusalem and Judah, and taken refuge in Moab, Ammon, and Edom. When Nebuchadnezzar has done his worst, they're in a position to come back and try to resume their lives. The same applies to the men of fighting age who had managed to avoid being captured.

So in this section there's the following cast: 1) Gedaliah and his associates, Judahites who have been trusted by the Babylonians to take over the country's administration; 2) Judahite fighters and returning refugees led by Johanan, who's prepared to join Gedaliah and accept Babylonian **authority**; and 3) Judahite fighters and returning refugees led by Ishmael, who is of the Davidic line, can see himself as ruler of Judah, sees Gedaliah as a collaborator, and has Ammonite support in seeking to continue an anti-Babylonian resistance movement.

We can already guess at tensions that will arise among the Judahites. By definition the fighters are people who've taken Zedekiah's stance in resisting the Babylonians. Gedaliah comes from the family of Ahiqam and Shaphan, who had supported and protected Jeremiah with his message of submission to Babylon. Putting two and two together, it's no coincidence that Gedaliah is the Babylonians' appointee as governor, any more than that the Babylonians were protective of Jeremiah. So Gedaliah is now urging people to accept Babylonian authority. It's not surprising that the fighters are divided about whether to accept this advice. It also wouldn't be surprising if people such as the Ammonites saw that it was in their interests to discourage the development of a stable administration in Judah, and it isn't surprising if Ishmael as a member of the royal family opposes Gedaliah's regime. Gedaliah doesn't belong to the royal family; Ishmael does. He could claim that he is the kind of person who should be leading the country, in light of God's promise to David. His attempting to take the king's daughters with him fits with his ambitions; marrying the king's daughter is a good political move. Nor is it surprising that Johanan later thinks they'd better run for their lives.

The surprise is that Gedaliah is so naive as to have no suspicion that Johanan could be right and then to expose himself to Ishmael and his supporters. After Gedaliah's assassination, it is also surprising to hear of people from farther north in **Ephraim** coming to pray in the devastated temple. It's an incidental indication of a persistence in Ephraim of commitment to **Yahweh** and recognition of Jerusalem as the place where Yahweh dwelt and was to be worshiped.

JEREMIAH 42:1–43:7

Things Can't Get Worse (Can They?) (2)

[1]All the officers in the forces, Johanan son of Qareah, Jezaniah son of Hosha'iah, and the entire company, great and small,

approached [2]and said to Jeremiah the prophet, "May our prayer for grace come before you; plead on our behalf with Yahweh your God on behalf of all these remains, because we remain a few out of many, as your eyes do see us. [3]May Yahweh your God tell us the way by which we should go and what we should do." [4]Jeremiah the prophet said to them, "I've listened. Here am I, I'm going to plead with Yahweh your God in accordance with your words. The entire message that Yahweh will reply regarding you, I'll tell you. I won't withhold anything from you." [5]They themselves said to Jeremiah, "May Yahweh be a true and truthful witness against us, if in accordance with the entire message that Yahweh your God sends you regarding us, we don't so act. [6]Whether good or bad, we'll listen to the voice of Yahweh our God to whom we are sending you, for the sake of what is good for us, because we listen to the voice of Yahweh our God."

[7]At the end of ten days Yahweh's message came to Jeremiah. [8]He called to Johanan son of Qareah and all the officers in the forces with him and the entire company, great and small, [9]and said to them: Yahweh, Israel's God, to whom you sent me to present your prayers before him, has said this: [10]If you go back to dwell in this country, I'll build you up and not overthrow, I'll plant you and not uproot, because I regret the evil that I did to you. [11]Don't be afraid of the king of Babylon, of whom you're afraid; don't be afraid of him (Yahweh's declaration) because I'm with you to deliver you and to rescue you from his hand. [12]I'll give [him] compassion for you, and he'll have compassion toward you and take you back to your land. [13]But if you're going to say, "We won't stay in this country" (so as not to listen to Yahweh your God's voice), [14]saying, "No, rather we'll come to the country of Egypt, where we won't see battle and hear the sound of the horn and be hungry for bread, and stay there": [15]now therefore listen to Yahweh's message, remains of Judah. Yahweh Armies, Israel's God, has said this: If you do set your faces to come to Egypt and come to sojourn there, [16]the sword that you're afraid of will overtake you there in the country of Egypt and the famine that you fear will stick to your heels there in Egypt, and you'll die there. [17]All the people

who set their faces to come to Egypt to sojourn there will die by sword, famine, or epidemic. There won't be survivors or remains in the face of the evil that I'm going to bring upon you. [18]Because Yahweh Armies, Israel's God has said this: As I poured out my anger and wrath on Jerusalem's residents, so I'll pour out my wrath on you when you come to Egypt. You'll become an oath, a devastation, a belittling, and an insult, and you won't again see this place. [19]Yahweh has spoken against you, remains of Israel. Don't come to Egypt. Acknowledge clearly that I've testified against you this day. [20]Because you were deceitful in your spirits when you sent me to Yahweh your God, saying, "Plead on our behalf to Yahweh our God, and in accordance with all that Yahweh our God says, so tell us and we'll act." [21]I've told you this day, but you haven't listened to the voice of Yahweh your God and to all that with which he sent me to you. [22]So now you must really acknowledge that you'll die by sword, famine, or epidemic in the place where you want to come to sojourn.

[43:1]When Jeremiah finished speaking to the entire people all the words of Yahweh their God that Yahweh their God had sent to them, all these words, [2]Azariah son of Hosha'iah, Johanan son of Qareah, and all the arrogant people were saying to Jeremiah, "You're speaking falsehood. Yahweh our God hasn't sent you to say, 'You're not to come to Egypt to sojourn there.' [3]Because Baruk son of Neraiah is inciting you against us so that you give us into the Kaldeans' hand to kill us or take us into exile in Babylon." [4]So Johanan son of Qareah and all the officers in the forces and the entire people didn't listen to Yahweh's voice so as to stay in the country of Judah. [5]Johanan son of Qareah and all the officers in the forces took the entire remains of Judah that had come back to sojourn in the country of Judah from all the nations where they had been driven— [6]men, women, children, the king's daughters, and every person whom Nebuzaradan the head of the guards had settled with Gedaliah son of Ahiqam son of Shaphan, and Jeremiah the prophet and Baruk son of Neraiah. [7]They came to Egypt because they didn't listen to Yahweh's voice.

So they came to Tahpanhes.

There's a story about a man who falls over the edge of a cliff but manages to grab the branch of a small tree and thus stop himself from falling hundreds of feet to his death. The tree saves him, but only temporarily, because he can't get back up the cliff. He can't afford to let go, but he also can't assume that the tree will stay rooted into the cliff. He shouts for help, asking, "Is there anyone there?" Eventually he hears a voice from the heavens that says, "Jump, I'll catch you." After a moment, he shouts again, "Is there anyone else there?"

The voice from the heavens is the voice that speaks out to Johanan and company. In most versions of that modern story, it wasn't the man's fault that he fell over the cliff. One sad aspect of the Jeremiah story is that Johanan had started off as the good guy over against Ishmael the bad guy, but somehow he's lost the plot. Or maybe his later actions provide a further instance of a dynamic that features in many a revolution, the way unity can easily fragment because it conceals deeper disagreements, or the way revolutionary good intentions are forgotten when someone tastes the elixir of power. If Ishmael was furthering his ambitions as a member of the royal family, which gave him a basis for seeking the throne, there's no reason to think Johanan would be sympathetic to that cause any more than he was sympathetic to the assassination of Gedaliah. But you can't blame Johanan for suspecting that the **Babylonians** were not going to be concerned to make too fine a distinction between members of the **Judahite** forces who had assassinated their appointee and members of those forces who deplored the action. So Johanan and company assumed they'd be wise to get out of here. The previous section ended by telling of their journey from the Mizpah and Gibeon area just north of Jerusalem to somewhere near Bethlehem just south of Jerusalem. They were close to the effective southern boundary of Judah on the road that led to Egypt, even though it was maybe only a couple of days' journey (in theory, though the story stresses the involvement of an entire community and the fact that the journey might involve quite an effort, with belongings and supplies to carry as well as old people, infants, and pregnant and nursing women to make allowance for).

So they've already set off toward Egypt when it suddenly occurs to them to wonder what **Yahweh** thinks they should do. Jeremiah himself hasn't been mentioned for a couple of chapters since he arrived in Mizpah to join Gedaliah, but he's evidently part of the group Johanan rounded up and marched south. So they ask him what they should do after they've already started doing it. That context makes the way Jeremiah has to wait ten days before he knows what Yahweh has to say about the situation more amusing. (The previous occasion when he had to wait was when Hananiah broke Jeremiah's yoke, which symbolized the subservience about to come on Judah, which was also an event with a solemn ending—see Jeremiah 28.)

A nice point the story makes, given that they've already set off, is that nevertheless it's not too late for them to change their minds. It seems there's no end to Yahweh's patience, even though he often says there is. The point is vividly made by his talk of regretting the tragedy he'd brought upon them. He doesn't mean he regrets the fact that he did it. He means he regrets the fact that he had to do it. He did it with a heavy heart, and one can speculate that his heart is getting heavier as the people threaten to turn down every opportunity to start again. So as they halt for those ten days on the way out of the promised land, he tells them that it's still not over until it's over. They just have to decide to turn around and go back. Yahweh repeats those promises about building and planting, not destroying or uprooting. He also repeats the promises that he gave Jeremiah personally that have been vindicated against all odds, given the people who've wanted to get rid of him, as if to say, "If I can preserve Jeremiah, I can preserve you."

As far as they can see, asking them to turn around is like asking them to let go of the branch of the tree and fall into the void, believing that God will catch them. They can't do it. They resume their journey and arrive at the first big city in Egypt, breathing a sigh of relief. Did they have heavy hearts, too?

JEREMIAH 43:8–44:14

Remains

[8]Yahweh's message came to Jeremiah at Tahpanhes: [9]Take some big stones in your hand and bury them in clay on the pavement at the entrance to Pharaoh's house at Tahpanhes, in the sight of the Judahites. [10]You're to say to them: Yahweh Armies, Israel's God, has said this: Here am I, I'm going to send and get Nebuchadrezzar, king of Babylon, my servant, and I shall set his throne above these stones that I've buried, and spread his canopy over them. [11]He'll come and strike the country of Egypt: the people destined for death, to death, the people destined for captivity, to captivity, the people destined for the sword, to the sword. [12]I shall set fire to the houses of the gods of Egypt and he'll burn them and take them captive. He'll delouse the country of Egypt as a shepherd delouses his coat, and he'll go out from there in well-being. [13]He'll break up the columns in the house of Sun in the country of Egypt, and he'll burn the houses of Egypt's gods with fire.

[44:1]The message that came to Jeremiah regarding all the Judahites living in the country of Egypt, living in Migdal, in Tahpanhes, in Memphis, and in the country of Patros. [2]Yahweh Armies, Israel's God, has said this: You've seen all the evil that I've brought on Jerusalem and on all Judah's cities. There they are, a desolation this day, there's no one living in them, [3]because of their evil that they did, so as to provoke me by going to burn sacrifices to serve other gods that they hadn't acknowledged—they or you or your ancestors. [4]I sent to you all my servants the prophets, sending them urgently, to say, Will you not do this outrageous thing, which I repudiate. [5]But they didn't listen, they didn't bend their ear, so as to turn back from their evil, so as not to burn sacrifices to other gods. [6]My wrath and anger poured out and burned against Judah's cities and against Jerusalem's streets, and they've become a devastation, a ruin, this very day.

[7]So now, Yahweh, God of Armies, Israel's God, has said this: Why are you going to do a great evil to yourselves and to cut off for yourselves man and woman, child and infant, from the midst of Judah, so as not to leave remains for yourselves? [8]To provoke me by the deeds of your hands, by burning sacrifices to other gods in the country of Egypt to which you're coming to sojourn there, so that you may cut them off for yourselves and so that you may become a belittling and an insult among all the nations on earth? [9]Have you disregarded the evil acts of your ancestors, of Judah's kings, of its wives, your own evil acts, and those of your wives, which they did in the country of Judah and in Jerusalem's streets? [10]They were not broken until this day, they were not in awe. They didn't walk by my teaching and by my laws that I put in front of you and in front of your ancestors.

[11]Therefore Yahweh Armies, Israel's God, has said this: Here am I, I'm going to set my face against you for evil and cut off all Judah. [12]I shall take the remains of Judah who set their faces to come to the country of Egypt to sojourn there, and they'll all come to an end in the country of Egypt. They'll fall through the sword and come to an end through famine. Great and small, by sword and famine they'll die. They'll be for an oath, a devastation, a belittling, and an insult. [13]I'll deal with the people living in the country of Egypt as I dealt with Jerusalem, by sword, famine, and epidemic. [14]There'll be no survivor or escapee of the remains of Judah who are coming to sojourn there in the country of Egypt, to go back to the country of Judah, when they lift up their hearts to go back to live there, because they won't go back (except survivors).

When we were children, our parents sent my sister and me off to Sunday school on a Sunday afternoon. I never asked why they did so. I imagine they appreciated an hour's quiet after

Sunday lunch, but I also suspect that though they didn't go to church, they somehow wanted us to get something out of the teaching we'd receive. What's strange is that decades later both of us are still involved with church. Yet we represent only a tiny proportion of all the youngsters who were sent off to Sunday school in this way in those days. Why did we survive? The church in the U.K. is much smaller than it was fifty years ago. Rather little remains.

The fact that little "**remains**" of **Judah** and that even less will shortly remain is a key emphasis in Jeremiah's thinking. The word appears on average about three times in each chapter of this part of the book. English translations of the Old Testament often use the word "**remnant**," which then becomes a theological technical term. It suggests the way that God's grace ensures that the people of God doesn't entirely disappear, despite its waywardness. It also suggests a challenge. The remnant, the people who survive and remain, are challenged to become a faithful remnant.

These stories in Jeremiah make clear that it's not the case that the remnant, the people who remain, are necessarily the people who are already faithful. Some people such as Jeremiah and Baruk are among the faithful, but other faithful servants of God perish. In chapter 26 there was the story of the unfortunate Uriah. The person who saved Jeremiah from Uriah's fate was Gedaliah's father Ahiqam, but neither Ahiqam's **faithfulness** nor Gedaliah's faithfulness saved Gedaliah. Likewise, while many faithless people perish in the course of the **Babylonian** invasion and capture of Jerusalem, many faithless people like Ishmael survive. The people who remain (like my sister and me) cannot congratulate ourselves as if our remaining proves our virtue. We have to take our remaining as our challenge to faithfulness.

God "has to" let some Judahites remain because God "cannot" let **Israel** go out of existence. His commitment to Israel was too unequivocal to make that possible. That dynamic is also the church's security. Yet God has to continue grabbing by the scruff of the neck the Judahite community that remains in order to get it to meet its challenge, to respond to its survival in the appropriate way. The story so far has made clear that the chances of its doing so are small. It seems committed to walking in the opposite direction from the one in which **Yahweh** points, just as the broader Judahite community did before the **exile**. The company's arrival at the Egyptian border marks another moment when it can appropriately be faced with the challenge, which has a warning attached. To adapt the story from the previous chapter about the man who has fallen over the cliff, the tree really is creaking and threatening to uproot. Egypt is simply not as safe as people think.

Nebuchadnezzar did invade Egypt a couple of decades later, but one should not be too literalistic in interpreting the warnings issued by prophets, any more than one should be literalistic in interpreting the warnings of parents ("I'll kill you if you do that again!"). The point is to provide a vivid picture of the risk they're undertaking, in this case accompanied by a symbolic action of the kind that Jeremiah has undertaken on previous occasions. The nice picture of Nebuchadnezzar delousing Egypt very thoroughly (half-hearted delousing is no use to anyone) illustrates the point.

Another indication that we should not be too literalistic is the contradiction that Jeremiah utters. He's capable of saying that the entire remaining people will perish but that some will also survive to return to Judah. The contradiction is a necessity. They need to face the fact that they deserve simply to disappear and that they risk Yahweh's ensuring that this happens in order to bring them to their senses. But there remains the commitment incumbent on Yahweh that comes from his own nature: to be faithful to his commitment even when his people are not faithful, to be unable finally to eliminate them (how amazing that we congratulate ourselves on our survival when it comes from God). Ironically, far from dying out, the Judahite community in Egypt later flourished and became a major center of Jewish learning. It was there that people translated the Scriptures into **Greek** and thus made them accessible to the Gentile world.

JEREMIAH 44:15–45:5

An Ambassador in Chains

[15]All the men who knew that their wives burned sacrifices to other gods, and all the wives standing by, a big congregation, and the entire company who were dwelling in the country of Egypt at Patros, answered Jeremiah, [16]"The message you've spoken to us in Yahweh's name—we are not listening to you. [17]Rather, we'll definitely perform every word that has gone out of our mouth, burning sacrifices to the Queen of Heaven and pouring libations to her, as we and our ancestors, our kings and our officials, did in Judah's cities and Jerusalem's streets, and had our fill of bread and were well off, and saw no evil. [18]From when we held off from burning sacrifices to the Queen of Heaven and pouring libations to her, we've lacked everything and we've come to an end by sword and famine. [19]And when we were burning sacrifices to the Queen of Heaven and pouring libations to her, was it without our husbands that we made cakes to image her and poured libations to her?"

[20]Jeremiah said to the entire company, to the men and women and the entire company who were giving him an answer, [21]"The sacrifices you burned in Judah's cities and Jerusalem's streets, you and your ancestors, your kings and your officials and the people of the country—has Yahweh not been mindful of them and brought them to mind? [22]Yahweh could no longer bear it, in the face of the evil of your deeds, in the face of the outrages that you committed, so the country became a desolation and a devastation and a belittling, so that there's no resident, this very day. [23]In the face of the way you burned sacrifices and committed offenses against Yahweh and didn't listen to Yahweh's voice and didn't walk by his teaching and

laws and declarations, therefore this evil has happened to you this very day."

[24]Jeremiah said to the entire company and to all the women, "Listen to Yahweh's message, all of Judah in the country of Egypt. [25]Yahweh Armies, Israel's God, has said this: You and your wives—you've spoken by your mouth and with your hands you've fulfilled it, saying, 'We'll definitely perform our vows that we've made, to burn sacrifices to the Queen of Heaven and pour libations to her.' You may indeed perform your vows. You may indeed act upon your vows. [26]Therefore listen to Yahweh's message, all Judah who live in the country of Egypt: Here am I: I'm swearing by my great name (Yahweh has said), if my name will anymore be proclaimed in the mouth of anyone from Judah, saying, 'As the Lord Yahweh lives,' in the country of Egypt. [27]Here am I: I'm going to watch over them for evil not for good. Everyone from Judah in the country of Egypt will come to an end by sword and famine until they're finished off. [28]The people who survive the sword will go back from the country of Egypt to the country of Judah few in number, and all the remains of Judah who are coming to the country of Egypt to sojourn there will acknowledge whose word will be performed, mine or theirs. [29]This will be the sign for you (Yahweh's declaration) that I am going to deal with you in this place, so that you may know that my words against you for evil will indeed be performed. [30]Yahweh has said this: Here am I; I'm going to give Pharaoh Hophra, king of Egypt, into the hand of his enemies and into the hand of the people who are seeking his life, as I gave Zedekiah, king of Judah, into the hand of Nebuchadrezzar, king of Babylon, his enemy and one seeking his life."

[45:1]The message that Jeremiah the prophet spoke to Baruk son of Neraiah when he wrote these messages on a scroll from Jeremiah's mouth in the fourth year of Jehoiaqim son of Josiah, king of Judah: [2]Yahweh, Israel's God, has said this to you, Baruk: [3]You said, "Oh, alas, for me, because Yahweh has added sorrow to my pain. I'm weary with my groaning. I haven't found rest." [4]You're to say to him, "Yahweh has said this: Now. What I've built, I'm overthrowing; what I planted,

> I'm uprooting (it's the entire country). [5]Do you seek great things for yourself? Don't seek them, because here am I, I'm going to bring evil on all flesh (Yahweh's declaration), but I'll give you your life as a trophy in all the places where you go."

When Paul was apparently in prison in Rome, he wrote letters to a number of churches. In church today I was struck by a passage in which he describes himself as an ambassador in chains and asks the Christians in Ephesus to pray for him so that he'd be bold in making the gospel message known there (among political prisoners, thugs, terrorists, psychotics, and so on). This seemed a surprising request. One might've thought that sitting in chains in a Roman prison he might want, for example, the gift of discretion, even the gift of keeping his mouth shut, or the gift of liberty. Boldness in making the gospel known was what brought him into prison. The usual view is that he was released but then rearrested and executed three or four years later.

His story overlaps with that of Jeremiah and that of Baruk. Although we are only four-fifths of the way through the book of Jeremiah, we are at the end of Jeremiah's story. The last we see of him, he's being coerced into joining the **Judahites**' self-imposed exile in Egypt, to accompany the group of fugitives who are intent on taking no notice of what he says to them (so should we worry less about people's taking little notice of us when we talk about Jesus?). In a strange way it's an appropriate end to what must have seemed like his wildly unsuccessful ministry. Yet here we are studying his message, as people have been studying it for 2,500 years. Evidently somebody listened to it and made sure that his words didn't get lost and eventually got the Judahite people in Jerusalem to make it part of their Scriptures.

Which takes us to Baruk, because he certainly listened, and it seems a fair guess that he was involved in making sure that

Jeremiah's words didn't get lost. The message to Baruk goes back to that occasion nearly twenty years' previously when Jeremiah had him write down all the messages Jeremiah had received. To judge from God's reply, Baruk's protest related not to trouble coming to him personally but to the trouble coming to his people that he'd had to record. God had told him not to expect great things for himself. Maybe as a scribe in Jerusalem he could at least have expected a decent house and a regular income. Nobody is going to have those. Indeed, many people are going to lose their lives. Baruk will at least keep his. And actually, he'll get a fame that has lasted for 2,500 years.

He was still with Jeremiah; Johanan's people have been suggesting (rather implausibly) that he was behind Jeremiah's negative message to them. Including at this point the promise to him from long ago suggests, "You see, God has kept his promise." It also implies that Baruk can surely take the risk of continuing to trust in God for the future, even when it looks bleak and when people are attacking him, and when some of them have little hesitation about taking the life of people they believe are leading others astray. Maybe Baruk was the person who wrote the story we've been reading for the past few chapters, and his closing it with this recollection is a way of saying, "Yes, God kept his promise."

The first part of the section concludes the argument between Jeremiah and the people with Johanan. Jeremiah earlier referred to people making offerings to the Queen of Heaven, whom they apparently thought of as **Yahweh**'s wife. Here they themselves refer to it unashamedly, claiming that their lives went better when they did make those offerings. Jeremiah's response includes the declaration that Yahweh won't "carry" their actions forever. The verb is the one most often translated "forgive." Forgiveness involves God's carrying responsibility for our sins, as if he were the guilty one. He doesn't make us bear responsibility; the relationship between God and us would

213

then break down. There's a sense in which there's no limit to Yahweh's capacity to carry responsibility for us in that way. Yet if God meets with no response from us, God can reach the point where he says he won't carry it forever.

JEREMIAH 46:1–24

Pharaoh the Windbag

¹ What came as Yahweh's message to Jeremiah the
prophet about the nations.

²Regarding Egypt, about the forces of Pharaoh Neco, king of Egypt, that were at the river Euphrates at Carchemish, which Nebuchadrezzar, king of Babylon, struck down in the fourth year of Jehoiaqim son of Josiah, king of Judah.

³ Get ready, buckler and shield; advance to battle;
⁴   harness horses; mount, horsemen!
Take your position with your helmets,
    polish lances, put on armor!
⁵ Why have I seen—they're shattered, they're turning
    back,
    their warriors are beaten down, they've fled, fled?
They haven't looked back;
    terror is all around (Yahweh's declaration).
⁶ The swift is not to flee,
    the warrior is not to escape.
To the north, by the side of the river Euphrates,
    they've collapsed and fallen.
⁷ Who is this rises like the Nile,
    like streams whose waters surge?
⁸ It is Egypt that rises like the Nile
    and like streams whose waters surge.
It said, "I'll rise, I'll cover the earth,
    I'll destroy a city and the people who live in it."
⁹ Rise, horses; rage, chariotry;
    warriors are to go out,

Ethiopia and Libya seizing shields,
  Ludites seizing and drawing the bow.
10 That day belongs to the Lord Yahweh Armies,
    a day of redress for taking redress on his
      adversaries.
The sword will consume, be full,
  soak in their bloodshed.
Because the Lord Yahweh Armies has a sacrifice
  in the northern country by the river Euphrates.
11 Go up to Gilead, get balm,
    young Ms. Egypt.
In vain you're multiplying healings—
  there's no restoration for you.
12 Nations are listening to your belittling;
    the earth is full of your scream.
Because warrior is collapsing on warrior;
  together both of them are falling.

13The message that Yahweh spoke to Jeremiah the prophet
about the coming of Nebuchadrezzar, king of Babylon, to
strike down the country of Egypt.

14 Tell it in Egypt, make it heard in Migdal,
    make it heard in Memphis and Tahpanhes.
Say: Take your position, get yourself ready,
  because the sword is consuming all around you.
15 Why has Apis fled, has your Bull not stood?—
    because Yahweh has thrust him down.
16 He's made many people collapse,
    yes, each one has fallen into his neighbor.
They said, "Get going,
  let's turn back to our people,
to the country of our birth,
  from the sword of the oppressor."
17 There they called Pharaoh, king of Egypt,
    "A noise who has let the appointed time pass."
18 As I live (a declaration of the King—
    Yahweh Armies is his name):

like Tabor at the mountains and Carmel at the sea,
    one will come.
19 Make for yourself bags for exile,
    you who dwell as Ms. Egypt.
Because Memphis will become a devastation,
    desolate without resident.
20 Egypt is a beautiful, beautiful heifer;
    a gadfly from the north is coming against her.
21 Her mercenaries in her midst, too,
    are like well-fed bullocks.
But they're turning, fleeing together,
    they're not taking a stand.
Because their day of disaster has come upon them,
    the time when they're dealt with.
22 Her sound is like a snake as it goes,
    because with forces they will go.
With axes they're coming to her,
    like fellers of trees.
23 They're cutting down her forest (Yahweh's
    declaration)
    when it cannot be measured,
because they're more than locusts;
    there's no numbering of them.
24 Ms. Egypt is being shamed;
    she's given into the hand of the northern people.

That passage from Ephesians 6 to which I referred in connection with Jeremiah 45 begins by talking about the fight that the church is engaged in and by reminding us of the enemy we are fighting and the armor (mostly if not entirely defensive) that we need to wear. We read it on a Sunday when instead of my preaching a sermon, we had a congregational discussion of the readings, and one person commented that the passage confronts our instinct to assume that we are responsible for fixing things and are capable of fixing things on our own. It tells us that our situation is tougher than we think but also that God provides us with the means of facing its toughness.

There are parallels with **Judah**'s situation, specifically in relation to Egypt. At the beginning of **Israel**'s story, Egypt features as the great oppressor, but in the time of Isaiah and Jeremiah, it's the great temptation. To the north and east, **Assyria** and **Babylonia** fight it out for the position of top dog, which carries with it having Judah as part of the empire. Egypt isn't quite in the same league as Assyria and Babylon, but it's capable of snapping at their heels and thus capable of supporting little Judah when it's trying to assert its independence.

Like Isaiah and Ezekiel, Jeremiah here, near the end of the book, incorporates a substantial collection of prophecies about the destiny of nations such as Egypt. They constitute an expansion on the general points about the world of nations that came in Jeremiah 25, at the book's midpoint. In both contexts such prophecies remind Judah that **Yahweh** is indeed sovereign in the world of nations as a whole. Judah should thus lift its head and think about the fact that Yahweh is God of the whole world, which is background to Jeremiah's having been called to be "a prophet concerning the nations." While Jeremiah would see Yahweh as sovereign in relation to (say) **Greece** or China, he doesn't mention such peoples because his focus lies on the nations that are significant for Judah. But for us, thinking about what he says about those nations helps us think about God's relationship with (say) the United States or the United Kingdom.

The prophecies begin with Egypt because of its key significance as a potential ally for Judah, and the key point about Egypt that Jeremiah wants to bring home is the double insight emerging from Ephesians 6: Don't think that your job is to look after your own destiny and that the resources that you can see are your means of doing so. Your job is to trust Yahweh for your destiny. And trusting Egypt is really stupid, because it's going to be Nebuchadnezzar's next victim.

The prophecy speaks as if it's addressed to Egypt, and prophecies about the different nations are commonly addressed to them in this way, but we don't get the impression that the prophets generally went around all these nations delivering them. More likely they delivered them in the temple courts like their other prophecies so that Judah could hear them. They're designed for home consumption. When Jeremiah gets taken off to Egypt, of course, he could deliver a prophecy about Egypt there. But the beginning of this prophecy gives us a date back in that crucial fourth year of Jehoiaqim, 604, the year Nebuchadnezzar defeated Egypt in a crucial battle at Carchemish in northern Syria and sealed Babylon's position as the controlling power in Judah's world.

In the first prophecy, Jeremiah ironically encourages the Egyptians to get ready for this battle, but he goes on to describe the way they're going to be defeated—as indeed happened. Jeremiah describes the disaster as if it's already happening—it's happening before the eyes of his imagination. The second prophecy presupposes a time somewhat later when Nebuchadnezzar is going to invade Egypt. It repeats the point Jeremiah made to the Judahite party on its way to Egypt (see chapter 44). The parallel provides a concrete example of the way prophecies about a foreign nation are given *to* Judah itself, to push God's people into thinking about political questions in the right way. Events will show that Yahweh is the real power in politics whereas Pharaoh is indeed just a windbag.

JEREMIAH 46:25–47:7

Spiritual Warfare and Shocking Sovereignty

[25]Yahweh Armies, Israel's God, has said, Here am I, dealing with Amon of Thebes and in connection with Pharaoh, Egypt, its gods, its kings—Pharaoh and the people who trust in him. [26]I'll give them into the hand of the people who seek their life, into the hand of Nebuchadrezzar, king of Babylon, and into the hand of his staff. But afterwards it will be inhabited as in former days (Yahweh's declaration).

²⁷ But you, don't be afraid, my servant Jacob;
    don't shatter, Israel.
Because here am I, I'm going to deliver you from
        far away,
    your offspring from the country of their
        captivity.
Jacob will again be still and calm,
    with no one disturbing him.
²⁸ You, don't be afraid, my servant Jacob (Yahweh's
        declaration),
    because I'm with you.
Because I'll make an end of all the nations where
        I've driven you,
    but of you I won't make an end,
though I've disciplined you in exercising authority,
    and not treated you as innocent.

⁴⁷:¹What came as Yahweh's message to Jeremiah the prophet
regarding the Philistines, before Pharaoh struck down Gaza.
²Yahweh has said this:

There, waters are rising from the north,
    and they'll become a raging torrent.
They'll flood the country and what fills it,
    the city and the people who live in it.
People will cry out,
    all the country's residents will howl,
³ at the sound of the pounding of his steeds' hooves,
    at the noise of his chariotry, the clatter of its
        wheels.
Fathers are not turning to children
    because of the weakness of their hands,
⁴ because of the day that's coming
    for the ravaging of all the Philistines,
for cutting off every surviving helper
    for Tyre and Sidon.
Because Yahweh is going to ravage the Philistines,
    the remains of Caphtor's shore.

⁵ The shaved head is coming to Gaza,
    Ashqelon is becoming silent.
You remains of their valley,
    how long will you gash yourself?
⁶ Oh, sword of Yahweh,
    for how long will you not be still?—
    gather up into your sheath, rest, be still.
⁷ How can you be still
    when Yahweh is commanding you?
Regarding Ashqelon and the seacoast
    he has set its appointment.

There's one more aspect of the comments about warfare in Ephesians 6 that links with these chapters in Jeremiah. One big reason that Paul wants the church to take its fight seriously is that it's not fighting mere flesh and blood. There are negative supernatural forces involved in earthly events, and the church needs not to underestimate the nature of the forces it battles against. That's why you need supernatural armor.

Jeremiah's prophecies about different nations make little reference to the reasons for the troubles that come to them—their defeats being judgment for their oppression of **Israel**, for example, or for other wrongdoing. The prophecy about Egypt does refer to one theological significance attaching to the event. Like the exodus story, it notes that Egypt's defeat implies the defeat of Egypt's gods, who are incapable of protecting their people. Yes, the battles involve spiritual forces, not just human ones, and they involve **Yahweh**'s showing who is the God who has real power over against those gods as well as Pharaoh. For Egypt that distinction between Pharaoh and the gods is fuzzy—Pharaoh is a kind of demigod. But Amon is the real deal, the great creator deity, the top god. Thebes is similarly the real deal of Egyptian cities; indeed, while Thebes is the name with which we are familiar, its Egyptian name, which Jeremiah actually uses, means "the city." Amon's great temple was there, at Karnak; you can still visit its remains. The

220

fact that Yahweh can declare that Egypt will be defeated by Nebuchadnezzar "my servant" is evidence that actually Yahweh is the real deal. It's stupid to fear or trust in other supernatural forces.

Yet Jeremiah knows that Egypt is as much the victim as offender in its trust in Pharaoh and its gods, so the defeat that demonstrates who is truly Lord will be succeeded by an act of restoration. Yahweh's way of relating to Egypt thus parallels his way of relating to Israel. Yes, Yahweh is driving the **Judahites** away; but he'll bring them back. They can afford to risk trusting the classic prophetic invitation and exhortation "Don't be afraid." There's a master-servant relationship between Yahweh and Israel, and even though Israel hasn't been much of a servant, this failure doesn't let Yahweh off the hook of being a reliable master.

Although the **Philistines** had been Israel's enemy centuries before and were then Judah's potential ally in Isaiah's day, they're now a shadow of their former self and of no direct significance for Judah as foe or friend. Gaza and Ashqelon are two of the Philistine cities. Caphtor is where the Philistines originally came from, across the Mediterranean (the name likely refers to Crete). Tyre and Sidon are cities 150 miles farther north, so reference to them sets the flood that's threatening Philistia in the context of the broader invasion that's coming to the coastal peoples.

A clue to the point of the prophecy is that it's a kind of appendage to the prophecy about Egypt, because in effect Philistia was now a dependency of Egypt, so its fate follows from Egypt's fate. The prophecy gives no reason of any kind for the disaster that's to come to it, which is a reminder that many events in world history have no real meaning, at least meaning that's accessible to us. Little nations get caught up in the fate of big nations as individuals get caught up in the fate of their communities. The striking assumption that runs through the Prophets is that events still happen within God's purpose. They'd rather assume that God's sovereignty works out in shocking ways than assume that God's sovereignty isn't operating.

JEREMIAH 48:1–27

A Complicated Neighborly and Family Relationship

¹ Concerning Moab. Yahweh Armies, Israel's God,
    has said this:
Oh, also for Nebo, that it's destroyed,
    Qiriataim is shamed, captured.
The stronghold is shamed, it has shattered.
²   Moab's praise is no more.
In Heshbon they intended evil against her:
    "Come, let's cut her down from being a nation!"
Madmenah, you'll be silent, too;
    the sword will follow you.
³ The sound of an outcry from Horonaim,
    destruction and great wounding!
⁴ Moab is broken,
    they've let the outcry be heard to Zoar.
⁵ Because the ascent to Luhit—
    with weeping one ascends, with weeping.
Because on the descent to Horonaim
    adversaries have heard the cry about the
        wounding.
⁶ Flee, save your lives,
    be like Aroer in the wilderness!
⁷ Because on account of your trust in what you've
        made,
    and in your treasures, you too will be captured.
Kemosh will go out into exile,
    his priests and officials together.
⁸ The destroyer will come to every city,
    no city will escape.
The valley will perish, the plain will be devastated,
    as Yahweh has said.

9 Give wings to Moab,
      because it's to fly, go out.
   Its cities will be for devastation,
      with no resident in them.
10 Cursed is the one who does Yahweh's work unreliably;
      cursed is the one who holds back his sword
         from bloodshed.
11 Moab has been relaxed from its youth;
      it's been still on its lees.
   It hasn't been poured from bowl to bowl;
      it hasn't gone into exile.
   Therefore its taste has stayed in it,
      its bouquet hasn't changed.
12 Therefore there—days are coming (Yahweh's
         declaration)
      when I'll send off decanters to it.
   They'll decant it and empty its bowls
      and smash its jugs.
13 Moab will be shamed because of Kemosh
      as Israel's household was shamed because of
         Bethel,
      the object of their trust.
14 How can you say, "We are warriors,
      men fit for the battle"?
15 Moab is destroyed,
      people have gone up to its cities.
   The best of its young men
      have gone down to the slaughter
   (the declaration of the King,
      Yahweh Armies is his name).
16 Moab's disaster is near to coming,
      its evil is hurrying quickly.
17 Condole with it, all you who are around it,
      all you who acknowledge its name.
   Say, "How has the strong club broken,
      the splendid mace!"
18 Come down from honor, sit on the thirsty ground,
      you who sit as Ms. Dibon.

> Because Moab's destroyer has come up against you;
>> he's devastated your fortresses.
> ¹⁹ Stand by the road and look out,
>> you who sit as Aroer.
> Ask the man who flees and the woman who escapes;
>> say, "What has happened?"
> ²⁰ Moab is shamed, because it has shattered—
>> howl and cry out;
>> tell at the Arnon that Moab is destroyed.

²¹A judgment has come regarding the country of the plain, regarding Holon and Jahzah, upon Mepha'at, ²²Dibon, Nebo, Bet-diblatayim, ²³Qiryatayim, Bet-gamul, Bet-me'on, ²⁴Qeriyyot, Bosrah, and all the cities in the country of Moab, far and near.

> ²⁵ Moab's horn is cut off,
>> its arm broken (Yahweh's declaration).
> ²⁶ Get it drunk, because it's made itself big against
>> Yahweh;
>> Moab will wallow in its vomit.
> It will be an object of ridicule, too:
> ²⁷ wasn't Israel an object of ridicule to you?
> Was he found among robbers,
>> that when you speak of him you shake your head?

The London Olympics have just finished. I didn't watch, but I did check the news each day because I was concerned not with the number of medals that Britain had won (I didn't expect it to be many, though I was wrong) but with what might be going wrong with the arrangements. Would the transport system collapse? Would there be security chaos? Would it rain for the whole time? The U.S. news had long been discussing such gloomy prospects. I thought this reflected the usual post-colonial mixed feelings about the former imperial masters, though eventually I discovered from a humorous piece about how things would've been if the games had happened in New York that New York had wanted the games.

There isn't much love lost between **Judah** and Moab, either. Whereas Egypt is a big power to the south, Moab is a little power nearer to hand, a neighbor just across the river Jordan, part of what is now the kingdom of Jordan. Judah's relationship with Moab is complicated, perhaps partly because it was a family relationship. Like the Judahites, the Moabites were descendants of Abraham, though an Israelite storyteller may have delighted in telling an unsavory tale about how they started (see Genesis 19). But another **Israelite** storyteller drives home the importance of being positive about individual Moabites, telling a story about a Judahite family that takes refuge in Moab during a famine, about a young Moabite widow called Ruth who takes care of her mother-in-law, about the welcome the people of Bethlehem give to this Moabite, and how she becomes David's great-grandmother.

One can imagine the scandal the story would arouse when people read it. The Moabites were people who hired a prophet to curse the Israelites at the end of their generation of wandering in the wilderness when they were about to enter Canaan (and had no designs on the Moabites' territory). They were people **Yahweh** sometimes let cause trouble to Israel because of Israel's own wrongdoing and about whom the Israelites told another scatological story about their overweight king Eglon. They were people whose gods Israel periodically fell into worshiping and whose troubled destiny Isaiah 15–16 describes in a prophecy that Jeremiah is here re-preaching. It is full of warnings but also implies some sadness at what lies ahead for them, and it has a vision of their being led to come and seek Yahweh in their trouble. Their country was one where Judahites took refuge when the **Babylonians** arrived. They were people whom Ezekiel imagines gloating when Judah is conquered by Babylon. Yes, it was a pretty complicated relationship, like that between the United States and the United Kingdom.

One context in which one can imagine Jeremiah's speaking to Judah about Moab is the incursions by Moab (among others) during Jehoiaqim's reign. Second Kings 24 sees these as inspired by Yahweh himself as an act of chastisement for Jehoiaqim's policies, but that fact wouldn't stop Yahweh from also seeing Moab as deserving punishment for its action. Another context is the similar circumstance in Zedekiah's reign, reported in Jeremiah 27, when Judah is inclined to rebel against Babylon. This time Moab is a potential ally, so the point of a message from Jeremiah about trouble coming for Moab would be to encourage Judah not to think of Moab as a useful ally. A third context is the way Moab became a refuge for Judahites, so Jeremiah's point would be to warn them not to think they can solve their problems that way.

Judah's attitude to Moab was thus complicated, and so was God's. You could say that God's attitude to Moab was as complicated as God's attitude to Israel itself. Here most of the focus is on the way judgment is appropriate for Moab, though there's no need to take the reference to condolence as merely cynical. One can imagine both Jeremiah and Yahweh grieving at the experience that's to come on Moab, even while affirming its necessity.

The bases for judgment on Moab are similar to the basis for judgment on Judah and **Ephraim** (who does get a mention). It's Moab's trust in things it has made and in its treasures—its divine images and its resources. It's Moab's unwise adherence to its god Kemosh, whom Yahweh will demonstrate to be powerless. Apparently the Moabites should have known better. Maybe they should have paid more attention to what Yahweh had been doing with Israel since way back.

JEREMIAH 48:28–49:6

The Arrogance of Power

²⁸ Abandon the cities, stay in the crag,
    residents of Moab,

Be like a pigeon that nests
    in the sides of the mouth of a chasm.
29 We've heard of Moab's majesty
    (it's very majestic),
its height and majesty and exaltation,
    and the loftiness of its mind.
30 I myself know (Yahweh's declaration) its fury;
    its trivialities are not upright, they haven't acted
      uprightly.
31 Therefore I'll howl for Moab, I'll cry out regarding
      Moab, all of it,
concerning the people of Qir-heres I'll moan.
32 With more weeping than for Ja'zer I'll weep for
    you,
    vine of Sibnah.
Your tendrils crossed the sea,
    to the sea of Ja'zer they reached.
Upon your summer fruit and your grapes
    a destroyer has fallen.
33 Celebration and rejoicing gather up
    from the farmland and the country of Moab.
I've made wine cease from the presses;
    no one treads with a shout; the shout is no shout.
34 From the outcry of Heshbon as far as Ele'alah,
    as far as Jahaz they're giving their voice,
from Zoar to Horonayim, Eglat-shelishiyyah,
    because the waters of Nimrim, too, will become
      desolation.
35 I'll stop (Yahweh's declaration) anyone ascending to
    the shrine for Moab,
anyone burning sacrifices to its gods.
36 Therefore my heart moans for Moab like a flute,
    my heart moans for the people of Qir-heres like
      a flute.
Therefore the profit it made—they've perished;
37   because every head is shaved, every beard cut off.
On all hands there are gashes,
    around waists there's sackcloth.

38 On Moab's roofs and in its squares,
   all of it, is lamentation,
because I've broken Moab
   like a jar no one wants (Yahweh's declaration).
39 How it's shattered—wail, all of you;
   Moab has turned its back in shame.
Moab will be an object of ridicule,
   an object of horror to all the people around it.
40 Because Yahweh has said this:
   There, one swoops like an eagle
   and spreads his wings toward Moab!
41 Qeriyyot has been captured,
   the strongholds have been seized.
The mind of Moab's warriors on that day
   is like the mind of a woman in labor.
42 Moab has been destroyed from being a people
   because it made itself big against Yahweh.
43 A terror and a pit and a trap
   are against you who live in Moab (Yahweh's
      declaration).
44 The one who flees from the face of the terror
   will fall into the pit.
The one who climbs out of the pit
   will be captured by the trap.
Because I'll bring to it, to Moab,
   the year of my dealing with it (Yahweh's
      declaration).
45 In Heshbon's shelter people who are fleeing stop,
   being out of strength.
Because fire has gone out from Heshbon,
   a flame from the midst of Sihon.
It has consumed Moab's forehead,
   the skull of the people of Sha'on.
46 Oh, alas for you, Moab,
   the people of Kemosh have perished.
Because your sons have been taken into
      captivity,
   your daughters into captivity.

⁴⁷ But I'll restore Moab's fortunes at the end of the days
    (Yahweh's declaration).
As far as here is the decision for Moab.

^{49:1} Regarding the Ammonites. Yahweh has said this:
Has Israel no sons,
    or no one to enter into possession?
Why has Malkam dispossessed Gad
    and its people dwelt in its cities?
² Therefore—there, days are coming
    (Yahweh's declaration)
when I'll make the battle alarm heard
    concerning Rabbah of the Ammonites.
It will become a devastated tell;
    its daughter cities will be set on fire.
Israel will dispossess the people who dispossessed it
    (Yahweh has said).
³ Howl, Heshbon,
    because Ai is destroyed!
Cry out, daughter cities of Rabbah,
    put on sackcloth, lament.
Run to and fro in the enclosures,
    because Malkam is to go out into exile,
    his priests and his officials.
⁴ Why do you boast of the valleys?—
    your valley is flowing away.
Miss-who-turns-away, you who trust in your
        treasures,
    [saying,] "Who will come against me?"—
⁵ Here am I, I'm going to bring a terror against you
    (a declaration of the Lord Yahweh Armies)
    from all those around you.
You'll be driven each person straight ahead;
    there will be no one drawing together the
        fugitive.
⁶ But afterwards I'll restore the fortunes of the
        Ammonites
    (Yahweh's declaration).

As we drank our morning tea my wife told me that some foreign banks had announced that they were pulling out of Greece during its economic crisis, and we wondered what this meant for people who had accounts at those banks. Huge numbers of refugees were also crossing into Turkey from Syria, where there's civil war. At the other end of Turkey, Greeks and Turks are shooting each other. They'll be using weapons made in the United States, I speculated, having been reading about the United States being the supplier of 80 percent of the world's weapons. "Well, at least one of our manufacturing industries is flourishing," my wife responded. Actually tensions between Turkey and Greece have eased, but they go back millennia, to the time of Alexander. All these news items seem important to us because we are due to go to Greece and Turkey in three weeks.

Tensions today between nations that are related or are neighbors again parallel tensions in Jeremiah. Ammon started off life as Moab's half-brother. The Ammonites are thus further members of Abraham and Sarah's family. They too live across the Jordan from **Israel**, north of Moab in the northern part of what is now the kingdom of Jordan, between Moab and Syria. As the name implies, the Jordanian capital of Amman lies in what was once their land. They too had land allocated to them by **Yahweh** that the Israelites were told not to attempt to possess. There was no basis for treating them as under God's judgment, unlike the Canaanites west of the Jordan, but to complicate that question, the Israelites did take over from the Canaanites land that the Canaanites had already captured from Ammon. So Ammon, too, became a people with whom Israel lived in tension. Its gods were a temptation to Israelites; sometimes God used Ammon to chastise Israel. In a notorious story the Ammonites threatened to gouge out the eyes of Israelites living on the land they saw as theirs, and in another notorious story, it was the Ammonites whom Israel was fighting when David stayed home and went for an unwise stroll on his roof

(2 Samuel 11). Like Moab, Ammon was a place where **Judahites** took refuge during the **Babylonian** invasion.

Within Jeremiah's lifetime, the same three backgrounds could apply to Ammon as applied to Moab. It had been attacker, ally, and refuge. The complication in the history of the Ammonites' territory could mean that they felt quite justified in annexing land that had been occupied by Gad, one of the clans that formed part of **Ephraim**. So Israel here refers to Ephraim and nicely takes for granted that the mere fact that Ephraim had been destroyed by the **Assyrians** a century before didn't mean that members of Ephraim's clans were never going to be occupying Ammon's land again. It's another indication that God hasn't abandoned his people—even that long-gone Northern Kingdom.

The point in prophesying about one of Judah's neighbors is again to get Judah to look at Ammon from Yahweh's angle, not from an angle that leaves Yahweh out. Judah is invited to share in God's mixed feelings about Ammon, which again parallel God's mixed feelings about Judah as well as about Moab. As a matter of fact, Ammon is going to be subjected to terrible devastation by the Babylonians, and Yahweh is willing to associate himself with that action by Nebuchadnezzar "my servant." Again the prophecy's focus lies on the nature and consequences of this devastation, to rub Judah's noses in the facts. Again it emphasizes that Yahweh's action will show who is really God—here it's the Ammonites' god Malkam who's put in his place (the name usually appears as Milkom; Jeremiah's spelling reflects that it's probably understood more as a title, "their king," than as a name). At the same time, Jeremiah and Yahweh are aware of the horror and suffering that events will bring, and they grieve over it. Further, as with Moab, destruction won't be the end of the story. The image of restoring a people's fortunes is a distinctive feature of Jeremiah's; he applies it to Moab and Ammon as well as to Judah.

The stress on putting down Moab's majesty also parallels the prophets' warnings to Judah, especially in Isaiah. Moab occupied a physically exalted position in the mountains east of the Jordan that becomes a figure for its exaltedness as a people. Majesty and power are not wrong in themselves, but they constitute an all-but-irresistible temptation to arrogance and wrongdoing. On one hand, they tempt Moab (like Judah) to "make itself big against Yahweh." On the other, they tempt Moab to be oppressive in relation to other peoples.

JEREMIAH 49:7–27

The Wisdom That Fails

> ⁷ Regarding Edom. Yahweh Armies has said this:
> Is there no longer any wisdom in Teman;
>   has planning perished from the discerning?
> Has their wisdom gone stale?
> ⁸   Flee, turn around, lie low, residents of Dedan,
> because I'm bringing Edom's disaster upon it,
>   the time when I deal with it.
> ⁹ If grape-pickers came to you,
>   would they not let gleanings remain?
> If robbers [came] by night
>   they'd destroy [only] what they needed.
> ¹⁰ But it's I who've stripped Esau,
>   bared his hiding place.
> He can't hide; his offspring is destroyed,
>   his brothers and his neighbors, and there's no one.
> ¹¹ Abandon your orphans, I'll give them life;
>   your widows may trust in me.

¹²Because Yahweh has said this: The people for whom there has been no decision that they should drink the glass: if they'll certainly drink it, are you one to go totally innocent? You won't go innocent, you'll certainly drink it. ¹³Because by myself I've sworn (Yahweh's declaration) that Bosrah will be for

devastation, for insult, for desolation, for humiliation, and all its cities will be for desolations forever.

¹⁴ I've heard news from Yahweh,
    and an envoy is sent among the nations.
  Draw together and come to it,
    rise up for battle!
¹⁵ Because there—I'm making you small among the
      nations,
    despised among people.
¹⁶ Your dreadfulness has deceived you,
    your arrogance of mind.
  You who dwell in the clefts of the crag,
    you who seize the height of the hill,
  if you make your nest high like an eagle,
    I'll bring you down from there (Yahweh's
      declaration).

¹⁷Edom will become a devastation, everyone who passes by it will be devastated. He'll whistle at all its injuries, ¹⁸as at the overthrow of Sodom and Gomorrah and their neighbors (Yahweh has said). No one will live there, no human being will sojourn there.¹⁹There, it will be as when a lion comes up from the Jordan jungle into an enduring abode, because in a moment I'll hurry him out of it, and whoever is chosen I'll appoint for him. Because who is like me, who can subpoena me, who is the shepherd who can stand before me? ²⁰Therefore listen to Yahweh's plan which he's devised for Edom, his intentions which he's formulated for the residents of Teman.

  If the flock's boys don't drag them away,
    if their abode isn't devastated at them . . .
²¹ At the sound of their fall the earth shakes,
    the outcry makes its sound heard at the Sea of Reeds.
²² There, like an eagle he goes up and swoops,
    spreads his wings against Bosrah.
  On that day the mind of Edom's warriors
    will be like the mind of a woman in labor.

²³ Regarding Damascus.
Hamat and Arpah are shamed, because they've
    heard evil news,
they toss like the sea with anxiety; it cannot be still.
²⁴ Damascus is weak,
    it has turned around to flee.
Panic has gripped it,
    anguish and labor like a woman giving birth.
²⁵ How has the praiseworthy city not been abandoned,
    the city in which I rejoiced?
²⁶ Therefore its choice men will fall in its squares
    and all its fighting men will become silent on
        that day
    (a declaration of Yahweh Armies).
²⁷ I shall set fire to the wall of Damascus;
    it will consume the strongholds of Ben-hadad.

For next year the United States president has proposed to Congress a budget of $52.6 billion to cover intelligence agencies, including the CIA. Yet we aren't clear what to do about some major international questions that impact the United States, such as Iran's development of nuclear weapons, and we know that our enormous venture in invading Iraq that cost us so much in lives and resources was based on misleading intelligence. The budget for the U.K. intelligence services is about $3 billion (U.K. and U.S. billions used to be different, but I think they're now the same). Do we get value for the money?

It's the question Jeremiah asks when he moves from Moab and Ammon to Edom. Edom is the people to the south and southeast of the Dead Sea, the other side of the Moabites from the Ammonites. Bosrah was its capital, and Teman is also a term for Edom, while Dedan is to the south of Edom. Edom, too, is part of the family. Indeed, it's closer to **Israel**, because Edom was Esau's other name, as Israel was Jacob's other name—Edom and Israel were brothers. The relationship got onto a bad foot as Jacob cheated Esau of his blessing. Otherwise, similar characteristics apply to Israel's relationship with Edom as apply in connection with Moab and Ammon. Israel was also forbidden by **Yahweh** to attempt to conquer Edom's territory, though Edom's attitude to Israel was nevertheless less than friendly. Yahweh also used Edom to chastise Israel, and Israel for a while controlled Edom as part of its little empire. Edom, too, is potential ally and potential temptation, as well as refuge.

Arguably there's even less love lost between Edom and Israel than between Moab or Ammon and Israel, to judge from the sharpness of the treatment of Edom by prophets other than Jeremiah. Maybe one piece of background is that because Edom was itself under pressure from Arab peoples, the Edomites gradually advanced into southern **Judah** and took control of much of this territory. They're later referred to as Idumeans; Herod the Great was an Idumean, but by this time the Idumeans had been converted to Judaism.

Edom evidently had a reputation for wisdom. In the Old Testament, wisdom includes practical skill and expertise, and the Edomites may have had their reputation because they were skilled at metalwork. Jeremiah jumps from there to the question of their skill in international politics, about which they were clueless. It's not that they were any less wise than Moab and Ammon; it's just that their reputation for insight makes their cluelessness the more ironic. Like Moab and Ammon (and the United States and the United Kingdom) they assumed they could control their destinies if they thought hard and did the requisite research. The trouble is, they left Yahweh out of the picture. It was a fatal error because Yahweh makes plans and formulates intentions, and human wisdom lacks the means of accessing them. Edom's position in high mountain country, higher than Judah, won't help it.

There's no promise of restoring Edom's fortunes as there is for Moab and Ammon, though there's again a note of sadness at the fate of the vulnerable in the line about orphans and widows, which includes an invitation: "Keep, ancient land, your storied pomp," Yahweh almost says. "Give me your tired, your poor . . . the wretched refuse of your teeming shore. Send these, the homeless, tempest-tossed, to me."

Damascus, then as now, is the capital of Syria, so once again Jeremiah has moved north, to the nation that lives beyond Ammon. The Syrians or Arameans lie further back in Israel's family history; they're part of the wider family of Abraham rather than being his descendants. Once more they were sometimes allies, sometimes foes, sometimes underlings. They too were a people in whose destiny Yahweh was involved in a positive way—Amos 9 refers to Yahweh's giving them their land as he gave Israel its land. They were a more numerous people than the others Jeremiah has spoken of, but it won't exempt them. So Judah should neither trust nor fear them either.

JEREMIAH 49:28–50:13

The Promise of a Future

²⁸Regarding Qedar and the kingdoms of Hazor, which Nebuchadrezzar, king of Babylon, struck down. Yahweh has said this:

> Rise up, go up to Qedar,
> destroy the Qedemites!
> ²⁹ People will take their tents and their flocks,
> their tent cloths and all their things.
> They'll carry off their camels for themselves;
> they'll proclaim against them, "Terror is all
> around."
> ³⁰ Flee, go way away, lie low,
> residents of Hazor (Yahweh's declaration).
> Because Nebuchadrezzar, king of Babylon,
> has devised a plan against you,
> has formulated an intention against you.

³¹ Rise up, go up, to a quiet nation,
    dwelling with assurance (Yahweh's declaration).
It has no gates, no bars;
    they stay alone.
³² Their camels will become spoil,
    the abundance of their cattle plunder.
I shall scatter to the winds the people shaved at the
        forehead,
    from all sides I shall bring about their disaster
    (Yahweh's declaration).
³³ Hazor will become a refuge for jackals,
    a devastation forever.
No one will live there;
    no human being will sojourn there.

³⁴What came as Yahweh's message to Jeremiah the prophet
regarding Elam at the beginning of the reign of Zedekiah, king
of Judah. ³⁵Yahweh Armies has said this:

Here am I, I'm about to break Elam's bow,
    the foundation of their strength.
³⁶ I'll bring to Elam four winds
    from the four corners of the heavens
I'll scatter them to these four winds;
    the nation won't exist where Elam's fugitives
        don't come.
³⁷ I'll shatter Elam before its enemies,
    and before the people who seek their life.
I'll bring evil upon them,
    my angry blazing (Yahweh's declaration).
I'll send the sword off after them
    until I've finished them off.
³⁸ I'll put my throne in Elam
    and cause king and officials to perish from there
    (Yahweh's declaration).
³⁹ But at the end of the days I'll restore Elam's
        fortunes
    (Yahweh's declaration).

^{50:1}The message Yahweh spoke regarding Babylon, regarding the Kaldeans' country, by the hand of Jeremiah the prophet:

2   Tell among the nations,
     make it heard; lift a banner, make it heard.
   Don't hide it, say, "Babylon is captured,
     Bel is shamed, Merodak has shattered."
   Its idols are shamed,
     its fetishes have shattered.
3   Because the northern nation has gone up against it,
     it will make its country a devastation.
   There'll be no one living in it;
     human being and animal have fled, gone.

4   In those days and at that time
     (Yahweh's declaration)
   the Israelites will come,
     they and the Judahites together.
   They'll go, and weep as they go,
     and seek help from Yahweh their God.
5   They'll ask the way to Zion,
     and their faces will be toward there,
   [saying,] "Come, join yourselves to Yahweh
     by a lasting covenant that won't be disregarded."
6   My people was a flock that were lost;
     their shepherds had led them astray.
   On the mountains they turned them back,
     from mountain to hill they went,
     they disregarded their resting place.
7   All the people who found them consumed them;
     their adversaries said, "We won't be guilty,
   on account of the fact that they offended against
      Yahweh,
     the faithful abode, their ancestors' hope, Yahweh."

8   Flee from the midst of Babylon,
     go out of the Kaldeans' country,
     be like the he-goats at the front of the flock.

9 Because here—I'm going to arouse
    and cause to go up against Babylon
a congregation of great nations
    from the northern country.
They'll dispose themselves against it;
    from there it will be captured.
Its arrows like those of a successful warrior
    won't turn back empty-handed.
10 The Kaldeans will be plunder;
    all its plunderers will be full (Yahweh's declaration).
11 Because you celebrate, because you exult,
    despoilers of my possession.
Because you jump like a heifer with grain,
    you bellow like stallions.
12 Your mother is very shamed,
    the one who bore you is disgraced.
There—the end of the nations:
    wilderness, dry land, steppe.
13 Because of Yahweh's wrath it won't be inhabited,
    it will be a devastation, all of it.
Everyone who passes by Babel will be devastated
    and will whistle at all its injuries.

It's been a year since I became priest-in-charge at our church, when we could no longer afford a paid pastor. That fact was a sign that the church is getting smaller, and it wasn't clear how long we'd be viable at all. Indeed, we've had two funerals in the past three weeks. Yet we've also had a new couple join; another woman has become a regular; and a member of another church family started coming because we sometimes sing in Spanish, her first language. I've thus let myself have the tiniest hope that we are not bound to decline until we die.

If you were a sixth-century **Judahite** prophet, you could be tempted to think that your nation was bound to decline until it died. This prophecy about **Babylon** declares that it's not so. Judah has hope for the future, partly because **Yahweh** is bringing judgment on its overlord.

The book of Jeremiah virtually ends with a gargantuan prophecy about Babylon. It's the longest prophecy about a foreign people in the Bible, and it occupies the longest pair of chapters in the Bible. There's good reason why it should be so. The Babylonians are Judah's political overlords and the people responsible for Judah's most terrible experiences. They deposed, maimed, and exiled Judah's rulers. They besieged, captured, and burned down its capital, caused the death of many of its people, and transported many others. How are Judahites to think of Babylon? How does God think of it? What is God's intention for it? Its own day is going to come, the prophecy declares. You could think that its chief god, Merodak or Marduk (alternative spellings of his name) or Bel (his title, "Lord"), had defeated Yahweh, but the fall of Babylon will signify that Marduk isn't such a great god.

The fall of Babylon won't actually bring the destruction and depopulation that the prophecy describes. This doesn't stop the book of Ezra from reporting Babylon's fall to **Persia** as a fulfillment of this prophecy (Ezra 1); it evidently knew that you don't have to be literalistic in interpreting prophecy. Prophecy is poetry. The expressions Jeremiah uses to describe Babylon's fall (destruction and depopulation) are standard ones, which he's used in connection with Moab and Edom. Babylon's conqueror won't come from the geographical north; the next chapter will speak more literally. The discrediting of Babylon's gods will take a distinctive form, too. In the midst of the crisis, they changed sides and gave their support to Cyrus, the Persian conqueror.

In this opening part of the Babylon prophecy, Jeremiah emphasizes its significance for Judah. No, the **exile** doesn't mean Judah is going to decline and die. The fall of Babylon will lead to **Israelites**' and Judahites' having recourse to Yahweh. Set over against Judahites, the term *Israelites* implies **Ephraimites**. You might definitely have thought they were finished, but Jeremiah has made clear a number of times that it's not so. The story in Ezra indeed portrays Judahites coming to Jerusalem, weeping and rejoicing as they start rebuilding the temple. Do they weep with joy, with sadness at its destruction and the realization of how it used to be, or with sorrow at the waywardness that led to its destruction and the suffering they've gone through as a consequence of their waywardness? Maybe they have all those feelings.

Whichever it is, they do have hope for the future, and they commit themselves to a lasting covenant. It's the kind Jeremiah 31 referred to when speaking of a new covenant that would involve Yahweh's expectations being written into their minds and wills. They'll now have new memories to reshape their thinking. They won't disregard this new covenant, and neither will Yahweh. They couldn't complain that the exile had happened. While they had been the victims of their leaders' neglect, Jeremiah imagines their invaders nevertheless able to defend their action on the basis of being Yahweh's agents in bringing Yahweh's judgment to Judah. Now the tables are to be turned, not in the sense that Judah will get its revenge on Babylon but that Babylon is victim in the way Judah had once been. It's Judah's cue to leave now, like Lot's family leaving Sodom as its moment arrives.

The prophecies about Qedar and Elam concern peoples that were nothing to do with Judah. They were not neighbors or enemies. Maybe the point lies here. Yahweh's sovereignty in the world affected affairs way beyond Judah. It covered wandering Bedouin peoples and a far-off people in Iran. These peoples, too, were Nebuchadnezzar's victims; but here, too, Nebuchadnezzar was under the direction of a higher **authority**. Yahweh is the global God, and therefore Jeremiah is a global prophet. And what Yahweh is doing needs to be told "among the nations." Judgment isn't a private business between an individual and God or even a community and God. It's a public business. Jeremiah talks a lot about shame. There are no secrets. Yet the aim isn't merely to shame people but to let the whole world know what it needs to know about right and wrong and about the manner of God's involvement in the world. And there's liberation in knowing that all your secrets are out and you have no exposure to fear.

JEREMIAH 50:14–40

Death and Life Interweave

¹⁴ Dispose yourselves against Babylon around about,
    all you who direct the bow.
Shoot at it, don't hold back in connection with an
    arrow,
    because it has offended against Yahweh.
¹⁵ Shout against it round about, it's giving itself up,
    its towers are falling,
its walls are being thrown down,
    because it's Yahweh's redress.
Take redress upon it;
    as it has done, do to it.
¹⁶ Cut off sower from Babylon,
    and seizer of sickle at harvest time.
Before the oppressor's sword
    they'll turn, each one, to his people,
    they'll flee, each one, to his country.
¹⁷ Israel is scattered sheep,
    whom lions have driven away.
First the king of Assyria devoured him,
    then later Nebuchadrezzar crushed his bones.
¹⁸ Therefore Yahweh Armies,
    Israel's God, has said this:
Here am I,
    I'm going to deal with the king of Babylon and
      his country
    as I dealt with the king of Assyria.
¹⁹ I'll take Israel back to its abode,
    and it will graze in Carmel and Bashan.
In the mountains of Ephraim and Gilead
    he'll eat his fill.

²⁰ In those days and at that time
  (Yahweh's declaration),
Israel's waywardness will be inquired after—and
    there'll be none;
  Judah's offenses—and they won't be present,
  because I'll pardon the people I let remain.

²¹ Concerning the country of Meratayim:
Go up against her,
  and to the residents of Pekud.
Put to the sword and devote the last of them
  (Yahweh's declaration),
  do in accordance with all that I've commanded you.
²² The sound of battle in the country,
  a great wounding!
²³ How the hammer of the whole earth
  has severed and broken!
How Babylon has become
  a devastation among the nations!
²⁴ I trapped you and yes, you were captured, Babylon,
  and you didn't know it.
You were caught and seized,
  because you challenged Yahweh.
²⁵ Yahweh opened his storehouse
  and brought out the instruments of his wrath,
because that's the work of the Lord Yahweh Armies
  in the Kaldeans' country.
²⁶ Come to it from afar, open its granaries,
  pile it up like heaps,
  devote it, there must be no remains of it.
²⁷ Put to the sword all its bullocks,
  they must go down for slaughter.
Oh, alas for them, because their day is coming,
  the time when they're dealt with.
²⁸ The sound of fugitives and escapees
  from the country of Babylon,
to tell in Zion of the redress of Yahweh our God,
  redress for his palace!

²⁹ Make it heard to the archers against Babylon,
   to all those who draw the bow!
Camp against it around about,
   there must not be people who escape.
Repay it for its actions,
   do to it in accordance with all that it did,
because it asserted itself against Yahweh,
   Israel's holy one.

³⁰ Therefore its choice men will fall in the squares,
   and all its fighting men will be stilled on that day
   (Yahweh's declaration).

³¹ Here am I regarding you, insolent one
   (a declaration of the Lord, Yahweh Armies).
Because your day is coming,
   the time when I deal with you.

³² The insolent one will collapse, and fall,
   and no one will raise him up.
I shall set fire to his cities
   and it will consume all around him.

³³ Yahweh Armies has said this:
   The Israelites and the Judahites
   are oppressed together.
All their captors have taken hold of them
   and refused to let them go.

³⁴ Their restorer is strong,
   Yahweh Armies is his name.
He'll contend their case strongly
   so that he may quiet the country
   and shake up Babylon's residents.

³⁵ A sword against the Kaldeans (Yahweh's
      declaration),
   to Babylon's residents, its officials, and its experts!

³⁶ A sword to the diviners so they become fools,
   a sword to its warriors so they shatter!

³⁷ A sword to its horses and its chariotry
   and all the mob in its midst, so they become
      women!
A sword to its storehouses, so they're plundered;

³⁸   a drought to its waters, so they dry up!
Because it's a country of images,
    so that through their dreadful objects they'll
      go mad.
³⁹ Therefore wildcats will live with jackals,
    and ostriches will live in it.
It won't be lived in again forever,
    it won't be dwelt in for generation after generation.
⁴⁰ Like God's overthrow of Sodom, Gomorrah, and
      their neighbors
    (Yahweh's declaration),
no one will live there,
    no human being will sojourn there.

Death and new life interweave. Last night we went to a concert by jazz and swing artist Steve Tyrell, who told us early in his set that it had been a most significant day for him. Eight hours previously, back in New York, his daughter had had a baby, his first grandchild. He then closed the set with a series of songs by Burt Bacharach and Hal David, whom he described as his great mentor and friend, and he then told us the other reason why it had been such a significant day. Seconds before receiving the message about his grandchild, he'd received another message: this great mentor had just died. He didn't know what to make of this collocation of events, he commented. In the midst of life we are in death.

Before and during the **exile**, there has been life and flourishing for **Babylon** but subjugation and then death for **Judah**. Whichever is your lot, it's tempting to assume it will continue forever. Like any superpower, Babylon assumes it will hold its position permanently. Like any afflicted people, Judah assumes its position will continue permanently. A prophet's vocation is regularly to tell both parties that they're wrong, which makes the prophet unpopular with both.

Jeremiah's exhortations to people such as bowmen are not addressed to Judah, which anyway has no bowmen. In light of history, we know that in effect it's addressed to the army of Cyrus the **Persian**; at least, these are the bowmen who unconsciously heard the commission and came to conquer Babylon. They'll be the unwitting agents whereby **Yahweh** responds to Babylon's people, who've turned themselves into God. Yahweh doesn't think it's appropriate simply to shrug shoulders at this action. People who challenge God can't simply be ignored. It's inappropriate to ignore the destruction of the palace that was the divine king's home (the temple). It's inappropriate to shrug shoulders at such insolence. It's the holy one of **Israel** that we are talking about.

Alongside the affront to the real God is the death-bringing action in relation to Israel—what Jeremiah pictures as the scattering of a flock of sheep, which would bring death to the sheep. Indeed, they've been devoured by **Assyrian** and Babylonian lions. It's tempting to think that the world needs a superpower to keep it in order, and the story of the Middle East (e.g., Assyria, Babylon, and Persia) shows that the existence of a superpower, the "insolent one," does ensure a certain kind of order. But it also means that little powers suffer a lot, and it's not obvious that the gain is worth the cost.

The Judahites are nevertheless going to begin a new life on the rich pasturage of Mount Carmel and Bashan (the Golan Heights) and in the hill country either side of the Jordan. Once again Jeremiah speaks of **Ephraim** and not just Judah; indeed, all four of those areas are Ephraim rather than Judah. The mere fact that death came well over a century ago doesn't mean new life is impossible. So another reason why action needs to be taken against Babylon is that Ephraimites and Judahites are both subject to oppression by Babylon. But Israel has a "restorer" (English translations usually have the word "redeemer"). A restorer is a member of your family who has resources that you lack and who's therefore in a position to expend these resources on your behalf when you're in trouble—an example is Boaz acting as restorer for Naomi and Ruth. Yahweh regards

Israel as a member of his family, and he will use some of his infinite resources to restore Israel. As was the case with Boaz, sometimes this involves going through legal procedures on behalf of the person in need; here, Jeremiah imagines Yahweh appearing in court on Israel's behalf, "contending" strongly for Israel, arguing that Babylon has to let his people go.

Maybe even more exciting is what Jeremiah has to say about Ephraim's and Judah's wrongdoing, about which Jeremiah has spoken so much, so loudly, and so vividly. He pictures someone inquiring about their waywardness and imagines puzzlement on the part of the person who's asked. "No, I don't know anything about wrongdoing by them." "Excuse me?" Well, you see, Jeremiah explains, Yahweh has pardoned it, and when Yahweh pardons something, it ceases to exist. One can think of it as analogous to a criminal record. When the court pardons, the record is actually expunged. So it's a serious and sad business when someone who has been forgiven thinks and/or acts as if he or she has not. My wife has just sprayed stain remover on a footstool where I spilled some wine. The stain is gone. Not only so, but a stain that had been there for years as a result of some earlier accident is also gone. That's how it is when Yahweh pardons. There's no evidence that once there was any wrongdoing. It's gone.

JEREMIAH 50:41–51:19

Wounds Too Severe for Treatment

41 There, a people is coming from the north,
  a great nation and many kings
  are aroused from earth's farthest reaches.
42 They grasp bow and spear;
  they're violent and they don't show compassion.
  Their sound is like the sea that roars;
  they ride on horses.
  Like someone disposed for battle
  they're against you, Ms. Babylon.

43 The king of Babylon has heard the news of them,
    his hands have become weak.
Anguish has taken hold of him,
    labor like a woman giving birth.
44 There, it will be as when a lion comes up
    from the Jordan jungle into an enduring abode,
because in a moment I'll hurry him out of it,
    and someone chosen I'll appoint for it.
Because who is like me, who can subpoena me,
    who is the shepherd who can stand before me?
45 Therefore listen to Yahweh's plan
    which he's devised for Babylon,
his intentions which he's formulated
    for the Kaldeans' country.
If the flock's boys don't drag them away,
    if the abode isn't devastated at them . . .
46 At the sound of the seizing of Babylon the earth
        shakes,
    the outcry makes itself heard among the nations.

51:1 Yahweh has said this:
Here am I, I'm rousing against Babylon
    and the residents of Leb-qamay a destructive
        wind.
2 I shall send strangers off to Babylon
    so they'll winnow it and strip its country,
because they're against it all around,
    on the day of evil.
3 The one who bends his bow isn't to bend it
    and isn't to stand in his armor.
Don't spare its choice men;
    devote its entire army.
4 People are to fall slain in the Kaldeans' country,
    thrust through in its streets.
5 Because Israel and Judah are not widowed
    by their God, Yahweh Armies.
Rather their country was full of guilt
    before Israel's holy one.

6 Flee from the midst of Babylon;
 each of you, save his life.
Don't be stilled because of its waywardness,
 because this is the time of Yahweh's redress;
 he's repaying recompense to it.
7 Babylon was a gold chalice in Yahweh's hand,
 making the entire earth drunk.
The nations drank from its wine;
 therefore the nations go mad.
8 Suddenly Babylon has fallen and broken;
 howl over it.
Get balm for its injuries,
 perhaps it may heal.
9 People say, "We are healing Babylon but it hasn't
 healed;
 abandon it, let's go each to his country."
Because its sentence has reached to the heavens,
 lifted to the skies.
10 Yahweh has brought out faithfulness for us;
 come, let's recount in Zion
 the action of Yahweh our God.

11 Polish the arrows, fill the quivers,
 Yahweh has aroused the spirit of Media's
  kings.
Because his scheme against Babylon
 is to destroy it.
Because it's Yahweh's redress,
 redress for his palace.
12 To Babylon's walls lift up a banner, make a strong
 watch,
 set up watchmen, prepare ambushes.
Because Yahweh is both scheming and doing
 what he spoke regarding Babylon's residents.
13 You who dwell by many waters, abundant in
 storehouses,
 your end has come, the time for your cutting
  off.

¹⁴ Yahweh Armies has sworn by his life:
I'm filling you with people like a locust swarm;
they'll raise a shout over you.
¹⁵ One who made the earth by his might,
established the world by his expertise,
by his understanding stretched out the heavens—
¹⁶ at his giving voice,
there was a roaring of the waters in the heavens—
he brought up clouds from the end of the earth,
made lightning for the rain,
brought out wind from his storehouses.
¹⁷ Every human being proves dense, without
knowledge;
every goldsmith is put to shame by the image,
because his figure is a falsehood,
and there's no breath in them.
¹⁸ They're emptiness, a work for mockery;
at the time they're dealt with, they'll perish.
¹⁹ Not like these is the one who belongs to Jacob,
because he's the one who formed everything.
It is the clan he possesses;
Yahweh Armies is his name.

Days after the publication of his memoir, the writer Christopher Hitchens was struck down by cancer. He died eighteen months later, but through his illness he kept writing because that's what writers do. In one piece he recalls the way he'd spoken of "the stupendous importance of love, friendship, and solidarity," and he now notes how this point "has been made immensely more vivid to me by recent experience. I can't hope to convey the full effect of the embraces and avowals, but I can perhaps offer a crumb of counsel. If there is anybody known to you who might benefit from a letter or a visit, don't *on any account* postpone the writing or the making of it. The difference made will almost certainly be more than you've calculated" (*New York Times*, Sept. 12, 2012, p. BR 1).

At one level Jeremiah has little sympathy for **Babylon** and its king in what he knows are their death throes, but he shows some awareness of how horrifying their demise will be. Their destroyers and slaughterers are people who will have no compassion. Ironically, this is the critique of Babylon itself in Isaiah 47, but it's a horrifying fact that Babylon is to be treated the way it treated others. Babylon's king is pictured as so scared he can't raise his hands to lift his weapons (someone who has lacked all compassion can imagine his own fate all too easily). In the event, Nabonidus, Babylon's last king, will abandon his city by the time its conquerors get near. Jeremiah depicts people wanting to tend to Babylon's wounds, but the wounds are too severe. The picture recalls a scene from a war movie when a soldier's buddy desperately tries to staunch the bleeding from his wounds but knows the attempt is futile and that telling him, "You're going to be all right; you're going to make it" is a lie.

So Jeremiah is aware of the horrific nature of what Babylon is to experience, but he doesn't protest about it. There's such a thing as punishment, as redress for wrongdoing, and Babylon is to receive it. As prophet to the nations, Jeremiah is aware not merely of the wrong Babylon has done to **Judah**. As the superpower, the global power over the Middle East, Babylon has made many peoples drink its poisoned chalice. The fact that its potential destroyers are even more ruthless than Babylon is frightening, but it will contribute to the efficiency of the event. These destroyers will be put down in due course. Behind their action is the action of God himself, the fierce lion. No, God isn't a tame lion, nor a gentle one.

Further, it's the putting down of Babylon that will make it possible for the Judahites to go home. In a nice and bold image Jeremiah declares that **Ephraim** and Judah are not a group of people who've been widowed by God. The prophets more often speak of their being divorced, but the result is the same. In a society where men hold the power, a woman who has been abandoned or whose husband has died (like Naomi and Ruth) is as vulnerable as a child without a father. That isn't **Israel**'s position. Her husband isn't dead. They couldn't complain if he'd abandoned them—their country is full of guilt before **Yahweh**. But their husband is still alive and intends to be their protector and rescuer.

Is it implausible to think that Babylon would fall? In Jeremiah's day there was no political basis for declaring that it would do so. Jeremiah's basis for his declarations is theological, not political. It lies in who Yahweh is. Jeremiah repeats declarations about God from his earlier ridicule of gods who can be represented by images. There's such a contrast between that kind of god and the one who's the creator, and there's an equivalent contrast between the wisdom of people who trust in Yahweh and the stupidity of people who worship by means of an image that has no breath in it. Yahweh isn't just some wood-and-metal god but the God of life and death.

JEREMIAH 51:20–44

In the Interests of the Living

> ²⁰ You [Babylon] were my club,
>   my battle instruments.
> I clubbed nations with you,
>   I destroyed kingdoms with you.
> ²¹ I clubbed horse and its rider with you,
>   I clubbed chariot and its rider with you.
> ²² I clubbed man and woman with you,
>   I clubbed elder and youth with you.
> I clubbed young man and girl with you,
> ²³   I clubbed shepherd and his flock with you.
> I clubbed plowman and his pair with you,
>   I clubbed governors and overseers with you.
> ²⁴ But I'll repay Babylon and all Kaldea's residents
>   for all the evil that they did

to Zion before your eyes [Judahites]
  (Yahweh's declaration).
²⁵ Here am I in relation to you,
  mountain of the destroyer (Yahweh's declaration),
  destroyer of the entire earth!
I'm spreading out my hand against you;
  I'll roll you from the crags
  and make you a burnt mountain.
²⁶ They won't get a corner stone or foundation stone
      from you,
  because you'll be a total devastation forever
  (Yahweh's declaration).

²⁷ Lift up a banner in the earth,
  sound a horn among the nations.
Sanctify nations against it,
  make [the horn] heard to kingdoms against it,
Ararat, Minni, Ashkenaz: appoint a marshal
      against it,
  bring up horses like swarming locusts.
²⁸ Sanctify nations against it,
  the kings of Media,
its governors, all its overseers,
  every country it rules.
²⁹ The earth is shaking and writhing
  because Yahweh's intentions are performed
      against Babylon
to make the country of Babylon
  a devastation without resident.
³⁰ Babylon's warriors are holding back from doing
      battle;
  they're staying in the fortresses.
Their strength has failed,
  they've turned into women.
People have set fire to its dwellings,
  its gate bars have broken.
³¹ Runner runs to meet runner,
  messenger to meet messenger,

to tell the king of Babylon
    that his city has been captured at one end.
³² The fords have been seized,
    people have set the marshes on fire,
    the fighting men are panicking.
³³ Because Yahweh Armies, Israel's God, has said this:
Ms. Babylon is like a threshing floor at the time of
    its treading:
    yet a little while and the time of its harvest will
    come.

³⁴ "He devoured me, crushed me,
    Nebuchadrezzar, king of Babylon,
    put me down an empty dish.
He swallowed me like a dragon,
    filled his belly with my tasty things, threw me up.
³⁵ The violence done to me and my body be on
    Babylon!"
    says the one who dwells on Zion.
"My blood be on Kaldea's residents!"
    says Jerusalem.
³⁶ Therefore Yahweh says this:
    Here am I, contending your case.
I'll exact redress for you.
    I'll wither its sea and dry up its spring.
³⁷ Babylon will become heaps of rubble,
    the dwelling of jackals,
a devastation, something to whistle at,
    with no resident.
³⁸ Together, like lions they roar,
    they've growled like the whelps of cougars.
³⁹ When they've been made hot I'll set out their
    drink,
    and get them drunk so they may exult,
and sleep an everlasting sleep
    and not wake up (Yahweh's declaration).
⁴⁰ I'll take them down like lambs to slaughter,
    like rams along with goats.

⁴¹   How Sheshak has been captured,
         the praise of the entire earth has been seized!
     How Babylon has become
         something devastating among the nations!
⁴²   The sea has gone up over Babylon;
         it's covered by the roaring of its waves.
⁴³   Its cities have become a devastation,
         its country desert and steppe,
     a country where no one lives in them,
         where a human being doesn't pass through them.
⁴⁴   I shall deal with Bel in Babylon
         and make what he's swallowed come out of his
             mouth.
     Nations will no more flood to him;
         even Babylon's wall is falling.

A woman recently inherited a diary her mother kept during the last months of her life. It showed a side of her mother she hadn't seen before—angry, afraid, self-recriminatory. It was upsetting to read. She asked the *New York Times* "Ethicist" columnist whether she should burn the diary rather than show her siblings. It seems likely that the mother didn't intend anyone to read it—she wrote it for herself. But the column writer noted that the siblings might gain something from reading it—maybe some new, more adult understanding of their mother. So maybe the woman should share it with them. The principle was "The interests of the living must outweigh the interests of the dead."

We've noted that both **Yahweh** and Jeremiah imply some sympathy for **Babylon** as for Moab, Ammon, and the other victims of calamity that these chapters describe. But these other peoples' interests are not up front in the chapters' thinking when they're still alive, and certainly not when they are dead and gone. The prophecies about Babylon are meant for **Judah** in Jeremiah's day and in the subsequent decades that saw their fulfillment. They're then meant for Judah in succeeding centuries when they were preserved in the book of Jeremiah, and also eventually for later readers like us.

In the way the poetry works, the prophecy begins by addressing Babylon but soon makes a transition to addressing the Judahites who've seen what Babylon did to **Zion**. The phrase "before your eyes" points to the pain of the Judahites who hear this message. So first, the prophecy reaffirms that Babylon has been God's agent, God's means of bringing judgment to peoples who deserved it. But once again it assumes that the superpower wasn't consciously accepting a commission to be God's servant. It was pursuing its own ends, and it will pay for the devastation it brought on Zion.

Jeremiah goes on to summon far-off nations whose identity or location would be little known to his actual hearers, which is the point. They're mysterious, distant peoples to the far north and far east, way beyond the immediate horizon (like Moab, Ammon, and so on) and the intermediate horizon (like Babylon, **Assyria**, and so on). Yes, Yahweh is lord over the whole world and can use all these nations to fulfill his purpose. There's another vivid, imaginative picture of the unthinkable fall of Babylon, designed to bring home its possibility to the Judahites, to help them (and us) envisage this implausible event.

In the third paragraph Zion itself speaks, externalizing the hurt of its people, who are the prophecy's immediate listeners. I want to see Babylon punished, Zion says in its hurt. God's response isn't to say, "You should be forgiving" but to say, "Yes, you'll see it." As the Bible assumes throughout, God is one who brings redress. Zion doesn't seek to do it. It knows that redress is God's business and that God can be trusted to do the right thing. If the superpower were listening, the prophecy would be fearful to hear. If pathetic little Zion says, "I'm going to get my own back," Babylon could just laugh. But if God says, "I'm going to give the superpower what for," it has reason to be scared.

With poetic justice, the judgment on Babylon is described in terms similar to ones used of both Judah and little powers such as Moab; it will be made desolate and empty of people. Sometimes the prophets make the point that Judah is treated just the same as other peoples; it gets no remission on the basis of **Israelite** exceptionalism. Sometimes they make the point that the agent of such destruction can also be the victim of it. Sometimes they make the point that the bigger you are, the harder you fall; on the day of destruction Babylon is no different from Moab or Judah (Sheshak is a cipher for Babylon that Jeremiah has used earlier, possibly some kind of insult). Once again Yahweh notes that the city's fall will mean the discrediting of the so-called gods in which it trusted.

If only the living will pay attention!

JEREMIAH 51:45–52:34

If Someone Disciplines You, It Implies Loving You

45 Get out from its midst, my people;
    each of you, save his life from Yahweh's angry blaze.
46 Beware that your spirit doesn't faint or you become afraid
    at the news that makes itself heard in the country.
News may come one year
    and afterwards news may come another year,
violence in the country
    and ruler against ruler.
47 Therefore, now: days are coming
    when I shall deal with Babylon's images.
Its entire country will be shamed;
    all its slain will fall in its midst.
48 The heavens and the earth and all that's in them
    will resound over Babylon.
Because from the north the destroyers will come to it
    (Yahweh's declaration).

⁴⁹ Yes, Babylon, for the falling of Israel's slain—
   yes, for Babylon all earth's slain have fallen.
⁵⁰ Survivors of the sword, go,
      don't stand there.
   Be mindful of Yahweh from afar;
      Jerusalem is to come up into your spirit:
⁵¹ "We were shamed, because we heard insult,
      disgrace covered our faces
   because strangers came into the sacred places
      in Yahweh's house."
⁵² Therefore, now: days are coming (Yahweh's
         declaration)
      when I'll deal with its images;
      in the entire country the wounded person
         will groan.
⁵³ If Babylon goes up to the heavens,
      if it fortifies its strong height,
   destroyers will come to it from me
      (Yahweh's declaration).
⁵⁴ The sound of a cry from Babylon,
      a great wounding from the Kaldeans'
         country!
⁵⁵ Because Yahweh is destroying Babylon,
      terminating the loud voice from it.
   Their waves are thundering like mighty waters;
      the roar of their voice is raised.
⁵⁶ Because a destroyer is coming against it,
      against Babylon.
   Its warriors will be captured;
      their bows will be shattered.
   Because Yahweh is a God of requital;
      he definitely repays.
⁵⁷ I shall make its officials and experts drunk,
      its governors and overseers and warriors.
   They'll sleep an everlasting sleep and not
         wake up
      (a declaration of the King,
      whose name is Yahweh Armies).

⁵⁸ Yahweh Armies has said this:
      Babylon's wall, broad, will be totally leveled,
         its high gates burned with fire.
   Peoples will have toiled for naught,
      nations will have got weary for fire.

⁵⁹The message that Jeremiah the prophet issued to Seraiah son of Neraiah son of Mahseiah when [Seraiah] went with Zedekiah, king of Judah, to Babylon in the fourth year of his reign; Seraiah was staff officer. ⁶⁰Jeremiah wrote down all the evil that would come to Babylon on a single scroll, all these messages that are written concerning Babylon. ⁶¹Jeremiah said to Seraiah, "When you come to Babylon, you're to see that you read out all these messages. ⁶²And you're to say, 'Yahweh, you yourself have spoken concerning this place that you'll cut it off, so that there won't be anyone dwelling in it, human being or animal, because it's to be devastation forever.' ⁶³When you've finished reading this scroll out, you're to tie a stone to it and throw it into the middle of the Euphrates. ⁶⁴You're to say, 'In this way Babylon will sink and not rise up because of the evil I'm bringing upon it. They'll have got weary.'"

   Until here are the messages of Jeremiah.

^{52:1}Zedekiah was twenty-one years old when he became king; he reigned eleven years in Jerusalem. His mother's name was Limutal daughter of Jeremiah of Libnah. ²He did what was evil in Yahweh's eyes in accordance with all that Jehoiaqim had done. ³Because through Yahweh's anger it came about in Jerusalem and Judah that he threw them out of his presence. . . . ²⁸This is the company that Nebuchadrezzar exiled in the seventh year: 3,023 Judahites; ²⁹in Nebuchadrezzar's eighteenth year: 832 people from Jerusalem; ³⁰in Nebuchadrezzar's twenty-third year, Nebuzaradan the head of the guards exiled 745 Judahites. All the people were 4,600.

³¹But in the thirty-seventh year of the exile of Jehoiakin, king of Judah, on the twenty-fifth day of the twelfth month, Ewil-merodak, king of Babylon, in the year he became king, elevated Jehoiakin, king of Judah. He released him from confinement ³²and spoke of good things with him. He gave him a

seat above the seat of the kings who were with him in Babylon [33]and changed his prison clothes. [Jehoiakin] ate with him regularly for his whole life, [34]and his provision was given him as a regular provision from the king, an amount for each day, for his whole life.

In a television interview, the great tennis player Serena Williams was talking about an outburst she'd had at a lineswoman who claimed Serena had foot-faulted; Serena had been convinced she was wrong. "What bothered me most," she said, "was that I was representing my religion. I felt like anyone who knew I was a [Jehovah's] Witness was stumbled. And I really don't want to stumble anybody." By "stumbling" she means causing someone to fall away from the truth; Jesus warns about this possibility (Luke 17:1–2). As she expected, the Witnesses called Ms. Williams in for a dressing down. "But it's not bad," she went on, "because in the Bible it says God loves you, and if someone reprimands you, they love you."

You can get a pretty gloomy picture of the prophets, not least Jeremiah, who specialize in reprimanding. But he and they would nod at Serena's comment, and the way the book of Jeremiah closes confirms the point. We've seen that it's one of the considerations underlying the prophecies about the other nations, especially **Babylon. Yahweh** had made Babylon a means of issuing a reprimand that was more than mere words, but Yahweh also promises to put Babylon down so as to free **Judah** from its power. The Judahites in Babylon will therefore have no need to share the anxiety that will preoccupy Babylon, either in the context of the struggles for power that followed Nebuchadnezzar's death in 562 or in the context of Cyrus's advance on Babylon two decades later. They can know that the moment will come when Babylon is conquered and they can leave. You could say that these stories in Jeremiah (and the prophecies) have two main functions. They seek to generate second thoughts among the people in power, who need to ask whether they're fooling themselves in thinking they can get away with things, and to generate hope for people in situations where they can't see God acting.

If such people find it hard to hold onto that hope, the account of Jeremiah's commissioning the symbolic action by Seraiah is designed to bolster their hope. The diplomatic journey to Babylon will be a consequence of the plot to rebel against Babylon to which chapters 27–28 allude. Zedekiah goes to have his knuckles rapped. Ironically, the summons facilitates Jeremiah's declaring the judgment on Babylon that won't come in Zedekiah's time but will come in due course. People knew that Jeremiah's symbolic actions carried out against Judah had truly been the means of putting Yahweh's **decisions** into effect. Jeremiah put on a yoke; Jerusalem had a yoke imposed on it. They could therefore believe that symbolic actions carried out against Babylon could truly be the means of putting Yahweh's decisions into effect. The dynamic didn't depend on Jeremiah's being present in person. It worked not because he had mysterious power but because Yahweh did. Events will prove that the Babylonians have wasted their efforts in conscripting so much labor from subordinate foreign peoples to build their impressive wall, for it will turn out not to be impregnable to the destroyers from the mythical or literal north that Yahweh intends to send.

If Jeremiah kept a copy of these prophecies about Babylon, it wouldn't be surprising if it lies behind Jeremiah 50–51. The chapters close with the words "thus far the messages of Jeremiah." The final chapter of the book has nothing directly to do with him. The material mostly comes from the history in 2 Kings, though Jeremiah 39 has already told us some of the story. So why is it here? One aspect of its significance is that it shows that Jeremiah was indeed right in the warnings he gave Jerusalem. Things turned out as he said they would. The terrible events that came about in Jerusalem were the vindication of his message. The good news would once again be that the fulfillment of his warnings again provided a basis for trusting his promises.

The statistics appear only here, not in 2 Kings, and they make clear how inappropriate is an image of an **exile** that involves the transportation of the entire people. The Babylonians only bothered to take the important people. It turns out that Yahweh was much less tough than he'd threatened to be (as will be the case for Babylon when it falls). The reprimands indeed were after all an expression of love. It's sometimes said you can only be truly wrathful about the people you deeply love (wrathful with them or on their behalf). But in wrath Yahweh remembers mercy, as Habakkuk had urged Yahweh to do.

The very last paragraph of the book also makes the point. Jeremiah had affirmed that Yahweh hasn't given up on his promise to David. The footnote about Jehoiakin relates to the time of political chaos in Babylon when Nebuchadnezzar's son and successor Ewil-merodak reigned for two years before being assassinated by his brother-in-law. He did have time to release Jehoiakin from prison in Babylon. It provides just a hint that Yahweh has indeed not forgotten David's line and that reprimand and discipline are indeed set in the context of love and commitment.

GLOSSARY

Assyria, Assyrians
The first great Middle Eastern superpower, the Assyrians spread their empire westward into Syria-Palestine in the eighth century, the time of Amos and Isaiah. They made **Ephraim** part of their empire; then when Ephraim kept trying to assert independence, they invaded Ephraim, destroyed its capital at Samaria, transported its people, and settled people from other parts of their empire in their place. They also invaded **Judah** and devastated much of the country, but they didn't take Jerusalem. Prophets such as Amos and Isaiah describe how **Yahweh** was thus using Assyria as a means of disciplining **Israel**.

authority, authoritative
English translations commonly translate the Hebrew *mishpat* with words such as *judgment* or *justice*, but the word suggests exercising authority and making decisions in a broader sense. It is a word for *government*. In principle, then, the word has positive implications, though it is quite possible for people in authority to make decisions in an unjust way. It is a king's job to exercise authority in accordance with **faithfulness** to God and people and in a way that brings deliverance. Exercising authority means making decisions and acting decisively on behalf of people in need and of people wronged by others. Thus speaking of God as judge implies good news (unless you are a major wrongdoer). God's "decisions" can also denote God's authoritative declarations concerning human behavior and about what he intends to do.

Babylon, Babylonians
Previously a minor power, Babylon took over as the regional superpower from **Assyria** in the time of Jeremiah and kept that position

for nearly a century until conquered by **Persia**. Prophets such as Jeremiah describe how **Yahweh** was using the Babylonians as a means of disciplining **Judah**. Their creation stories, law codes, and more philosophical writings help us understand aspects of the Old Testament's equivalent writings while their astrological religion also forms background to aspects of polemic in the Prophets.

Benjamin

Benjamin was the last of Jacob's twelve sons. The clan that traces its ancestry to Benjamin was a small one that received as its allocation a very small tract of land between **Ephraim** and **Judah**, though this land included Jerusalem itself. When the kingdom of Israel split into the two nation states of Ephraim and Judah, the Benjaminites are described as being associated with Judah, yet Ephraim had one of its sanctuaries at Bethel which had also been part of the land allocated to Benjamin. So there is some ambiguity about whether Benjamin naturally belongs with Judah or with Ephraim, and thus some ambiguity about Jeremiah's relationship with Jerusalem.

decision, see authority

Ephraim, Ephraimites

After the reign of David and Solomon, the nation of **Israel** split into two. Most of the twelve Israelite clans set up an independent state in the north, separate from **Judah** and Jerusalem and from the line of David. Because it was the bigger of the two states, politically it kept the name Israel, which is confusing because Israel is still the name of the whole people of God. In the Prophets, it is sometimes difficult to tell whether "Israel" refers to the people of God as a whole or just to the northern state. Sometimes the state is referred to by the name of Ephraim as one of its dominant clans, so I use this term to refer to that northern state to try to reduce the confusion.

evil

The Old Testament uses this word in a similar fashion to the way English uses the word *bad*—it can refer both to the bad things that people do and the bad things that happen to them, both to morally bad actions and to bad experiences. Jeremiah often uses the word with both connotations in the same context, pointing toward the fact that bad things often happen because people do bad things—though Jeremiah knows that this is not invariably so. Like other prophets, he can thus speak of God's doing evil in the sense of bringing calamity to people.

exile

At the end of the seventh century **Babylon** became the major power in **Judah**'s world, but Judah was inclined to rebel against its authority. As part of a successful campaign to get Judah to submit properly to its authority, in 597 and in 587 BC the Babylonians transported many people from Jerusalem to Babylon. They made a special point of transporting people in leadership positions, such as members of the royal family and the court, priests, and prophets (Ezekiel was one of them). These people were thus compelled to live in Babylonia for the next fifty years or so. Through the same period, people back in Judah were also under Babylonian authority. They were not physically in exile, but they were also living *in* the exile as a period of time.

faithfulness

In English Bibles this Hebrew word (*sedaqah*) is usually translated "righteousness," but it denotes a particular slant on what we might mean by righteousness. It means doing the right thing by the people with whom one is in a relationship, the members of one's community. Thus it is really closer to "faithfulness" than "righteousness."

Greece, Greek

In 336 BC Greek forces under Alexander the Great took control of the **Persian** Empire, but after Alexander's death in 333 his empire split up. The largest part, to the north and east of Palestine, was ruled by one of his generals, Seleucus, and his successors. **Judah** was under its control for much of the next two centuries, though it was at the extreme southwestern border of this empire and sometimes came under the control of the Ptolemaic Empire in Egypt (ruled by successors of another of Alexander's officers). In 167 the Seleucid ruler Antiochus Epiphanes attempted to ban observance of the **Torah** and persecuted the faithful community in Jerusalem, but they rebelled and experienced a great deliverance.

Israel, Israelites

Originally, Israel was the new name God gave Abraham's grandson, Jacob. His twelve sons were then forefathers of the twelve clans that comprise the people Israel. In the time of Saul and David these twelve clans became more of a political entity. So Israel was both the people of God and a nation or state like other nations or states. After Solomon's day, this state split into two separate states, **Ephraim** and **Judah**. Because Ephraim was far the bigger, it often continued to be referred to as Israel. So if one is thinking of the people of God, Judah is part of Israel. If one is thinking politically, Judah isn't part of Israel. Once Ephraim has gone out of existence, then for practical purposes Judah *is* Israel, as the people of God.

Judah, Judahites

One of the twelve sons of Jacob and the clan that traces its ancestry to him, then the dominant clan in the southern of the two states after the time of Solomon. Effectively Judah *was* Israel after the fall of **Ephraim**.

Kaldeans (Chaldeans)

Kaldea was an area southeast of **Babylon** from which the kings who ruled Babylonia came in the time Babylonia ruled **Judah**. Thus the Old Testament refers to the **Babylonians** as the Kaldeans.

Master, Masters

The Hebrew word is *ba'al*, an ordinary word for a master, lord, or owner, but the word is also used to describe a Canaanite god. It is thus parallel to the word *Lord*, used to describe **Yahweh**. So like *Lord*, *Master* can be a proper name, as it is treated in translations when they transliterate the word as *Baal*. The Old Testament generally uses *Master* for a Canaanite god and *Lord* for the real God, Yahweh, to make the difference clear. Like many other peoples, the Canaanites acknowledged a number of gods, and strictly the Master was simply one of them, though he was one of the most prominent, but the Old Testament also uses the plural *Masters* (*Baals*) to refer to other gods in general.

Persia, Persians

Persia was the third Middle Eastern superpower. Under the leadership of Cyrus the Great, the Persians took control of the **Babylonian** Empire in 539 BC. Ezra 1 sees **Yahweh** fulfill his promises in Jeremiah by raising up Cyrus as the means of restoring **Judah** after the **exile**. Judah and surrounding peoples such as Samaria, Ammon, and Ashdod were then Persian provinces or colonies. The Persians stayed in power for two centuries until defeated by **Greece**.

Philistia, Philistines

The Philistines were people who came from across the Mediterranean to settle in Canaan at the same time as the Israelites were establishing themselves in Canaan, so that the two peoples formed an accidental pincer movement on the existing inhabitants of the country and became each other's rivals for control of the area. By Jeremiah's day, like **Judah** they are a minor power.

remains, remnant

The Prophets warn that **Yahweh**'s chastisement will mean **Israel**'s (and other peoples') being cut down so that only small remains or a remainder or remnant will survive. But at least some remains of Israel will survive—so the idea of "remains" can become a sign of hope. It can also become a challenge—the few that remain are challenged to become faithful remains, a faithful remnant. See further the comment on 43:8–44:14.

Second Temple

The first temple was Solomon's, devastated by the **Babylonians** in 587 BC; the second temple was the one rebuilt seventy years later (see Ezra 5–6). It was vastly remodeled and expanded by Herod in Jesus' time but destroyed by the Romans in AD 70. The Second Temple period is thus the period from the late sixth century to New Testament times, the period when **Judah** was ruled by **Persia**, then **Greece**, then Rome.

Seleucids, see Greece

teaching see Torah

Torah

This Hebrew word is traditionally translated "law," but this gives the wrong impression, as the word covers instruction in a broader sense. The framework of "the Torah" (the books from Genesis to Deuteronomy) is the story of **Yahweh**'s relationship with the world and with **Israel**, though the Torah is dominated by instructions. "Teaching" is the nearest English word. The Hebrew word can thus apply to the teaching of people such as prophets as well as to the instructions in Genesis to Deuteronomy. It is sometimes not clear whether it refers to the Torah or to teaching in that wider sense.

well-being

The Hebrew word *shalom* can suggest peace after there has been conflict, but it often points to a richer notion of fullness of life. The KJV sometimes translates it "welfare," and modern translations use words such as "well-being" or "prosperity." It suggests that everything is going well for you.

Yahweh

In most English Bibles, the word "LORD" often comes in all capitals as does sometimes the word "GOD." These actually represent the name of God, Yahweh. In later Old Testament times, **Israelites** stopped using the name and started referring to **Yahweh** as "the Lord." There may be two reasons. They wanted other people to recognize that Yahweh was the one true God, but this strange foreign-sounding name could give the impression that Yahweh was just Israel's tribal god. A term such as "the Lord" was one anyone could recognize. In addition, they didn't want to fall foul of the warning in the Ten Commandments about misusing Yahweh's name. Translations into other languages then followed suit and substituted an expression such as "the Lord" for the name Yahweh. The downsides are that often the text refers to Yahweh and not some other (so-called) god or lord and that the practice obscures the fact that God wanted to be known by name and instead gives the impression that God is much more "lordly" and patriarchal than actually God is. (The form "Jehovah" isn't a real word but a mixture of the consonants of Yahweh and the vowels of that word for "Lord," to remind people in reading Scripture that they should say "the Lord" and not the actual name.)

Yahweh Armies

This title for God usually appears in English Bibles as "the LORD of Hosts," but it is a more puzzling expression than that implies. The word for Lord represents the name of God, Yahweh, and the word for Hosts is the regular Hebrew word for armies; it is the word that appears on the back of an Israeli military truck. More literally the expression thus means "Yahweh [of] Armies," which is as odd in Hebrew as "Goldingay of Armies" would be. Yet in general terms its likely implication is clear; it suggests that Yahweh is the embodiment of or controller of all war-making power, in heaven or on earth.

Zion

The word is an alternative name for the city of Jerusalem. Jerusalem is more a political name; other peoples would refer to the city as "Jerusalem." Zion is more a religious name, a designation of the city that focuses on its being the place where Yahweh dwells and is worshiped.